Ewen is a proud Western Australian, who grew up in Perth as a former high school teacher of 30 years, he has lived in several different areas of the state. He has two wonderful children, each now with families of their own. With a family history of service in the military, he has developed a keen interest in ensuring that the memories of these heroes are not forgotten. Much of his life has been dedicated to educating, whether it be in schools or through his work with St John Ambulance. This story continues that commitment.

This has been a long journey, with lots of downtime in between bursts of activity. It would follow a line of discovery for a while and then it would sit for some time. A little like making bread. Mix and knead and then let it sit for a while to "prove." This is not a time of nothing happening but a time when ideas grow, without the product growing. During these down times, lots of questioning and exploration would take place. It is during these times I would seek help from others. So, this book is not one of only my own work, but the coalescing of information from several sources.

Ewen Hill

WHATEVER IT TAKES

AUSTIN MACAULEY PUBLISHERS™

LONDON * CAMBRIDGE * NEW YORK * SHARJAH

A CIP catalogue record for this title is available from the British Library.

ISBN 9781398477261 (Paperback)
ISBN 9781398477278 (Hardback)
ISBN 9781398477292 (ePub e-book)
ISBN 9781398477285 (Audiobook)

www.austinmacauley.com

First Published 2023
Austin Macauley Publishers Ltd®
1 Canada Square
Canary Wharf
London
E14 5AA

Firstly, a huge thank you to my mother, who is the one who really inspired me along this journey. I could sense her pain at not knowing what had happened to her father and it was that, that spurred me on to find some answers.

There has not been a huge amount written on the Australian tunnellers, lots on the British, but not so much about the Aussies.

To John Reading and his team at www.tunnellers.net a big thank you, not only for the information and advice, but for the encouragement as well. Together the team at Tunnellers, endeavour to put up a comprehensive website, of information about the Australian Tunnelling Companies.

In Australia, the efforts of the National Archives (www.naa.gov.au) and the Australian War Memorial in Canberra, (www.awm.gov.au) have been amazing in preserving the memories of our heroes. Thank you to the AWM for the use of photos that have been collected from so many sources. Some from official sources like Frank Hurley, and many others drawn from many of the families of those that were there.

Thanks also, must got to Hazel Menzies, at the North Ayrshire Heritage centre in Irvine, Scotland, for details on Robert's service in the Ardrossan Volunteers and his apprenticeship at Wallace carpenters.

To J Bree (author), thanks for the advice and for the encouragement to "get back on the horse." With me not being one who had ever written a book before, it was great to have someone to turn to, to ask so many stupid questions. By the way, if you are into romance / mysteries / crime, that is one name you need to look up.

To my family, my brother and sisters and their spouses and children and my own children, I owe a huge debt of gratitude, for being such a wonderful bunch of people to grow up with. After putting up with all my spouting off, with newly discovered facts and theories, probably completely out of context, now you can see where all that information was going.

To my wife, thanks for the last few years listening to all my ramblings and at least looking interested even when you were half asleep. For the encouragement and support throughout this journey, a huge thanks.

Finally, to all those men and women of the Australian armed forces, St John Ambulance and Red Cross, without whom, none of us in this country would be enjoying the freedom we currently enjoy, a massive thank you. You deserve the undying gratitude of every man, woman and child in this country. You did your job to the best of your ability, against all odds. You are / were a small force who punch(ed) so very much above your weight and showed the world what a powerful bunch we can be, when you use your heads, not just your force.

FOR MY MOTHER ENID, AND MY GRANDMOTHER JEAN

Table of Contents

List of Figures

Prologue

This is the story of one man, an ordinary man, living an ordinary life, until he was called on to do extraordinary things. It is one story, out of many millions of stories, of other ordinary men and women, most of which will now, never be told. Each one of them deserves to be told, but with the passage of time and the generational limitations, most will pass into the ether. It is our duty to see that as many as possible do not disappear, but with that passage of time, it becomes increasingly difficult. So why this story? Well, why not?

It is the story of my grandfather, Robert Hood. A Scot who migrated to Australia and who then fought for his adopted country and no doubt in his mind, for his mother country as well. Much of this story is fact, but some has had to be extrapolated from company records and known methods of operation of the time. A number of characters in this story are real, and others are fictional. The significant real characters and their outcomes, are detailed at the end of the story.

I guess I should start at the beginning, except I really can't say where the beginning of this story is. So, let us start at one of the beginnings for me.

I was a baby boomer, born in the 1950s to a middle-working class family, in Perth Western Australia. My father had been in the RAAF as a communications technician from 1942, until the end of the Second World War, and my mother, worked for the Department of Agriculture through the war years. At one time, the shortage of space for business, meant that the secretarial pool she was a part of, was based in the ballroom of Government House in St Georges Terrace in Perth. After the war, she did as she was told at the time and stayed home to raise a family. We were far from wealthy, but we certainly were not poor. Like so many families of the time, we struggled through life with mum and dad working hard, to ensure my 2 sisters, my brother and I, had the absolute best upbringing they could provide. We all went on to complete 12 years of school, and each got university qualifications in our own areas.

I cannot recall when it was that I found out that my grandfather had died in the Great War other than it was early on. He had been a soldier with the Australian army. That was it. That was all I knew. End of story. Ok, so I don't have a grandfather. So, what? Lots of kids don't have a grandfather. I do have two grandmothers and I have a mother and father and that is something to be thankful for. Nothing to be concerned about, let us just get on with life. After a few years it dawned on me that my mother was born in 1920. The numbers do not add up. By this time, I was probably just in my early teens or maybe a little younger. So how could this be? So, I asked.

"No, your grandfather hadn't died IN the war, but he did die after mum was born, because of the war." To me, of course, this meant that he had died of wounds he received during the war. That worked. My grandfather was a war hero. Yes, that sits well. So, on we go with life. So many of us had no idea what had really happened with our fathers and grandfathers, during and because of those 2 wars. They had been told by their superiors, just to go back to ordinary life and forget about the war. Insanity really, isn't it? How could they possibly do that?

Probably 20 years later, I discovered that he in fact died at his own hand. Mum was only 1 month old, and he had committed suicide. WOW! That is a bit different. You must understand that in the 50s, 60s and 70s, suicide was a sin. Not only that, but it was also a crime. So that side of things had been hushed up. It was not talked about, hence the earlier story of his fate. In fact, it was not for many years after my mother was married, that she even discovered he had suicided. She had been told that he had died of heart failure, which probably was not that far from the truth, as you will find out.

So how did he do it? Why did he do it? Again, I am not sure if I was told he hanged himself or shot himself. I think it was the former but certain parts of the family in UK were of the understanding he shot himself. Why? Well, who knows? Whoever, really knows in these circumstances? "Well, it was the war, wasn't it", that seemed to be the logical answer.

In the later 1990s, I became involved in the Yellow Ribbon programme. This was a youth suicide prevention and outreach programme. By this time, I had been a high school teacher for about 20 years. I always felt the prime purpose of a teacher was the welfare and education of young people. This might sound obvious to most, but the reality in the education system is often somewhat different. As I was concerned with my students' welfare, I started to investigate why kids suicide and ways of defusing this. I had been involved with this for a year or two, when a presentation to one of my groups at school, asked me why I got involved with his particular cause. So, I explained about my commitment to my students and no sooner had I said that, than a picture of my grandfather popped into my head. I shared this experience with the group there and then, and we all understood.

In 2002, I went on trip to the UK and one of the things I did was to go to Edinburgh, Scotland, to meet my cousin, Janette. She is really my mother's cousin I guess, but that is kind of irrelevant. Janette's mother Ciss, was a sister to my mother's father, Robert. You will meet her in the story later on. Janette had been heavily involved in tracing the family tree. I was aware of this beforehand but when she started explaining all the relationships and branches of the tree, it dawned on me that maybe it would now be possible to find out a lot more information about my grandfather.

When I returned home, I asked my mother again. By this time, my father had passed away, so mum had more time on her own, to think and talk. She too had many questions unanswered about her father. She did not have much time left now, she figured, being 82, and she wanted answers too, so she told me what she could.

He was a tunneller (whatever that was), a sapper, and yes, he had suicided. She said she had his war service medals. "Would you like to see them?"

"Oh yes I sure would." She found them and I looked upon them with awe. My grandfather's war service medals. Just 2 of them. The Victory Medal and Great War service medal. All I had ever had contact with, from my grandfather. Pretty emotional I can tell you. There on the edge printed was "403 CQMS R HOOD. 1 TUN. COY AIF." WOW again! After a while she added that there was one other thing I might like to see. Whilst on service in France, he had made a jewellery box, out of the timbers of the ruined Ypres Cathedral. (Whilst this is a mistake, we were all under the impression that Ypres and Flanders were all a part of France. Of course, we are to discover later that Ypres and Flanders are, of course, in Belgium. Just shows how much we knew, does it not?)

She retired to find the box and bring it out. It is a surprisingly simple box, but with my training and experience in the woodworking field, I can appreciate the complexity and workmanship of this box. It is made from Oak and is about 250mm x125mm x 75mm. (10" x 5" x 3"). Dovetail joints in each corner, with the material being about 5mm (3/16") thick. Superb craftsmanship. It has a hinged, chamfered lid and an inset lock, perfectly fitted. On the top is a small silver scroll shaped metal plate, inset into the lid so that it forms one surface, so as not to snag anything. This plate is engraved, obviously by hand, so that it does indeed resemble a scroll. In the middle of this scroll is hand engraved the word 'YPRES'. He must have indeed been there. Here we have 2 tangible items from over 80 years ago, of the life of my grandfather. The biggest thing however for my mother was still, that he had committed suicide. "It is wrong." she would say. "It is a sin."

Because of his actions, she had been deprived of a father all her life. She had so many questions unanswered. In fact, she often blamed herself for his demise. She had not had an unhappy upbringing; in fact, it had been quite the opposite.

After my grandfather's suicide, my grandmother was looked after by friends for a short time, whilst my Great Grandmother trained to Sydney from Perth to collect her. They returned to Perth and lived in Florence St in West Perth. (My Great Grandmother used to dine out on the fact that she travelled in the train with Dame Nellie Melba, and met her and talked with her along the way). My mother was brought up in a loving family, where she had her mother, grandfather, grandmother, 3 aunties and 1 uncle, all close at hand, all involved with bringing her up. So, it was indeed, a happy upbringing. But something was always missing.

So it was that I commenced trying to find out as much as I could for my mother and the rest of the family who were, by now, also interested in the history.

*

Author's note. As most of this story takes place over a century ago now, the units of measurement used are of the Imperial system in most cases. I have provided approximate conversions to the metric system, for those who are more familiar with that. Interestingly, in some cases, the company diary records the action in the metric system, so reverse conversions have been included. Also, it was a much more racially ignorant time, and things were said and done then, that would not be acceptable now. However, to sanitise those remarks and opinions in this story, would be to alter history. No disrespect is implied or intended by the author towards any race or nationality by these inclusions.

Part 1

Chapter 1
Scotland

Saltcoats, Scotland, is a small town on the west coast of Scotland, in Ayrshire, about 25 miles (40 km) southwest of Glasgow and about 80 miles (130 km) north of the border with England. It is a beautiful part of the world, with the Isle of Arran just a short 12 mile (20 km) ferry ride across the Firth of Clyde. The rugged country of the Trossachs, can be seen just to the north and the similarly rugged area of the Galloway Forest Park to the south. Most of the west coast it is subject to the storms coming across the Atlantic Ocean, so can be bleak at times, but Saltcoats is nicely tucked in behind, and protected by, Ireland, the Isle of Arran, and the Mull of Kintyre. Its main claim to fame is… Well, that is a little difficult to say.

In times gone by, it was a source of salt, hence the name, for the Scottish people. Many of the small holdings along the coast made their income from producing salt on the banks of the Firth of Clyde. Later, in the C18th-C19th, it was a place of ship building producing about 70 ships over a period of less than 100 years, until most of that industry moved to Belfast. That saw the industry die off there completely, although it did continue longer in Ardrossan, but mostly small vessels. Saltcoats, along with the towns of Ardrossan and Stevenson, are more or less considered, as a single urban entity with the three towns occupying an area of only three miles wide and about 1 mile inland. The earliest recorded (modern) history in the area, was the construction of a castle at Canon Hill in the centre of Ardrossan, by Simon de Morville in c1140. It stood overlooking the town through a variety of occupiers until 1648 when Oliver Cromwell had his army destroyed it and transport the materials 12 mile southeast to Ayr. There, he built the citadel of Montgomerieston. The remains of that structure still exist in the centre of Ayr, with the imposing St John's Tower still being the centrepiece of the town.

Robert Hood was born in Saltcoats in Scotland 1st November 1887, to Hugh and Mary Hood. Hugh was a stone mason. Robert was the seventh of 13 children of which 11 survived childhood. Euphemia 1876-1955, Hugh 1877-1958, Alexander 1879-1967, Mary 1881-1949, Elizabeth 1884-1943, David 1886-1895 (Septic peritonitis), Robert 1887, Jemima 1889, James 1891-1891 (Diarrhoea), Marion (Known as Minnie) 1892 James 1894, Divina (Known as Ciss) 1895, David 1899.

He had 2 brothers, David, one dying at age 9 and 2 brothers James, the first of which survived less than 1 month. He had an ordinary upbringing for the time. When he left school, he became apprentice carpenter for 5 years to Mr J Wallace in Saltcoats, Ardrossan, Scotland.

When he was 18, he joined the Ardrossan volunteers. The Ardrossan volunteers were the forerunners of the Territorial Army (The Terries) or the reserve Army. In 1905, The Ardrossan Volunteers were a part of the 1st Ayrshire and Galloway Artillery Corps. This in turn was part of the 52nd (Lowland) Infantry Division. The 1st A and GAC corps was formed in 1859, in response to a perceived threat of invasion by France, and by 1863 had individual Corps in Irvine, Ayr, Largs, Ardrossan, Kilmarnock, Kirkcudbright, Stranraer, Port Patrick and Sandhead. This arrangement of units remained so until 1908, when a restructure took place, and it all became part of the Territorial Army, as a part of the Royal Artillery (RA). The corps was equipped with 4.7" (120mm) quick firing artillery pieces, a big upgrade from the 18 pounder RML (Rifled Muzzle Loaded) guns they had had since 1889. There was an artillery range at Irvine about 6 miles away, so all the gun practice took place there.

This was also the HQ of the 1st A and GAC. Additionally, a rifle range existed in Irvine as well, so the northern units of the Corps did their musketry practice there too. Their uniforms were, blue tunics with red collars, cuffs and piping, edged with black braid. There were 4 rows of this featured on the breast of the tunic. They wore dark blue trousers, with black stripes and piped with red. The peak caps were of a similar blue with black lace band, red piping and a silver grenade embossed centre front. The uniform was finished off with a black belt.

The most outstanding event in Robert's time with the Ardrossan, was on Monday 18th September 1905, when the whole of the Scottish Volunteer division was reviewed by His Majesty King George V, at Holyrood Park. A review of this nature had not taken place since Queen Victoria had reviewed the division last, in 1881. This was truly a big event, with in excess of 38 000 officers and recruits attending from all over Scotland. The 1st A and GAC contributed 23 officers and 581 other ranks to that total, of which Robert was one. In the week following the parade, the following message was conveyed to all those who had participated. It was from Col Davidson, Equerry in waiting, to his Majesty. It read:

Glenquoich Invergarry 8.35pm

The King commands me to convey to you, and all ranks under your command, His Majesty's great satisfaction with the fine appearance of the Scottish volunteer force review by him today.

The organisation by which so large a number of troops was conveyed from so many different quarters reflects the greatest credit on all concerned, and His Majesty fully recognises the patriotic spirit which has inspired the units of force to come long distances, in many cases at great personal inconvenience, in order to be present at the review.

His Majesty was greatly pleased with the physique and appearance of the troops and commands you to convey to all ranks his approval of their steadiness on parade and in marching past.

His Majesty highly appreciates the fine spirit which has resulted in the assembly of the magnificent force reviewed by him today, and heartily congratulates you on the success of the review, to which your untiring energy has so largely contributed.

The King had also said personally earlier in the day that "I would have travelled double the distance to see the very fine sight that I have seen this day. I am thoroughly proud of the Scottish volunteers."

It must have been a bit of a let-down, returning to everyday training after such a big day for them all. But return to training they did. A quick read of their training manual indicates that much of their time was spent on drilling. Section and platoon drill. Standing at attention, at ease, turning, opening and closing, wheeling, falling out, reforming and marching. They also included piling of arms (rifles), firing exercises, skirmishing etc. The troops quickly accomplished these and more mundane type of exercises, to the extent that before too long the drill manual had been discarded and the training became that of the regular army.

This was the beginning of Robert's military training, so when the great war finally arrived some 10 years later, he had a bit of a kick start on many of his fellow enlistees.

Times were tough in Scotland at that time. Just after the turn of the century there seemed little chance of improving one's situation. The economy was slow, job prospects were limited, and many Scotsmen left their homeland in search of better prospects. Many travelled to America, Canada, Australia, New Zealand and South Africa. So somewhere around 1910, Robert packed up and headed for South Africa. But he found South Africa was not to his liking, so he returned to Scotland. It was not long, before the old dissatisfactions arose again, and he got restless feet. This time he chose to try Australia, so in 1912 he set sail for Sydney aboard the P and O ship 'Geelong' arriving July 1912. This time he found things more to his liking so set up his trade in Hurstville, Sydney. Sydney was a boom town at this time, and he found no problem getting plenty of work so settled into his carpentry work again.

Chapter 2
Great War Commences

1914 came around and the Austrian Archduke Ferdinand was assassinated in Sarajevo, Serbia, in July. Eventually, the Austrian President sent an ultimatum to the Government of Serbia in response to this action, dictating the terms of retribution. These terms were crafted in such a way that there was no way Serbia could accept, short of handing over their own sovereignty. So, a state of war then existed between Austria-Hungary and Serbia. This was a war, just waiting for something to trigger it. Tensions had been in an extremely heightened state in Europe for a year or two and this assassination provided an excuse for all-out war.

Germany, being a close ally of Austria-Hungary, soon jumped into the fray as well as the Ottoman Turks. It was not long then until Great Britain, along with France and Belgium, declared war on Germany and the central powers. Germany had, for years, been planning for the possibility of an invasion of France. Ever since the Franco-Prussian war of 1870, an invasion of France had been contemplated. Count Alfred von Schlieffen was the Chief of Staff of the German Army from 1891-1906, and in his time as CoS, he developed a plan for this invasion. Many on the French side, expected that any invasion of France would take place through the Alsace or Ardennes regions of the border, so this is where the French fortified their defences. The border region with Belgium was not considered a high risk area, so defences here were light. Von Schlieffen proposed that any invasion, therefore, should take place through this region.

So it was that the German Army swept through Belgium in a wide anti-clockwise arc, and advanced on Paris from the north and northwest. It was so well rehearsed that their successes were rapid. Most of Belgium fell fairly quickly, and they advance to within 19miles (31km) of Paris. So close that the Parisiennes could clearly hear the battles. Had it not been for the timidity of some in command, and his now overstretched lines of supply, the Germans may well have been successful in taking Paris.

Because of both limiting factors, the combined forces of Belgium, France and Great Britain, were able to counterattack successfully and drive the German army back to a line, roughly equivalent to the Belgian-French border. It was along this line that the opposing armies dug in and thus we saw the commencement of the trench warfare. It was to last for 4 years, and cost millions of lives.

*

Robert considered enlistment, as many others were doing, but he had so much work on, he deferred. Australian troops left Australia via Albany and Fremantle in Western Australia, in the October / November of 1914 and headed for Egypt and then fatefully on to Gallipoli, Turkey, in April 1915. This is, of course, a story told extensively elsewhere. December 1915 and the Australian troops and the remainder of the allies withdrew from Gallipoli in their now famous bloodless, skilful withdrawal. Patriotic fervour reached fever pitch at home and Robert could no longer hold back. At the same time the government was calling for people from mining and associated technical industries background to enlist in the mining corps.

*

Sir John Norton-Griffiths was a mining engineer in England, at the time of the outbreak of war. He was also, currently, a Member of Parliament and a Major in the British Army. He saw in the mining industry, a way to assist the BEF in Europe by tunnelling under enemy lines and laying large charges, then detonating them to destroy large groups of enemy installations and personnel from below. He also felt it may be of use in intelligence gathering, installing listening posts under the enemy lines. He wrote to the War Office in December 1914, suggesting a method he was currently employing on the Liverpool sewers may be of some use in the clay of Flanders.

This 'clay kicking' entailed the digger lying on his back on an inclined timber which had been jammed between the floor and roof of the tunnel and by using the power of his legs, to force a narrow spade into the clay. He would remove the clay in wedges. He would then pass the sod backwards, to an assistant who would remove the spoils back down the tunnel. His attempts to persuade the hierarchy fell on deaf ears, however.

Just before Christmas that year, the Germans managed to dig a small tunnel between the lines and under an emplacement of the Indian Sirhind Brigade, where they detonated around 400kg (880lbs) of explosive in several charges. Between that explosion and the resultant German advance, the entire brigade of around 800 men was lost. No one even knew this tunnelling activity was even happening, and when further similar attacks occurred over the next month, the British commander wrote immediately to Lord Kitchener explaining the gravity of the situation they were finding themselves in. A change of heart, on the part of the British War Office, saw Norton-Griffiths immediately contacted and charged with raising companies of 'Tunnellers', although he preferred the term Moles.

Norton-Griffiths immediately started forming companies, firstly by raiding existing troops in infantry companies. He was, of course, looking for anyone who had mining experience. This did not fill all the positions he needed so he closed one of his own civil contracts down and drafted the unemployed miners into his companies. With further recruitment (mostly from the coal mining industry) he was able to get an operational company going within days. This proved a bit of a sore point with some of the military hierarchy as these were men with absolutely no military training, and a lack of all the disciplinary attributes expected of a soldier. At the same time a call was put out to the empire, to contribute to this enterprise and the Australian Government along with Canada and New Zealand all responded with Mining Companies.

In all, by the time all the companies had been formed there were 26 British companies, 170th-185th, 250th-258th, 8th Corps Mining Co, 3 Canadian companies, 1st 2nd and 3rd, a New Zealand Co, and 4 Australian companies, 1st, 2nd and 3rd Australian Tunnelling Companies, and the AEMM&BC Australian Electrical Mechanical Boring and Mining Company (known as the Alphabet company because there were so many letters in its name).

By employing the clay kicking technique, the British tunnellers were able to dig at about 3 times the rate that the German tunnellers were digging.

At that time, the Australian Infantry Force (AIF) was engaged in battle in the Dardanelles, Turkey, and all our efforts were concentrated on that futile theatre of war. We simply did not have enough people we could spare for tunnelling in

Europe. We were going to need them all for reinforcing Gallipoli it appeared. It was not until the decision was made to withdraw from Gallipoli that they could even think about fighting anywhere else. So it was that in late 1915, after the withdrawal of our troops from the Dardanelles, our government put out that call, to form a Mining Company. It was to be known as, the First Australian Mining Corps.

*

Robert took himself off to the local recruitment office after Christmas, applied and attended his medical at the Sydney town hall recruitment office on 3rd January 1916, and being found fit, enlisted, signing his attestation on 10th January 1916 at Casula, Sydney, New South Wales. From his medical examination we start to get a clearer picture of Robert. He stood 5'9" in height (175 cm), weighed 159 lbs (72 kg), was of a dark complexion, had black hair and blue eyes (piercing, light blue eyes to be precise) and he was of the Presbyterian faith.

His basic training was at the Casula army barracks and indeed was basic, consisting most likely of "this is a gun, this is the dangerous end, and this is how you make it go bang." Training at this time, was necessarily basic. Just enough to get started, place the recruit in a battalion and rely on the 6 weeks on the ocean to hone any other military type skills, particularly discipline. It was however, more than some of the early British units had received.

Robert was placed in Y Company of the depot battalion initially, and then transferred to the 1st reinforcements of the Australian Mining Corps on 15th February 1916 with his rank being that of Sapper.

Sapper has always been an interesting term. It comes from the name given to the trenches that our soldier fought, lived and died in. A sap is the name given to that trench, so the people who dig those trenches or saps were called sappers. It is a name or rank that continues to this day in the engineer corps even if they no longer dig trenches.

William Archibald McIvor was also an expat Scot. Born in Edinburgh, in August 1890, he enlisted on the same day, in the same place as Robert and listed his occupation as Plumber. William was also placed into the 1st reinforcements Australian Mining Company. These two would continue their friendship and support of each other throughout the conflict to come.

The big adventure began then, only 45 days later when they sailed for France aboard the HMAT A38 'Ulysses'.

At a civic parade in the Domain, Sydney on Saturday February 19, 1916, a large crowd of relations and friends of the departing Miners lined the four sides of the parade ground. Sixty police and 100 Garrison Military Police were on hand to keep the crowds within bounds. The scene was an inspiriting one. On the extreme right flank, facing the saluting base, were companies of the Rifle Club School; next came a detachment of the 4th King's Shropshire Light Infantry, then the bands of the Light Horse, Liverpool Depot, and the Miners' on the left, rank upon rank, the Miners' Battalion.

Report taken from Tunnellers.net.

So it was that on 20 February 1916, the Ulysses departed Sydney harbour and sailed for France. They planned to stop in along the way at Melbourne, to pick up equipment and supplies and Fremantle to pick up further troops, for the mining corps.

HMAT A38 Ulysses was formerly known as the SS Ulysses and was built in Belfast for the for the China Mutual SN Co, London, a Subsidiary owned by Alfred Holt (Blue Funnel Line) only 3 years prior in 1913. At 534' (171.7m) long and a beam of 45' (20.8m) and weighing in at 14499 ton, she was one of the largest of the transport ships leased by the Commonwealth Government to transport our troops to the war zones. She was powered by a triple expansion steam engine, turning twin screws and was capable of moving at up to 14 kt (25kph). The Commonwealth government had a lease on her until April 1917. The 'Ulysses' was one of the original transport ships responsible for taking our first load of troops departing Albany WA, 1st November 1915. (She went on serving this country until she was sunk by a German torpedo in WW2, 70mi (115km) off Cape Lookout, North Carolina USA, on 11th April 1942, whilst transporting a load of pig iron from NSW to Liverpool, England.)

On arrival in Melbourne, 22nd February, the troops encamped at the Broadmeadows Camp whilst the loading of the supplies took place. On their final day in Melbourne, 1st March, the Corps was paraded before, and inspected by, the Governor General as the Commander in Chief of the AIF. Later that day they set sail for Fremantle, arriving 7th March 1916. The local mining industry had promised to raise around 300 troops for the mining corps. In fact, they ended up recruiting well more than that and they joined the corps at Fremantle. By the time they left Fremantle they had amassed a total of 1303 officers, NCOs and ORs which made up the 1st Australian Mining Corps.

Australian Miners' Corps
Parade at Fremantle

At present at Fremantle, en route to the seat of war, are 1200 members of the Australian Miners' Corps, a body of military engineers which was recently formed throughout the mining centres of the Commonwealth. About 300 of the contingent enlisted on the Eastern goldfields of the Sate, and they form the biggest quota of any State. They are men of splendid physique, and are skilled in some special branch of engineering work. Colonel Fewster and other professional engineers are in command, and accompanying the contingent is Professor David, of Sydney University.

The whole force, with their band and equipment, will parade at Fremantle this morning, leaving Victoria Quay at 9.30 o'clock, and proceeding direct to the oval, where they will be met by the Mayor (Mr W.E. Wray), Senators Needham and Buzacott, and other representative citizens. At the special request of the Mayor of Kalgoorlie, Mr Wray will present an Australian flag to the corps on behalf of the residents of the Eastern goldfields of this State.

The West Australian 8 March 1916

Australian Miners' Corps
Presentation of Flag at Fremantle

An interesting event took place at Fremantle yesterday when the Mayor of Fremantle (Mr W. E. Wray), on behalf of the residents of Kalgoorlie, presented a flag to the Australian Mining Corps, which is about to leave for the front. This corps has been recruited from the whole of the Australian States, and is probably the finest body of men that has so far left the shores of Australia. Shortly before 10 o'clock yesterday morning the men, headed by their own band, marched through the principle streets and then proceeded to the Fremantle Oval, where a large concourse of people was awaiting them. Western Australia's contribution to this corps totals about 300 men, the majority who have been drawn from the Eastern Goldfields.

The mayor, in presenting the flag, stated that he had been requested by the Mayor of Kalgoorlie to hand it to the miners corps on behalf of the people of the goldfields. The men he said composed a core of skilled miners from every part of the Commonwealth and Western Australia had provided the largest quota numbering some 300 men. He was sure they would give a good account of themselves (applause). The officers themselves stood high up in the engineering and scientific world. Dignity was added to the corps by the attachment of Maj David better known to Australians is Prof David (applause), a very gallant, gentle man, who had done much for Australia, and indeed the whole world, in the realms of science.

He had to compliment the men of the mining corps on their manly bearing. He felt sure that it was the finest court that that had ever left Australia (hear hear). He hoped that the flag would bring them inspiration wherever they were stop it had not been consecrated by prelates, but it had been consecrated by the hearts of the people of Australia...

Senator Weedham stated that he had never witnessed a more inspiring site than he had that day, nor a more impressive and imposing one. He could bear out the remarks of the media in saying that this was the finest core that had ever left Australia. He desired to complement the men on the stand they took during the recent regretful Sydney riot (applause). They showed themselves as soldiers who would obey orders and he felt they would equip themselves well on the field of war.

Senator Buzacott, and Mr W.H. Carpenter MLA, also spoke. In a brief speech Lt Col A. C. Fewtrell received the flag and expressed the thanks of the core of the thoughtfulness of the Kalgoorlie people. He hoped to bring the flag back to the Federal capital as suggested by Mr Wray. Lt Col Fewtrell then called for three cheers for the Mayor of Kalgoorlie and three for the Mayor of Fremantle which were all heartily given.

The West Australian 9 March 1916

Their stopover in Fremantle was to be a quick one, with no more time available, than to allow for provisioning, parading for the locals to 'fly the flag' and load the troops from the goldfields, as well as 100 reinforcement troops from the 10th Light Horse Brigade. The men did get one day's shore leave and Robert decided to use it to go to the movies in Perth. He caught the train from Fremantle station into Perth and walked up to one of the picture theatres located in Hay St. While he was there, he got talking to the people sitting next to him at intermission time and walked out with them, still chatting, after the finish of the film.

Before they parted company outside, his new friends ran into some of their own friends, a Mrs Chappell and her 3 daughters. They were themselves Scots and they got talking with Robert and Mrs Chappell suggested he should come back to their home for dinner, before heading back to the ship. Robert was glad to find such lovely people and from his own homeland as well, so he accepted the invitation. It was really nice to experience home cooking again. The evening passed pleasantly but all too quickly, and before too long Robert found himself on the train back to Fremantle.

Thus, having arrived on March 7, they departed only a couple of days later. A huge crowd lined the North and South mole, at the exit from Fremantle harbour to wave them all goodbye and good luck. At the same time as they passed between the 2 moles, another ship was entering Fremantle Harbour by the same passage and each ship had to move further to their side, than normal. It appears that the 'Ulysses' pilot may have gone just a little too wide and unfortunately, they remained to the side just a fraction too long and struck an uncharted rock. One must remember that in 1916 Fremantle harbour had only been operating since the turn of the century, so a complete oceanographic survey had not yet been completed.

Whilst the outer hull plates of the ship had been extensively damaged, the inner skin had only minor damage, so she was not in danger sinking but she was taking water, all the same. Obviously, she was unable to continue the journey in her present condition, so HMAT A38 'Ulysses' put about and returned to Fremantle for substantial repairs and the men all de-shipped the following morning. Now, with 1303 troops on board, the authorities had a bit of a quandary on their hands. Having already bid farewell to the troops they now had to welcome them back and find something to do with them.

So now it was, that the 1st Australian Mining Corps got to spend almost a month in Perth, not on recreation leave, but entrained and marched to Blackboy Hill Camp in the foothills of the Darling Scarp, some 25 miles (40 km) to the northeast. Their time there was to be spent in further training. This turned out to be rather useful, as many of the later signed up troops, had in fact had little, or in some cases, no training.

Chapter 3
Blackboy Hill

Blackboy Hill had been set up previously to train men from Western Australia for the military, before they were posted to the various locations around Europe and the Middle East. It was so called, because the site, a small hill at base of the Darling Scarp, Greenmount, was covered in the local grass tree, Xanthorea Pressii, more commonly known as 'Blackboy' and had, in years gone by, been an Aboriginal hunting ground. It was called a blackboy, as the trunk of the grass tree is always blackened after a bushfire and it remains so from that time on. The leaves are more like brittle spikes up to several feet long but only ¼ inch (6mm) thick and square in cross section and hundreds of them radiating from the central trunk look like a grass dress. Its flower spike is often 6-8 feet (2-2.4m) long and stands up vertically from the tree.

Many said that the whole plant looked like an Aboriginal, standing on one leg, whilst holding a spear. The site of Blackboy Hill was chosen firstly, as it was remote from much of the metropolitan population but also because the Eastern Branch train line ran right past the site, with Helena Vale station being close by. As a result, it was easy to get troops to and from the camp to either the city or Fremantle Harbour.

The campsite was part of 4000 acres (1600 Ha) that had been granted to Captain James Stirling, the person asked by the British Government to establish the Swan River Colony (Perth) in 1829 and the first Governor of the State of WA. Captain A.N. Martin and Lieutenant F.A. Beale, of the Royal Australian Engineers, were tasked with the job of surveying and clearing the camp, ready for use, at the outbreak of war in 1914. The camp and a Post Office were built in 1914 and opened August 29th of that year. The camp was initially no more than a collection of bell tents and the early recruits, were all housed in these tents.

In 1915, a storm tore through the camp and destroyed all but one of the tents, so a group of workers from the Midland Railway Workshops was contracted, to build more substantial buildings of timber and concrete. Because the need for accommodation grew quite quickly, many other buildings were brought into the camp from all over the metropolitan area, to supplement the building programme. The site was closed November 30th, 1918 and this really defined the occupation of the site and its use for the Great War. It was used for the training of some 32 000 troops, notably the 11th Battalion but also for elements and reinforcements for the 12th, 16th, 24th and 28th Battalion.

The following year, the camp was turned over to the Health Department, by the Imperial forces, where it assisted with the Spanish Flu outbreak, by acting as a fever hospital. In 1919 this area, was still fairly remote, so had quarantine value. During the depression years, it was used by unemployed relief workers. It was not used by the military establishment, during the second world war as a training camp, but the buildings were dismantled and transported to other locations for use by the 2nd AIF. Locations would have included Karrakatta, Swanbourne and Northam Army barracks.

At least this unexpected stopover in WA had some plusses to it. Whilst it did, of course, delay the arrival and deployment of the men in France, it allowed for a month of military training that the troops would otherwise not have had. This may well have contributed to the overall success of the boys in France and Belgium, as they were asked to do a lot more over there, than digging holes and mining. We will discuss the type of mining the Corps would be asked to do at a later stage. In order not to overdo things troops were billeted out at weekends with volunteer members of the public, for some R and R. Members of the public had been canvassed to find those who could assist in times like this so any troops can get some relief and also experience, albeit briefly normal family life. Mr and Mrs Chappell of Florence St W. Perth were one such family who offered their home for billeting.

*

Robert Mack Chappell was a fifty something master baker who had arrived in Australia with his family in September 1912, from Edinburgh Scotland aboard the Aberdeen Shipping Company ship 'Gothic', having emigrated for much the same reasons as Robert Hood. Ironically, he and his family had tried South

Africa first as well, but 10 years before, and also found it not to his liking. On arriving in Australia, he took up a position as baker in a West Perth establishment. He was not just a baker, but a master baker and his skills became widely known in the district. He was accompanied by his wife Jemima (known as Mimey) and their 4 children, Jane (known as Jean) B. 1897, John (known as Jack and born in Johannesburg South Africa in 1899) Jessie, B. 1900, and Roberta (Berta) B 1904. Of course, Robert being the man of the house was also the master of the house but as his hours as a master baker were somewhat different to most peoples' working hours, it was actually Mimey who was the driver of activity in the house.

Initially, they set up home in Carr St, West Perth. They only spent about 3 years there before moving their home to 10 Florence St West Perth, not far from the business district of Perth in a quiet area and within easy walking distance of the train. They had a big backyard which contained two fig trees, an Adam and a Green Fig, a peach tree, a nectarine, a huge Mulberry tree at the bottom of the garden, grape vines scattered throughout and a Cape Lilac tree. In spring, the lilac tree would begin to shoot pale green tufts from the ends of its spindly branches, and as the weeks went on the tree would become darker and denser, as the leaves filled every available space.

Before the leaves had finished filling out, the buds would begin to show and then one day the air would be filled with the most wonderful perfume, as the lilac flowers burst their way through. Later as the berries formed, they would become fantastic projectiles for slingshots. This tree was well grown, large and with its multitude of rambling branches, and was just wonderful for any child lucky enough to be there to climb it. One could hide from the world in this wonderful tree or just sit there devouring the fruit from any of the fruit trees.

Having been built around the turn of the century, the house was typical of the Federation style houses that can still be found around the area today. It was a large house with 3 bedrooms, large dining room, large lounge room, complete with ornate fireplace, Jarrah timber mantlepiece and sides with an open wrought iron grate. It was next to this fire that Robert Chappell liked to sit and smoke his daily cigar, his one indulgence in life that he allowed himself. There were wide verandas around 3 sides which were covered in occasionally, to provide extra storage and rooms for outside sleeping in Perth's hot summers.

In fact, the kitchen had been built into the rear veranda of number 10. It also had an outside wash house or laundry. There were three steps down from the veranda, at the rear, to the wash house, which was provisioned with the concrete trough, cold water tap, wood fired copper and a mangle for squeezing the water from the clothing. They would then be hung out to dry, on the single line, tied between two poles at either side of the back yard and a long, angled pole, somewhere near the middle that could be used to raise and lower the line. From here you went on to the workshop and then the chook yard. For those unfamiliar with this term, 'chook' is a colloquial Australian word, used to denote hens or chickens. The chook yard was an area about 12' x 12' (4m x4m) with a small shelter of corrugated iron in one corner, where the chooks roosted for the night and where the eggs could be collected after being laid. The whole pen was surrounded by a fence about 6' high (1.8m) of chicken wire strung from poles of jarrah cut from the bush.

Of course, the loo (dunny, thunderbox, privy, W/C, toilet) was well outside the main house being towards the rear of the property. This structure was a brick building 3' wide and 6' long (1m x 2m) and was usually placed against the rear boundary of a property and there was a laneway that passed behind that the nightcart would travel along each night and collect the contents for disposal. There was always a small lift up hinged door on the back wall, about 2' x 1.5' (60cm x 45cm) that the nightcart man would lift, remove the can or thunderbox, as it was known, and empty it into his cart full of the nasty stuff, and then replace the can. The lane was therefore always known as the nightcart lane. Many of these lanes still exist today, although not for this reason anymore.

There was a vacant block behind number 10, so there was a large area available for the children to play. Interestingly, it was only 3 doors down from Sheridan's, a badges and engraving business, who would go on to make many war medals years later. During business hours there would always be the ker-thump, ker-thump, ker-thump of the presses as they punched our yet another run of badges. It was never annoyingly loud; it was just always there. The property was also only a fifteen minute walk from Hyde Park where you could picnic and sit and watch the ducks or Western Australia's famous black swans and all manner of other water birds on the lakes. Courting couples were regularly seen wandering dreamily around the lakes deep in conversation.

Picnics in Hyde Park were also a favourite pastime of the people of Perth as well, and being so close to the lake, the Chappells often found themselves reclining in the Sunday afternoon sun and relaxing on the grass on the slopes leading down to the lakes. The home in Florence St was also only a short 5-

minute walk from the West Perth railway station. The sounds of the steam trains plying back and forward from Perth station only 600 yards (550 m) to the east, to Fremantle, 11 miles (17 km) southwest, would fill the air day and night.

The hiss of the steam pump, the chuff, chuff, chuff, of the steam being vented through the exhaust stack, the blast of the steam whistle and the screeching of steel wheels on steel track as the train negotiated the curved sections, were all sounds which defined the era of steam. Today that all evokes a feeling of nostalgia, but then, it was just, plain, dirty. Coal dust and soot from the smoke stacks, pervaded the whole area for over a mile from the rail line.

*

Robert Hood found himself invited back to spend his billeting time at the home of the Chappells, who he had been introduced to, the other day at the film theatre. He was mightily relieved to have landed in the house of a fellow ex pat Scot. He immediately felt right at home. Although he was 10 years older, than the oldest of the children, it was nice to interact with the females here, of roughly his own age, after so long now with only male company. This weekend was spent talking, playing cards, walking, reminiscing about the old country as this was the term used to describe the country of their birth, Scotland. After lots of talk they discovered that they had both migrated to Australia the same year, only 2 months apart. Robert first in July and the Chappells in September.

Needless to say, the conversation would eventually get around to this war with Germany. That Australia had jumped into the war to back up the Motherland was great, but it was a shame so many would suffer because of it. It was now only 13 years since we had all been caught up in the Boer war in South Africa. They were all glad Robert was not heading to Europe to be on the front line fighting, but just digging holes and building shelters and things like that. He did not have the heart to tell them the likelihood was he would indeed be in the thick of it.

By the end of the weekend, Robert had built quite a friendship with them all, but especially young Jessie, who seemed to be the more outgoing of the 3 girls. She already had her eye well and truly on Robert. She thought he was really nice. He promised to return to them the following weekend if the billeting arrangements were to be allowed again. Back on the train now heading for Helena Vale station, which was the closest to the Blackboy Hill Camp, Robert recounted his experiences of a wonderful weekend to another of the Mining Corps returning to camp. He started taking about the feeling of homeliness, peacefulness and excitement all at the same time.

The weekend had been just so good, and Mr and Mrs Chappell were really lovely people originating from his homeland though they are maybe a little old fashioned. The food was fantastic after what they were used to on the ship and in camp, especially the pastries. Oh, the pastries. Mr Chappell was really a fantastic baker. On a more personal level he told of how the girls were all wonderful and the two older ones specifically. Berta would only have been about 12 at the time so was not really, as far as partnering goes, on the radar. Whereas Jack was 17 and great to knock around with, talking about things more blokey, the war, what it meant to be in it, and the sorts of things Robert was expecting to get involved in.

He thought Jessie was definitely the more outgoing of the two older ones and was certainly a lot of fun. But on the other hand, Jean was closer to his age and was quite strikingly beautiful. Both appeared intelligent and understanding of what was going on in the world and able to hold an intelligent conversation. Both were prepared to voice their own opinions on things and not just agree. Jessie probably dominated the conversation a little, but that was because she was the more outgoing of the two.

Chapter 4
Training Begins

Late Sunday afternoon, the train passed though Midland and onto the Helena Vale station. This station, and the branch line it was on, closed permanently in 1966 when a better route through the Darling Scarp was opened. The old route is still there as a walk trail, however. It was only a short 300 yard (270 m) walk to the camp from Helena Vale station. The troops all trickled back to camp on that warm, lazy March afternoon and the mood around camp was certainly upbeat for everyone had at last experienced something of a normal existence for the weekend, something that they had not had, for anything from 2 to 4 months. The mess hut was alive with conversation throughout the evening meal but was brought to a standstill at the end when the RSM called the group to quiet for the details of this coming week. Collective sigh... back to the grind of the army life. Route marches, kit inspections, weapons inspections, rifle drill, parade ground drill, guard duty, kitchen duty, latrine duty, lectures on cleanliness, the progress of the war, living in foreign lands, etc., etc.

A typical day in camp would start with reveille at:

0600 Morning roll call parade
0610 each platoon would get their orders for the day
0615 dismiss
0800 breakfast mess and clean-up
0900 Parade and inspection
0930-1030 1st training session
1030-1045 morning tea
1045-1145 2nd training session
1215 lunch
1315-1400 3rd training session

1400-1500 4th Training session
1500-1515 afternoon tea
1515-1615 5th Training session
1700 kit maintenance
1800 evening meal
2000 evening parade and lecture
2130 dismiss
2200 Lights out

As many of the Mining Corps had no previous military training, and some had truly little preliminary training at Casula, the officers and NCOs really had their work cut out turning this mob into a cohesive, disciplined Mining Corps. Miners were usually a rough group, as they answered to no man, as a rule, except maybe the boss, and even then, reluctantly. A hard living, hard drinking, undisciplined mob. That was the reputation of miners at that time. This time in WA was going to be extremely useful, although at this stage, they did not know how long they would have, so they packed as much as possible into their days.

They learnt that care of their rifle was paramount. It was to be looked after at all costs. It was not a gun (calling it that incurred an automatic 10 pushups on the spot) but a rifle. A Lee Enfield.303 bolt action repeating rifle, known as an SMLE Mark III. (Short Magazine Lee Enfield Mk III). The SMLE Mk III, affectionately known as the 'smelly' was a rifle released in 1907 and was a leap ahead in rifle technology. The SMLE Mk III* was a 1915 upgrade, which was aimed at making the rifle easier to manufacture, maintain and use and stayed in production until 1957. It had a 10 round magazine loaded by 5 round stripper clips and had a fire rate in capable hands, of around 20-30 shots per minute, and muzzle velocity of around 2400 ft/sec (730 m/s). It was accurate over around 500 yards (450 m) but was capable of firing up to 2 miles (3.2 km). They learnt how to strip it down, clean it and reassemble it, to the point that they could do it in their sleep.

They learnt what discipline was, and how it was essential in a cohesive force. They learnt what the structure of the line of command was. What the different insignias of rank were. They learnt how to march (Ad Nauseum), perform faultless drill (although many failed to find the point of this) and how to salute officers, i.e., anyone of First Lieutenant or higher rank. They learnt how to stalk an enemy, what a defensive battle plan was, what an offensive battleplan was.

They learnt about explosives, large and small. They learnt about trenching systems, machinegun pits, communication trenches and communications. And so, it went on day after day, but slowly they started to come together as a group.

*

William Archibald McIvor was born in Edinburgh Scotland in August 1890. His mother was Catherine McIvor, and he lists his occupation as Plumber. He lived in Belbour St, Kogarah, Sydney NSW.

Robert had known William McIvor before they enlisted, although not all that well. Now being together in the same unit, and both being Scotsmen, having enlisted on the same day in Sydney, they naturally bonded and a strong friendship grew. He was Bill and Robert soon became Bob as Australians have a real knack of shortening everyone's name, although occasionally, an attempt at shortening somebody's name ends up with the name being longer. For example, Tom becomes Tommy, John becomes Johnno, Roy becomes Roy the boy, Frank becomes Frankie and so on. Bob and Bill were both allotted palliasses in the same hut and chose to bunk alongside each other. With both a part of the 1st reinforcements, they also participated in their training sessions alongside each other too.

One of the characteristics of the Australian way of conflict, is what most people might call the buddy system. In Australia it is called mateship. The entire country is built on the premise of mateship. If you are in trouble your mate will give you a helping hand. If you need help on a job, call a mate. If you are in a trench fighting an enemy, a mate will be alongside you. Each of you will look out for the other.

26 years later, our troops would again be in a conflict, this time in a war against Japan, and fighting for their lives and their country in the jungles of New Guinea. The Japanese forces were thought to be almost invincible, by the way they had blitzed their way down the Malayan peninsular, through Singapore and the Dutch East Indies (now Indonesia). The Japanese Imperial Army suffered their first 2 defeats on land at the hands of the Australian forces. First at Milne Bay and then on the Kokoda Trail / Track. In both cases the JIA was beaten by a much smaller force. On the Kokoda Track, the Australian forces were outnumbered up to10 to 1, but still sent the JIA into 'an advance to the rear' (there was no word in Japanese for retreat).

One of the biggest differences between the IJA and the AIF has been shown to be that of mateship. The IJA soldiers were individuals, who blindly followed their orders to the death. To die for the emperor was the ultimate sacrifice and the ultimate honour. The AIF soldiers backed each other up (mateship) and fought, and sometimes died, together. You did everything and anything for your mate, then hopefully you survived together and celebrated together. This difference was apparent even with the construction of their fox holes. The IJA foxholes were big enough only for 1 soldier to fit in, whereas the Australian pits were always big enough for two. You and your mate.

*

Bob and Bill both learnt about backing each other all the way. They trained together and learnt together. With Bob having spent 2 years with the Ardrossan Volunteers in Scotland he already had fairly extensive military training, so this helped him immeasurably, not only with the parade ground type skills but also with the discipline and his ability to follow orders. With Bill alongside, with his 3 years in the Terries, the two of them shone in their training and soon found that they cruised through, where others, who tried to fight the discipline and the regimentation, found themselves on all sorts of penal duties, 'on a Fizzer'. Things like fines, extra kitchen duties, guard duty, extra latrine duty, cancellation of weekend leave, and for more serious breaches, in camp detention.

The second leave came around and the troops once again found themselves billeted around Perth once again. Naturally, Bob was true to his promise and headed for Florence St, West Perth where he was welcomed with open arms. They were all extremely glad to see him again. News had been released, saying the 'Ulysses' was going to be at least another week and possibly two, before she would be ready for another sea voyage. So, it also looked like they would have another weekend at least, yet. The time started with what happened this week and then progressed into an evening of cards, until late in the evening.

By the time they all retired for the night, there were only 3 remaining, Bob, Jessie and Jean. When Bob did retire, his thoughts turned over in his head. Sleep came slowly. He started to think that maybe he had been a little hasty with his preference. Sure, Jessie was the outgoing, vivacious one, but Jean, she was something else. Very attractive, quieter, but seemingly quite intelligent. Anyway, tomorrow will surely help him sort out his mind. Next thing, he finds himself thinking this is ridiculous. "I'm off to a war and I'm thinking about love? Crazy! Drop the idea." But how do you do that when it is all that occupies you mind?

The following day, they loaded up a picnic and headed for the jewel in Perth's crown, King's Park. This is a 1.5 sq. mile (just over 4 sq. km) park, right in the south western edge of the Perth CBD. It boasts an elevated position overlooking the city of Perth, the Swan River and across the water to the Shenton's Mill ruins and South Perth. It has sweeping views of the young city, across the South Perth area right around to Melville water and the Canning Bridge in the distance. At the base of Mt Eliza (the hill King's Park is built on), Mounts Bay Rd runs from Perth city, around to the right hugging the cliffs and on to Fremantle running past the University of Western Australia and joining the highway which in 1930, would be named Stirling Highway, so named after WA's first Governor, Capt. James Stirling.

Also, alongside Mounts Bay Rd, is the tram running along the water's edge past Crawley baths to the University of WA, Nedlands baths and back to the city on the western side of Kings Park. On the opposite (south) side of 'The Narrows' is a swampy low-lying area known as Mill Point, so called as Perth's first flour grinding mill, Shenton's Mill, is situated just near the point. This mill has been preserved and is still there now, although it is somewhat dwarfed now by the passing Kwinana Freeway and Narrows interchange. King's Park is a spectacularly picturesque area, boasting large areas of lawn to sit and picnic on with these fantastic views of the city. There are lovely tearooms for those that would like to dine a little more exclusively, as well as the state's Botanic Gardens.

The Chappells and Bob, set up their picnic, overlooking the river and the afternoon consisted of eating, drinking tea, talking, walking around the magnificent gardens and trails, and just sitting basking in the early autumn sun. March days were starting to shorten, but the sun was still warm enough, the temperature hovering around the 78 degree F(25 deg C) mark. They sat and talked of all manner of things, solving many of the world's problems. There was certainly plenty of discussion of Prime Minister Hughes' ideas on conscription. Most of the Aussie soldiers were against it.

The feeling was, they would not want to be working or fighting alongside someone who was there in the firing line, because he was forced to be. All the Australian troops were volunteers in this conflict and there were certainly significantly polarised views, on this subject within the community. Mr Hughes' advocacy for conscription, flew in the face of most of the rest of his (Labor) party, and many of the community felt that perhaps Australia was not quite ready for conscription.

The afternoon passed quite pleasurably, and Bob had lots of time observing both Jessie and Jean. Jessie was the life of the party. She was always the one wanting to follow this track or that to find where it went. They found lots of new parts on the escarpment face this way. She was the one wanting to run here or there. Whereas Jean, was the more circumspect. More inclined for slow walks and to take time to look and really see what was there, whatever it was. His preferences were now definitely changing. Sure, Jessie was a lot of fun. She had the ability to make any situation light but at the same time she was sort of frivolous. Jean was, well, more mature. By the time they packed up and headed home, Bob's mind was made up. His attentions would favour Jean. This was made especially clear after they stood around the wishing well and tossed a farthing, up into the bell and into the well. Who knows what each of them was wishing for?

They arrived back at the Chappells' house around 5. They all helped unpack the T Ford Tourer and headed inside. There was a couple of hours before dinner and Bob sat most of that time talking with Jean. Yes, she was nice. Better than nice actually. He had not really noticed before just how nice. After dinner was cards again for a while. Robert snr sat in the corner reading whilst Mimey, Jessie, Jean and Bob played cards.

Mrs Chappell was already starting to see a change in Bob and her suspicions were being aroused. Maybe she is seeing a little more than just friendship? "He is a wonderful man even from what we have seen in this short time. He would make a good husband," she was thinking, but, of course, not saying.

Sunday broke and everyone was up early for a good old-fashioned Scottish breakfast. Porridge, with salt naturally, eggs from their own chickens, bacon, sausages and, of course, the ever-present fresh bread. Plenty of hot tea was to follow. After breakfast Bob and the 4 Chappell children headed off for Hyde Park, a short three quarters of a mile (1km) away along Vincent St. They wanted to walk down together and just walk and talk, wander around and see and experience the lakes, the birdlife and the serenity of the place.

*

Hyde Park had only been so named for just 17 years at that time. There had been a series of swamps and lakes, around the northern side of Perth, stretching from Claisebrook cove to the east, on the Swan River, through an area known as the third swamp, through to what is now Lake Monger and Herdsman lake in the west. The whole wetland region was known as the Great Lakes District. Much of this has now been drained and filled but in 1897, an area of 39 acres (15.5 Ha), of the area named Third Swamp, was set aside as a public park. In 1899 it was named Hyde Park and over the ensuing few years the land was sculpted, and the swamps were defined into 2 distinct lakes. Moreton Bay figs, Norfolk Island pines, Jacaranda trees and Plane trees were planted, along with retaining some of the area's natural Eucalypt and Melaleuca species. The area had already become a haven for water birds like the Australian White Ibis, Black Swans and all manner of ducks.

*

The jolly group were in high spirits when they arrived at the park. The walk along Vincent St had been fun each trying to outdo the other with car spotting. Who could spot the newest model on the road? There were plenty of Model T Fords, a couple of Buicks, a couple of Dodges, even one Cadillac and, of course, a few Chevrolets and Chryslers. It is still early days of motoring in Perth. The population is only around 130 000 at this time and the numbers of cars or horseless carriages as some are still wanting to call them, are still small in numbers, so there is still novelty value attached. There is great interest with every new make and model that hits the streets of Perth.

It does not take long, once they reach the park for the hustle and bustle to be left behind. Once in the park, the quiet envelops our little band of friends. They have brought some of last week's bread to feed to the ducks and swans. The group head down to the lake and Berta is keen to feed the ducks first. She grabs the bag of bread and starts to cast it to the amassing throng of water birds. The ducks hang back and take what is thrown to them, but the swans keep trying to take it straight from her hand. Jack and Bob step in to keep the swans at bay and feed them separately. It is all fun though. Each of them has a turn at feeding, but Bob makes sure he is at hand when Jean is throwing out to the ducks and is there to laugh with her and enjoy the moment with her.

Jack has a fairly good idea what is happening now, and he likes Bob a lot, so he tries to take Jessie and Berta and leave Bob and Jean to themselves; at least as far as is possible in this situation. Bob and Jean take the opportunity and take a walk around the lake and across the bank that divides the two lakes. The divide is a little like a dam bank and its sides are kind of steep. Whilst strolling across the bank, Jean slipped on the slippery soil and almost took a tumble. Bob, reflexes as sharp as a cheetah, reached out and grabbed her by the arm and stopped her hitting the ground. "Careful there, Jean. Ye dinnae wannae end up in the loch dae ye?" Bob was quick with the comment.

"Thank ye, Robert. I feel a wee bit silly really. It's noe the first time I've slipped here." Jean's face was bright red as she said it.

As soon as it was over, he held onto her hand to steady her. This was the first time he had even made contact with her. He soaked up the moment as they just looked at each other. He led her up to more level ground and then relinquished his hold on her hand. Inwardly, he was glad she had slipped. He had gained the chance to hold her hand, and she had not tried to shy away. He was delighted. Jean did not let on how she felt, but she too was thrilled at the incident. This all happened out of sight of the others so there was nothing to report to Mum and Dad when they all returned home.

The group joined up and walked back to Florence St where lunch was waiting. They reported they had a pleasant morning with the ducks and swans and generally relaxing in the park, which was growing nicely and there was now quite a lot of cover and shade in parts. They also reported the sighting of the Cadillac, complete with white wall tyres, not a regular sight at that time. Much discussion ensues on this wonderful sight. Compared to their Model T tourer, the Caddy is an amazing sighting. When all the excitement subsides Mrs Chappell, spreads lunch on the table and they all tuck in, still discussing the mornings proceedings. Once lunch is over, the mood quickly declines as it is apparent that Bob must head back to camp soon. That will bring everyone back to reality and back to the routine of ordinary life.

"*Ordinary life*? What is that these days anyway? Everything is changing. Why do we have to go through this all again? Haven't we learnt that this kind of thing does not solve anything?" These were common questions at that time. It was only 13 years since the end of the Boer War in South Africa. But still we go, and still, we must go and back up what we think is the right thing to do. After all, the mother country is in need of help, so we will assist.

Chapter 5
Last Week at Blackboy

In 1916, the Federated nation of Australia was only 15 years old, so there was still a huge tie to "The Mother Country"—England. Australia, at this time, was still really just an outpost of the British Empire, at least in the minds of most Australians. We were almost all, still of British descent and migration as a large scale happening, had not yet commenced apart from UK-based arrivals. The "White Australia Policy" was still in force, and saw to this. It was introduced into Australian law as the "Immigration Restriction Act", in the Federation year of 1901.

The aim being, in the words of later Prime Minister John Curtin, that "This country shall remain forever the home of the descendants of those people who came here in peace in order, to establish in the South Seas an outpost of the British race." The relaxing of this edict did not start occurring until 1949-1966, and then only to western Europeans. The complete abandonment of the policy did not happen until the Whitlam Labor government of 1973. In fact, in 1975 the second Whitlam government introduced the "Racial Discrimination Act", which made it illegal to discriminate on the grounds of race.

So, once again, go we did, and what is more, all were volunteers. Hundreds of thousands of us. From all walks of life. Not just the miners and associates of the Mining Corps, but accountants, lawyers, clerks, teachers, doctors, nurses, tradesmen, bank clerks, farm workers, labourers, unemployed, even clergymen. Every vocation you care to name was represented in these volunteers. Since the conflict and withdrawal at Gallipoli, the recruitment process had a renewed fervour, and many more volunteers had signed on, so that the losses would not be in vain. After all it was our duty, to serve our country in its hour of need.

This was again the topic of conversation after lunch. All were agreed that whilst the idea of going to war was repulsive, it was still necessary, as we cannot allow the oppressors to dominate this world. It was the duty of every able man, to do his bit. The outbreak of war in 1914 had been met with a great deal of enthusiasm by the Australian people. For the men, it was an opportunity for adventure and travel at the expense of the government of the day. For the women, it meant up to 4 years of worry. The best they could hope for was that their men would return in one piece. (Little did they know that would not necessarily be cause for relief.)

Initial enlistments were met with a rush followed by a lull when the first flush had passed. Throughout 1915 the enlistment rate dropped right off. It was necessary in subsequent years to campaign and recruit, in order to raise enough volunteers. It was due to this that Prime Minister Hughes, had suggested the introduction of conscription. England had introduced it, so we probably should. The Australian population in 1916 was a shade under 5 million, so it was to be a difficult task to raise enough men to mount a credible force. So far, we had done well enough, with the force sent to the middle east, in an attempt to counter the Ottoman (Turkish) involvement, but now that had fallen in a hole, the focus was to turn to the Western Front, i.e., France and Belgium. The conversation to and froed on the pros and cons of the involvement in the first place and then the possibility of conscription again. Mostly it was the men in favour and the women not so much.

By the end of the war, we had a tally of 416 809 men enlisted for military service. That was equivalent of almost 10% of our population at that time. This was an herculean effort, considering that they were all volunteers. Every one of them.

After a lazy afternoon spent discussing and drinking cups of tea, Bob made for the train station for his journey back to camp. This time it was set up that Jean would be the only one to accompany him to the train station. West Perth station is only a ten minute walk from Florence St, but Bob and Jean made it last a little longer. They wandered slowly down to the West Perth subway and then along Railway St, to the station opposite the Perth Metropolitan Markets. The smell of the fresh produce is an ever-present aroma in this area. The markets basically supply all the fresh produce for the city of Perth and her suburbs and although it is Sunday there is still activity preparing for the early morning opening tomorrow. They sat on the bench together discussing little of importance. Just to be there with only each other was a real bonus. The train arrived, too soon for them and Bob was on his way, hanging out the window of the carriage to say goodbye and wave, as Jean slowly faded into the distance.

He sat down in the seat, contemplative and quiet. What a wonderful time he had had on this leave. Perth central station was only a mile along the track, and he had to change to the midland line there. Central station was again awash with soldiers waiting for their train to return to Blackboy. It was also rather noisy with everyone discussing their exploits on leave. Many had spent their time 'on the town' so were a little worse for wear, shall we say. Most of the corps were miners and used to living the hard life. This usually meant wine women and song, or a variation of that. Ironically, that meant many of the men spent at least part of their weekend not far from where Bob spent his.

On the north side of the railway line between Perth Station and West Perth Station was Roe St, an extension of Railway St. This area was well known as the street of ill repute. The Roe St brothels had been in operation since the last century and were 'tolerated' by the establishment, despite being illegal, provided they were well fenced. They continued uninterrupted through until their closure in 1958.

Bob, of course, being of good Presbyterian background would have none of this and tended to not associate with those who were desirous of this sort of entertainment, unless he absolutely had to. He looked around the station for Bill and eventually found him. It was good to be back with his mate. At least now he did not feel out of place by being on his own whilst everyone else was in groups laughing and carrying on. The journey back to Helena Vale was slow, with lots of stops and a change of train at Midland. The train from Midland was almost entirely soldiers.

By the time they made it back to Blackboy, the noise had died down substantially, with all the men realising it was now back to the slog. More of the same. More Drill, more weapons training, more duties, more, more, more. Strangely though, it did not seem as difficult as it did initially. Maybe they were getting better at it. Maybe the training was actually working.

0600 and reveille came around way too soon for them all. It is now late March, so the mornings are starting to get a bitc to them. They all stumble out into the morning chill and count off. Anyone missing, of course, will face disciplinary action. Usually just missing morning muster will entail the loss of two days' pay. Missing return to camp is seen as a much more serious infraction, depending on circumstances and time the person is AWL. Bob and Bill were never in any danger of being involved in anything like that. They both had too much respect for the officers and the system as a whole.

This morning they are all told that there will be no leave this weekend. The men all groan in unison. The OIC deliberately waits for the noise to die down, and with a wry smile on his face, tells the men that HMAT 'Ulysses', will be ready for the crossing by the end of next week. They are aiming to leave on April 1st. The men gave a cheer and the conversation later, considers this to be an appropriate date, April Fool's Day, for the 'Ulysses' has now been re-christened the 'Useless' by the men. The OIC continues that they will all be entitled to a 3 day leave pass as of Tuesday. This is followed by more cheering. The men are expected back in Camp by 1800 Thursday day evening, with Friday required for packing up ready for transport to Fremantle on Saturday and departure. First however, will be 8 straight days intensive training, but the end of the beginning is in sight.

The men were starting to get tired of the waiting, so this was great news for them. The excitement was palpable around the parade ground, but first, there is this week to get through, was the thinking. It turned out that getting through this week would be harder than they had planned. Day 1 for Bob and Bill was preparing and building the practice shelters for machine gun pits, command pits and communication huts. Having done this, they pulled them down and started all over again. Bob found working with this West Australian Jarrah a bit different from the timbers he was used to. It was similar in style and figure to the red timber of the Red River Gum from the Eastern States but was harder and had a tighter grain.

Once you got used to it, it was a wonderful timber to work with. He would hope he would get the opportunity to use it again when (if) he got back home after the Western Front. The miners would dig, the carpenters would timber and the electricians would wire. This went on all day until the commanders were satisfied with the results.

Day 2 dawned with the hope of an easier day. For the next 3 years they would hope the next day would be easier, but like today, they were most often disappointed. Before breakfast today the men were paraded for a route march. Off they went, almost all the 1300, carrying their rifles which weighed around 10 lb. (nearly 5 kg), practice ammunition, kit, and water. All up, around 40 lb. (18 kg) was carried by the men. The first stage of the march took them north around 5 miles (8km) to a pre-arranged farm where breakfast was provided.

From here the corps marched a further 8 miles (13km) with regular breaks until lunch, which was held in the Swan Valley.

After lunch, they headed for the camp again, but this, of course, was, by now, some ten miles (16km) away. They made it home by 1730, exhausted but also proud that they had accomplished such a feat. They had been on long marches in the earlier weeks but nothing like this. Nothing this long and arduous. Naturally, they all wanted to know the purpose of such an exercise, and naturally there was no answer forthcoming. They were awfully glad that they did not challenge the record set in 1914 by the 3rd Field Ambulance when they marched thirty two miles (50km) in one day. Little did they know, that, for what was to come, they would need that physical strength, toughness and endurance, as well as mental toughness. This march was just part of the process.

Dinner that night was a noticeably quiet affair, as most were just too tired to be bothered. The evening session was not a taxing one. There was just a lecture and the men were left to themselves after that. Most just went back to their hut and went to bed. Bob went back to his hut and checked through his equipment. He identified the items needing attention and cleaned it ready for tomorrow. He understood one way to get the Sergeant offside, was to go on parade with unclean equipment. Boots, webbing, brass, rifle and hat. As tired as he was, he also realised that care of your equipment was paramount and made your life a lot easier on parade, but could also save your life in conflict, by everything being in good order and ready to use. So, he polished, brushed and oiled until he could go no further. Keeping him going though, was Bill. Once again, the two of them were working together, to ensure that they made it through. After all, what are mates for? Sleep came quickly for them both. No one heard the last post that night.

Day 3 commenced normally for the 1st Australian Mining Corps. Morning muster, breakfast and morning parade and inspection. Only today, the men were told to parade at 9.30am with full kit, including water bottle, filled and blanket roll. The men instinctively knew what was in store for them today, a route march. And sure enough, after muster and roll check, "Parade will advance in column of route…Right turn. Parade… by the left, quick march." They were off on a route march alright. All the way, to Mundaring Weir, almost twelve miles (20km) away. But not just any twelve miles. twelve miles, uphill.

Blackboy Hill was at the foot of the Darling Scarp. Anywhere to the east, was uphill, a steep hill at that. They marched off down Innaminca Road to the

York Road, now known as Great Eastern Highway, Perth's road link to the Eastern States. After just half a mile march (800m) the RSM called a left wheel and they commenced their climb. It is a winding climb, not high by world standards, but if you are on foot, and carrying a 40lb pack (18Kg) and carrying a 10lb rifle (4.5kg) and wearing, heavy studded boots, and dressed head to toe in a wool tunic and breeches, well, anything above flat would be steep.

Onwards and upwards they trudged, passing nothing much other that the occasional vehicle but lots of scrub, trees and flies. Oh, the flies. They landed on your back and took turns at flying around into your face, particularly your eyes and nose. You knew they covered your back because you could see them on everybody else's back. It did not matter, how many you swatted, there were always plenty to fill their place. Some of the locally sourced troops, dealt with that situation by breaking off a small branch from any of the plentiful scrub and marched with that in front of their face. It was not long before most of the guys had done the same. Sergeants and officers turned a blind eye to this rather nonmilitary equipment, as they knew too, just how bad the flies were. At the twomile mark, they passed Darlington Road, but still the road in front continued to climb.

Mostly, the road was quite wide, but there were bits where the road had been carved from the granite, and they were a bit narrower, so they did not want to meet traffic in those places. Mile three passed, and the road started to level out and they all gave a sigh of relief. There were even a few downhill parts, but they were always followed by another uphill section. At least it gave their muscles a chance to recuperate. This section of the road was a beautiful section. The trees were larger and offered more shade. The temperature was around the 75° F (24° C) mark, so was certainly warm enough that the shade was a welcome relief. The road wound on through sweeping bends and up and down until at 1pm the boss called a halt. 1 hour lunch break, and what a welcome break it was. They had covered almost six miles since the 10am start. Not a bad effort for troops carrying packs and uphill. They sheltered in a valley in the shade of the trees, a small distance away from the Mahogany Creek Inn.

One of the locals told the story that "Moondyne Joe" had holed out in the roof of the Inn, on one of his many breakouts. 'Moondyne Joe', whose real name was Joseph Bolitho Johns, was an English copper miner, who came to Australia in the mid-19th century. He set up farming fifty miles (80km) to the east of their present location around York, in an area now known as Moondyne. He once trapped a horse that had no brand, so he put his own brand on it, which was effectively horse stealing, for which he was arrested. He broke out of the Today Goal that night and re-stole the horse and rode off into the night. He later killed the horse and cut his brand out so there was no evidence to convict him of horse stealing. He was recaptured and only charged with escaping custody, receiving a short sentence for that.

Some years later, he was arrested again for cattle stealing and received a ten year, hard labour sentence. He loudly protested his innocence of this crime, for the rest of his life. He gained notoriety due to his plentiful escapes from prison, and on one of his freedom jaunts, he hid from the police in the ceiling of the 'Mahogany Inn'. He became one of Western Australia's most notorious Bushrangers, although his crimes were all crimes of property, not personal injury. His escapes were so prolific that they even built a special cell for him in Fremantle Prison. It was lined with Jarrah sleepers 6" thick (150mm).

Jarrah is a particularly hard wood, but if that was not enough, the sleepers were then impaled with hundreds of steel nails, so effectively he was incarcerated in a wall of hardwood and steel. He still escaped. At this point the miners who had been listening to this story all cheered. Not too fond of the law, were the miners, overall. Anyway, apparently, he sort of faded away in the end, succumbing to insanity or something and passed away in his 70s as an inmate at the Fremantle mental asylum.

The men just sat and listened intently, to the recounting of this wonderful story. The discussion that followed contained opinions from, being glad he got away, through to the police need more public support. There would never be complete agreement other than it was a great story. Either way it whiled away the lunch break, not that they were in any hurry to get back on the road.

Lunch now being over, it was time to reform and continue the onward march to the Weir. Not yet quite halfway there yet, there was a collective groan when the order to reform was given by Lt Woodward. They still had two miles (3km) to go on the York Road before getting to Mundaring, where they would turn towards the Weir. After lunch, and a rest, the pace quickened as there was no big climb to negotiate. So, not before too long, they found themselves marching through the small settlement of Mundaring, a town set up to service the construction of the Dam fifteen years previously.

As the town was on the main road east, it has remained as a service town for the region. It is a quaint little town with a mixture of old English and colonial architecture. A right wheel and the troops swung to the south, crossed the railway line and headed off through the bush to the Dam site, still another 4 miles (6.5km) away. By 5pm the dam was well and truly in sight and so was the end of their route march. No sooner had they arrived and had another break, when the order came to set up the bivouac. The men set about setting the tents and moving in, when Lt Woodward called for a group of previously trained men, to practice advanced Guard duty. This involved those with prior military training, so that included Bill and Bob. This practice lasted for an hour and was pretty hard going all round, not the least because it was actually a case of the blind leading the blind. Most of the officers were just as raw as their recruits.

Eventually, they mastered the basics of forming and executing the guard. The officers finally came to agreement on what the book was telling them and managed to get it across to the men. Truth be told, the men being taught, had more military training and experience than the officers at that stage, so between them all, they managed a relatively good guard.

*

Mundaring Weir was completed only thirteen years ago, but most of the fellows had heard of it. It was part of an extremely ambitious scheme, proposed a few years prior, by a Western Australian engineer named Charles Yelverton O'Connor. O'Connor was in fact the engineer behind the Fremantle harbour that their ship the Useless, was being repaired in currently. With the discovery of gold in Coolgardie in 1892 and the subsequent finds in Kalgoorlie, the population of the two towns skyrocketed, Coolgardie's population alone, peaked out at 16,000 during the goldrush and Kalgoorlie went way over that.

The main problem for these people at the time was the lack of water. There was no fresh water available in the area. The government then set up condensers to distil drinking water, from the abundant salt water that was available in the region. However, this was an expensive solution and the amount of wood needed to fire the condensers was rapidly denuding the area, an area where the growth was already slow due to the lack of rain.

O'Connor proposed building a dam in the hills of Perth, on the Helena River and pumping the water via a pipeline 330 miles (530 km) to Kalgoorlie. It would also be used to provide water for settlements along the way. O'Connor met a huge amount of criticism for this outrageous scheme, but he was determined to accomplish it. He convinced the government of the day, to agree to the scheme and it was commenced in 1896. His plan was to build the dam on the Helena River, a small river that feeds into the Swan River, in order to provide a water supply. Then by a series of 8 pumping stations, pump the water through a 30" (760 mm) pipeline all the way to the Mt Charlotte reservoir in Kalgoorlie. This was to cost an estimated 2.5 million pounds (5 million dollars). The dam, when completed in 1902, was the highest overflow dam in the world and was raised by a further nine metres, this being completed in 1951.

O'Connor was hounded by certain sectors of the press and some members of parliament. His principal opponent was the editor of the Sunday Times, Thomas Walker, and he published many an editorial lambasting O'Connor and the scheme. "The gold will dry up and we will be left with a white elephant scheme, even if it works, which I doubt" was the sort of comments regularly printed. One particularly vehement article was published on 9th February 1902 and read in part:

And apart from any distinct charge of corruption this man has exhibited such gross blundering or something worse, in his management of great public works it is no exaggeration to say that he has robbed the taxpayer of this state of many millions of money...This crocodile imposter has been backed up in all his reckless extravagant juggling with public funds, in all his nefarious machinations behind the scenes by the kindred-souled editor of The West Australian. Sunday Times 9/2/1902

Of course, the gold did not run out. Large quantities of gold are still mined at Kalgoorlie and its surrounding areas, and the scheme did work and continues to work to this day. Also, a commission of inquiry found absolutely no evidence of corruption in the scheme. The pumps were started at Mundaring Weir on 22nd January 1903 and two days later water flowed into the reservoir in Kalgoorlie. O'Connor was not there to see it, however. Following the Sunday Times article above, on 10th March O'Connor took his horse for a ride into the surf just south of Fremantle and shot himself. The man was a genius and ahead of his time. His two major projects, Fremantle Harbour and the Goldfields Water Supply Scheme, were both projects he was told were impossible.

*

Dinner was followed by a short break, which gave the men time to explore the Weir and the surrounds, some even went swimming.

After this, the evening consisted of a rather impromptu concert which was a load of fun as nothing was either rehearsed or scripted. Everyone turned in early tonight as it was to be an early start tomorrow. Early start did I say? Reveille was at 2am, followed by breakfast and break camp. March off occurred at 4am with the newly practiced No 1 Company Guard leading the way. Back they went all the way to Mundaring, where they arrived at 7am and were granted a two hour break. The guard led off again at 9, headed towards Blackboy Hill, only this time they all knew it was downhill once they got to the top of the scarp. Oh, so much easier than yesterday they thought, but yesterday's difficult was destined to become tomorrow's easy, even though tomorrow was still a few months away.

The weary men arrived back at Blackboy Hill Camp at midday, and as soon as lunch was over, they were all given the afternoon off. After cleaning their gear, sleep was the priority.

The next day was split, with half the company in the morning on weapons drill and the other half on camp maintenance. The second half of the day is then reversed. The weapons drill included dismantling, deep cleaning and reassembling all the different weapons. For most of the men that is their Lee Enfield .303 Mk III or III* (SMLE). It was simple in its construction but works best, naturally, when it is clean. So, clean it they did. Over and over again. Pull it apart. Put it together. Pull it apart. Put it together. They did it so often they could just about do it with their eyes closed, which, of course, is the whole idea.

In the heat of battle, the men need to be able to clear and fix a jammed weapon, without having to think about it. They learned how to protect their weapon from sand and mud. How valuable a lesson for them, this was, they did not realise, but they would find out shortly. Perhaps if they did know they would have packed up right there and then and headed home. This was then followed by practice firing exercises, using dummy ammunition. Live firing was still to come.

The other half of the day entailed the clearing of hut sites, as the buildings were still being erected following last year's storm, erecting huts, general clean up and maintenance and digging of rubbish pits; after all, if miners can't dig a hole, then who can? As a carpenter, Bob found his skills of use in the construction area as most of the buildings were of course, timber and Bill was able to put his plumbing into practice as well. At least today the guys all felt more at home with the work they were being asked to do.

Day six saw a four way split of the company between half day on camp maintenance / building again and a half day split between weapons training and live firing on the rifle range. Finally, the men got to actually fire their weapon. For many of the men this was a first time live firing a rifle and for many more they were hoping it would also be their last, although they mostly realised this would be a vain hope. After all they were in the army even though they still mostly considered themselves as a group of miners on special assignment first and soldiers second. Some of them even got to see what happens when you live fire a .303 if it has not been cleaned properly. It could kick like a mule and if you were not ready for it. It could really turn a shoulder black and blue. It was certainly incentive to ensure the barrel of your weapon was clean.

That evening, the men attended an evening of entertainment at the YMCA hall. A concert had been arranged, primarily on their behalf, to wish them well, for their onward journey. An excerpt, from the Daily News of the following Tuesday, gave a report of the evening's entertainment.

Y.M.C.A. MILITARY WORK

A Soldier's Own Night was held in the YMCA hall, at Blackboy Hill on Saturday evening, and attracted the large crowd of men. Mr J. V. Wederburn presided. A lengthy and varied program, including songs, recitations, piano forte selections, and exhibitions of weightlifting, was gone through. The novelty of the entertainment was greatly appreciated, and the efforts of the numerous artists quite delighted the audience. The following took part in the program: Privates M Hancock, McKenzie, Cockerill, Martin, Percy Trotter, Snell, McGrath, Marlow, Morris and Sorensen.

The Daily News, Tuesday, 28 March 1916

Day seven and only two days before final leave, but who is counting? Today the men are all to be involved with field exercises. Whilst the Mining Corps is unlikely to be engaged in infantry style tactics, the CO thinks it will be good, if they understand a little of how they work. Besides, who knows what may befall the men of the Mining Corps when they are on the Western Front. They may be required for combat if things do not go to plan. Ordinarily, the men of the 1st

Mining Corps would not be expected to be involved with infantry style combat, as they were primarily there only to prepare the ground for the troops to fight, not to actually do the fighting. However, in war things do not always go to plan, so it was best to have the men prepared, just in case they were needed to fight.

The men were not disappointed at the day's programme for a change. At least it was not a route march. Anyway, this was more like playing games. It is just that with these games learning to do it properly can save your life and the lives of your mates. The men were divided into platoon-sized groups and spread around the campsite and many different techniques were discussed and practiced. The British way of battle of the time, was basically jump up over the trench wall and charge down the enemy regardless of the level of enemy fire. Men were expendable and the army with the most men would win. 'Collateral Damage' is the term used to describe such a needless loss of life, but to the British command structure, drawn almost exclusively from the upper class, as distinct from progressing through the army ranks, the loss of lower class life, the troops, was a necessary, if unfortunate situation.

The advantage of the Australian way of life, is that basically everyone is an equal. We have no class structure, well at least no formal class structure. As such, where the General, or the Lieutenant for that matter, is of the same social standing as the man he is ordering to do something, more consideration is given to the humanity of the order. This does have a downside though. If the soldier does not agree with the officer, he is just as likely to tell him to "get stuffed" or worse, a disposition that has got many an Aussie digger into hot water over the years, especially with the British establishment. To many of the British Officers, Aussies troops were uncouth, untrained and undisciplined colonials.

The Australian command had a different attitude to combat strategy, and they were going to make sure our troops did not fall into the same tragic strategies of the British. We had learned something in the Dardanelles of combat and the pitfalls of the current thinking. It had not been a total loss. Little did they know that despite their convictions, command on the Western Front would be dominated by British Military strategies, whether they liked it or not. After all, when the British had millions of men and the Australians had 300 000 it would be natural for the British to be in command. It took an Australian General, Monash, to take over late in the war, to change this attitude to battle strategy.

So, our men would try some of these different approaches in the camp and allow the officers to evaluate the effectiveness of the differing strategies. It was good for both the men and the officers to try something different, instead of the same old things. Times are changing, war is changing so ideas and strategies must change. For one thing, mechanisation is now starting to influence the battlefields. The tank is on the horizon, bigger and faster machine guns and artillery and the aircraft warfare, is about to make its presence felt. The other good thing about today's proceedings, was that there were plenty of breaks between exercises, as the officers set up the next scenario. Not much to do except sit back under the trees and wait. From the camp, which is no more than 100 ft above the Perth coastal plain, the men would have sweeping 180° views right through to the city some fifteen miles (25km) distant. The men thought this was a good way to spend their days.

By the time the evening mess came around, the mood in the camp was once again upbeat. Whilst the men were tired having to put in another full day, they were satisfied that they had at least done something today, where they could see a point to it. In their own minds though, they were also hoping that they would never have to get involved in combat. The overwhelming feeling Bob had on this day, was that of fear. Fear that they would have to confront all sorts of horrible situations. After all, war is about death. Killing more of the other guys than they can kill, of your mates.

Bob looked around the room. Would we all make it home? How many of these guys will we leave behind? How much actual conflict will we be a part of? Ok, we may be the Mining Corps, but we won't be underground all the time, will we? So many questions, with so few answers. Once they were all underground, they would feel a lot more at home, and safer, or so they thought.

Day eight, Monday and the camp is alive with excitement. The intercompany sports day has arrived. The six teams involved were the 1st, 2nd, and 3rd Miners (Tunnellers), Infantry and 10th Light Horse. With Morning inspection and Breakfast out of the way the troops from all the different Battalions at Blackboy Hill, were hard in preparation for the afternoon sports. A look around the camp and so many different activities were evident. There were men preparing for boxing, there were five different classes to be contested, field events like standing long jump, hop, step and jump, high jump, novelty events like the Sack race, Wheelbarrow race, Tug of War, running events and even a Parade Drill competition. The competition was to take place down at the Helena Vale racecourse just a short march away from the camp, on the other side of the railway line.

Many relatives and friends were expected to be in attendance for this day as it was one of the few opportunities, they got to see the men in action together. It would also be the swansong for the men of the mining corps, as they were due to be leaving shortly and it would give the people of WA an opportunity to say, goodbye, again, and good luck, as there was to be no departure parade through the streets, as this had already happened when they left the first time, 3 weeks ago. It would be a little embarrassing to repeat what had already been done.

Bob and Bill decided their part in the day was to be in the Drill, so they spent the morning running through the sequences they were using in their display, with the rest of the team. Many of the men of the mining battalion were involved and were taking things seriously as much pride depended on success, in these competitions. Once there is a competition between men in these situations, things become serious. There are many bragging rights attached to wins, in these circumstances. So, the training had been slow to start with but once the idea of bragging rights became obvious, it turned serious. The men were ready for battle. Bring it on.

After a quick lunch, the men were all marched down to the racecourse and the competitions got under way. The camp commandant, Lt Col Battye was present along with other dignitaries, to observe the afternoon's proceedings. The event of the afternoon was the inter battalion Tug of War. The No 1 Miners (Bob's mob) beat the tunnellers, The No 2 Miners beat the Infantry and the No 3 Miners beat the Light Horse. The overall winners in this event were the No 2 Miners after the semis and final. So, the Mining company had well and truly stamped their authority on this test of strength.

In the boxing events, there were three rings set up, and all bouts in all divisions were limited to three rounds. The mining corps again did well but the eventual winners in each of the weight divisions were named but their battalion origins were not recorded. The West Australian newspaper of the 29th of March listed the results of the day.

Heavy-weight	1st Judd	2nd Birrell
Middle-weight	1st Jobson	2nd Flatt
Light-weight	1st Hickling	2nd Purcell
9 Stone	1st Summers	2nd Hincks
8 Stone	1st Claudius	

We have been able to determine the details of most of these men.

Judd was probably, 153 Daniel Sydney Judd, 32, of the 1st Mining Corps, a metalworker, possibly from Cobar NSW. He was Returned to Australia 23rd September 1918 suffering from Cardiovascular debility.

Birrell was 923 Nicholas Henry Birrell (eventually Sgt) 44, 1st Mining Corps, from Melbourne Vic. He listed his occupation as Miner, Norseman WA. He was RTA 21st July 1918 having been gassed in May and classified, premature senility.

Jobson. There does not appear to be any possible matches within the AIF to this name being at Blackboy Hill camp, so it is probable this was a typographical error. The likely misspell would be for the name Hobson, to which there is a match. It is probable then that this was, 89 Roy Napoleon Hobson, 18, 44th Battalion AIF, a railway porter of Fremantle WA. He was twice WIA in January 1917, October 1917 then KIA April 1918.

Flatt was 2817 Charles Edwin Flatt, 20, 10th Light Horse. He was WIA in Gaza and taken POW. He was RTA 5th March 1919.

Hickling was probably 25400 Ernest Hickling, 25, 3rd Divisional Ammunition Column. He lists his occupation as fireman and was from East Perth WA. RTA 16th January 1919.

Purcell was probably 5457 Peter Purcell, 39, 11th Battalion AIF, a labourer from Perth WA. (Ex-Kilkenny Ireland). Peter was RTA 28th August 1917, ill with tachycardia.

Summers was probably Lt Lionel Logan Summers MC, 28, 11th Battalion AIF, a railway transport officer, of Perth WA. Lt Summers DOW 12th November 1917.

Hincks was 134 Thomas Hincks, 22, 1st Mining Corps, a miner of New Lamton NSW. Repatriated to English hospital 30th August 1918 and RTA 8th January 1919.

Claudius, was 24573 Leslie C Claudius, 21, 3rd DAC, a fitter from North Perth. He was RTA 23rd July 1919.

In the track and field events 5 different competitions tested the men. There was the standing long jump, the high jump and the hop, step and jump (triple jump). Results of these again courtesy of "The West".

Standing long jump	1st McAuley	2nd Allcorn	3rd Monkhouse
High jump	1st Wilkinson 5ft (1.52m)	2nd Plunkett	3rd Grogan
Hop, Step and jump	1st Wilkinson 44ft (13.38m)	2nd McAuley	
Running 100 Yards	1st Robinson	2nd Brown	3rd Wisbey
Running 440 Yds (400m)	1st A R Brown	2nd Liddelow	3rd Truran

McAuley. There are no McAuleys registered with the AIF that could be possibly our man, so it is again assumed there is a spelling error in the name. This was probably 599 Sgt Donald Macaulay, DCM, MM, 22, C coy 44th Battalion, AIF Labourer, Perth WA. Born Stornaway Scotland, discharged in England Medically unfit, GSW right forearm, amputated above the elbow. He appears to have remained in the UK after discharge. His name was even misspelt several times on his own record papers.

Allcorn (Again looks to be an issue with the spelling of this name) was probably 2818 Raymond Leslie Alcorn, 35, Initially 1st Mining Corps (at the time of this event at Blackboy Hill) and later 5th Battalion AIF, a miner of North Perth WA. RTA invalid, 21st July 1918.

Monkhouse was 5156 George Monkhouse, MM, 20, 11th Battalion AIF, later 3rd Divisional Signal Co., Electrical Engineer of East Fremantle WA. RTA 3rd September 1919.

Wilkinson was 4580 Robert Hooper Wilkinson, 28, 28th Battalion AIF, Farmhand from Cranbrook WA. Sick to hospital twice. WIA twice. GSW arm, chest, neck. Shell shocked. RTA 9th July 1917

Plunket, 1127 John, 33, 3rd Mining Corps, Miner, Kalgoorlie WA. DOW (Gas) 3rd April 1917

Wisbey, 5463 John Edward, 22, 16th Battalion AIF, Horse driver, from Bayswater WA. RTA sick, trench foot, nephritis 10th April 1917.

Brown A R, one of two possibilities. Probably 26921 Alexander Robert, 27, 11th Battalion AIF, later 13th FAB, Clerk, Perth WA. RTA 1st June 1919.

However, it may have been 672 Aubrey Ralph Thomas (later Cpl) MSM, MID, 34, 11th Battalion AIF, Public servant, from West Swan WA, RTA 21st June 1919.

Liddelow, 2472 Thomas Leslie, 3rd MGS 10th Light Horse, Farmhand of Perth WA. RTA 10th July 1919

Truran, Thomas Charles, 38, 58th Depot (Blackboy Hill camp), never allocated to an AIF battalion, Farmhand, Bunbury WA. Discharged medically unfit 20th June 1916.

There were also two novelty events that afternoon as well. There was the sack race and the wheelbarrow race. These brought a great deal of mirth to the afternoon. Some took these seriously, but most looked upon them as a moment for some fun and levity. The sack race saw some of the contestants tumble and roll and some others made sure some of their mates did not make the finish line, at least not still in their sack anyway. Much sabotage seemed to be the order of the day. Similarly, the wheelbarrow race was plagued with subterfuge. In this race, there are two contestants on each team. One member is face down standing on his hands and his partner is standing holding the first's legs, like the handles of a wheelbarrow. As many of the mining corps were, of course, miners, they were well acquainted with the pushing of the wheelbarrow around the goldfields.

The goldrush in Western Australia occurred predominantly in the 1890s with the discovery of gold in Coolgardie by Arthur Bayley and William Ford in 1892 and Paddy Hannan in Kalgoorlie in 1893 and the state's population exploded in the ten or so years after. Many of the miners of this era walked hundreds of miles pushing their wheelbarrow and digging tools from all parts of the state to the goldfields to be a part of this goldrush. As a result, the wheelbarrow race held special significance for many of the men of the mining corps.

Whilst the men of the Mining Corps may have claimed superiority around the wheelbarrow race, it became a source of considerable embarrassment that it was won by a team from the infantry.

Sack race   1st Buck   2nd Shacklock   3rd Milne
Wheelbarrow   1st Monkhouse and Truran
race   2nd Shacklock and Potter
        3rd Kelly and Thomas

Buck, was 1630 Arthur Victor Buck, 24, 51st Battalion AIF, and was a wheelwright of Perth WA. He was KIA 2nd April 1917.

Shacklock was Lt Ernest Frederick Shacklock, 27 (Pte at the time) 11th Battalion AIF, an accountant of Subiaco WA. RTA invalid, 30th May 1919.

Milne was probably 4845 Henry Joseph Milne, 39, 51st Battalion AIF, a dairy hand of Armadale WA. RTA 1st February 1919, debility.

Monkhouse is probably 5156 Spr George Monkhouse MM, 20, 11th Battalion AIF, eventually Aust. Corps Signals Coy, RTA 19th October 1919.

Truran, Thomas Charles, described previously.

Kelly, is 5035A Arthur Charles Kelly, later CQMS, 26, 44th Battalion AIF, a store manager of Narabri NSW. WIA (Mustard Gassed) RTA 16th December 1918.

Potter, is likely 2281 Albert Richard Potter, 33, 44th Battalion AIF, a Jeweller of Perth, WA. RTA 4th November 1919

Thomas, is likely 2991 Frederick Reginald Thomas, later Sgt, 29, 3rd Pioneer Battalion AIF, a Wine and Spirit merchant originally from Kiama NSW. WIA by GSW right foot, 6th September 1918. RTA 3rd March 1919

The final events were the bandsmen's race and the O'Grady Drill. The Mining Corps had a sort of unofficial band, made up of members with a musical background. This had formed whilst they were still in Liverpool camp in Sydney. It was a few men who discovered they had a common interest in music. Their instruments were accumulated from a range of their own and a few donated ones. This band had formed themselves but were taken on by the Corps as their own. (Sadly, once they arrived in England the instruments were pawned to provide for more weapons for the Corps.) The band was immensely popular and provided many musical interludes throughout the day's proceedings.

As for the drill demonstration Bob and Bill and their team, were soundly beaten by the men of the 10th Light Horse.

Bandsmen's race 1st J Knox   2nd A Pumfrey 3rd J Bourke

O'Grady Drill 1st Fullerton, Humphries, Henderson, Reynolds, Stewart, Martin

Knox was 1366 James Knox, 29, AEMM&BC and was a carpenter of Grafton NSW. RTA 5t March 1919

A. Pumfrey was 1384 Cpl Albert Pumfrey, 26, AEMM&BC, hairdresser of Sydney NSW. RTA 12 May 1919.

Bourke was 1342 L/Cpl John Patrick, 25, AEMM&BC, hairdresser of Wellington NSW. RTA 11 May 1919.

Fullerton was 2816 William John Fullerton 31, 10th Light Horse, a clerk from Subiaco WA. RTA 5 February 1918, debility.

Humphries was 2467 Bertie Connick Humphries 25, 10th Light Horse, a boiler maker from Mt Lawley WA. RTA 17 July 1916, invalid.

Henderson was 24254 Arthur Norman Henderson 20, 10th Light Horse, a school teacher of Geraldton WA. RTA 5 July 1919.

Reynolds looks to be 2481 Bert Reynolds, 21, 10th Light Horse (initially, then to the Camel Corps later), a labourer of York WA. KIA 6 November 1917, GSW head

Of the 33 possible identities here, 13 were either wounded, or too ill to continue and 5 dead. 18 out of 33 of the men, who on this day, were there for the fun of the event, either never came home or were affected for the rest of their lives. Not to mention the ones who came home mentally affected and never recorded.

Every single one of these men, has their own story to be told, as well. They should be told too, but the sad fact is that many of them will not be told and thus will be lost to history and to us all forever. Whilst it is never too late to start, much of the information is now, lost forever. Sometimes the value of this information is not recognised, by us, until it is too late.

The day was kept moving quickly, with up to four events in progress at any one time. At the same time, the band from the Mining Corps continued to provide entertainment, for those who were more inclined to the musical side of life. There is also mention of an artillery drive demonstration by two six horse teams, out of Guildford and this added yet another dimension to the day. There was a need at the time to bolster recruitment, so whilst the day was an outlet for the men of the camp, it was also an opportunity to promote further recruitment.

The day appears to have been a roaring success, and the camp commander, Lt Col Battye, congratulated the men on their performance and took the opportunity to wish the men of the 1st Australian Mining Corps, the best of luck as they embark for France in just four days. After the awards were presented to the winners and runners up, the men regrouped and were marched back to the camp, as high as kites. The standard of the march started off beautifully, but soon deteriorated, as the high spirits took hold and they got away from the audience at the racecourse. For the men of the Mining Corps, this day, meant the end of their time in camp and three days leave before sailing for France.

Chapter 6
Final Family Weekend

Tuesday morning and there were no complaints about rising today. Morning muster, Breakfast and inspection done and dusted, and the men marched for the train station. It was going to take more than one train to move this lot today. Midland first stop, Perth second stop and then they were all going in different directions. Bob caught the next Fremantle line train, just the one station and walked up to Florence St; well almost ran. He did not have to knock on the door as Jessie was sitting by the window "reading a book." She was really just watching out for Bob to arrive. Even though she knew by now he was in love with Jean, she was still smitten by him. Great excitement was exclaimed when he came into view. They all rushed out to greet him as they were aware this was the last opportunity before embarkation. Well, almost all anyway. Jean did not need to rush out, she already knew who Bob was coming to see. She just casually wandered to the door and greeted him quite formally.

"Good morning, Mr Hood!"—somewhat tongue in cheek. Then Bob made a point of greeting Mimey personally, Robert of course, being already hard at work in the bakery in Carr St. Jack too was absent, as this being a Tuesday, he was at work too, in the law office. That morning was spent just discussing the week's proceedings and enjoying the garden. So much had gone on this week, but all Bob wanted to do was get away with Jean and have some time together alone.

The girls had some shopping needing to be done, so they all trained to Perth central after lunch and spent the afternoon plying the shops in Hay St, Murray St, Barrack and William St. Bob was just content, being the chaperone for the ladies, if it meant walking with Jean. He became the pack horse carrying the ladies' shopping. He still managed to get away to check out some of the men's shops, but really, he was just along for the walk. His only respite came when they all decided to stop off for tea, at the cafeteria on the upper floor, of Boan's department store.

This was one of the best cafeterias in Perth at the time, commanding a third floor position overlooking the train station and Wellington St. It was so nice to sit down and just enjoy the time with Jean, even if Jessie and Berta were both there. After the last couple of weeks training and route marching, this was an exceedingly pleasant interlude. He was rather fond of both the younger ladies, but he desperately wanted to spend some alone time with Jean. He knew however that this was unlikely to happen, so he learnt to enjoy the time as he had it.

Inevitably, the conversation centred around yesterday afternoon's newspaper article about the foundering of the Useless on exiting Fremantle harbour. Although the ship was not mentioned by name, most likely for security reasons, it was obvious to which incident it referred. The ship's master and officers were cleared of any wrongdoing and the blame was clearly placed on the Fremantle Port Authority Pilot, Capt. Williamson.

Many of the men on board the ship at the time had already formed their own opinion and it was not that of pilot blame. It was clear that the shallower water was not properly marked, and the pilot had been forced wide by the entering ship, S.S. Indarra. The pilot did admit being further from the centre line than he had intended but believed he was still safe. A letter to the editor of "The Daily News" paper that afternoon summarised the feelings of the Mining Corps in general.

FAIR PLAY (To the Editor)

Sir, I am one of the soldiers in camp at Blackboy and we have all been feeling proud to think that we are, soon going away to fight for our King and our glorious country of freedom and justice. But all our gladness received a check when we took up your paper this afternoon and read your account of a vessel grounding. We have been following this case. I was a seafaring man before enlisting and was on the spot when the vessel struck. I challenge any sailor in Fremantle to prove that there was known foul ground at that spot. The whole facts lie in a nutshell. Why hold back the truth? The vessel struck an uncharted rock, and they are making the individual suffer for the Port.

Mr Scaddan came to our camp and spoke to us, promising us that when we return, he would see that we were put before anyone else in the matter of work, but now we feel downhearted. Should we return, wounded or maimed, shall we receive West Australian justice as shown in the case mentioned? Will some of your correspondents reply to prevent our going away with a wrong impression of our country men's sense of justice?—

Yours, etc., A SOLDIER. 27 March 1916.

They continued the discussion with all sorts of things, mostly superficial but Bob was simply happy to be there, so he joined in on topics like the price of bread now, the latest motor cars, how busy it was becoming in Perth now and how much they are being expected to do to assist Father in the shop. All the while Bob was wondering what the future would hold for him. In 3 days, he would be off to war. He was putting his life on the line for the "Empire," and it just made him think how silly these discussions were. They were really not of much significance, given the context of the times. They were issues however that were important to people at that time.

To the average person in Australia, the war was a world away and was not therefore having much impact on them. That was, unless they had a son or brother or father serving in the AIF. Those people were acutely aware of the impact of the war, on their everyday living. Scanning the papers every day, looking for familiar names on the casualty lists. Dreading the postie who delivered the telegrams. Praying he would ride on by to, well, anywhere else.

"Anywhere else but here... Please don't stop here...Keep going, keep going ... Thank God he didn't stop here." This was something the Chappells were going to learn about first-hand soon enough.

Late afternoon and the four of them, rose from their tea and headed for the station, only a couple of hundred yards away. Spirits were still high, and Berta was chirping and skipping back and forward, all the way through Forrest Place, past the GPO to the train station. After about 10 minutes, they were already walking up the slope to Florence St, Bob still carrying all the shopping. Jean was thinking what a handsome figure he was in his AIF tunic and breeches. Arriving back at No 10, Robert was already home and greeted them at the door. He could hear them coming up the street. He was glad to see Bob, he liked him a lot. For someone, he had only known for 2-3 weeks, it was strange how much he admired and respected him. The feeling, by the way, was completely mutual. Bob felt he had found a friend in Robert and Mimey Chappell.

With dinner over, Robert headed off to bed. He had to be up again at 1 am to start the bread for that day. So, he bid them all goodnight and left them for a quiet evening of cards and reading. Jack had arrived home as well, and he and Bob spent some time together discussing the state of the war. Much had been written in the papers about the current situation. Both were concerned about the reports of the success of the German submarines on allied shipping. Upward of 20 ships had been sunk in the last month by these subs, of which half were British. A sobering thought given that within the next 3 days Bob would be on one of those ships that would be considered a target by the Germans. That the British supremacy on the sea was being challenged, by the German Navy, meant that another dimension had been added to the conflict, and a worrying dimension at that it was. Whether the 'Ulysses' was up to it or not, the boys agreed that the hastily needed repairs would probably not help. That made Bob rather nervous. Another story in today's paper indicated that the British had detonated a mine under the German trenches, destroying a large section of their system.

Bob commented on this, "Well I guess tha' will be ma lot befoor too long Jack. Tha's if this war is still goin' on by the time we get there."

"Aye I suppose that's true enough Bob. How dae ye feel aboot that?" Jack asked.

"Actually, I dinnae rightly knaw," Bob replied. "I mean, par' o' me wants it tae still be goin' on, but the other par' says, I want it done wi' ba then. I dinnae, I guess it would be a shame if it were over, all this would be for nothin'." However, he now felt he had a reason to come home safely. He went on, "I'm noe really a fightin' man, dae ye ken? Bu' at the same time, I cannae abide this bullyin' ba these darn Huns. Soe I guess someone has tae step up and stop 'em in their tracks."

"Aye, Bob, they do. I think Australia wouldn't be there unless the British were there though, dae ye?" asked Jack.

"Och noe, not a chance man," answered Bob. "There is the New Guinea and Bougainville issue, bu' that's only the by and by. Noe, we're in it because the British are in there. Le's face it, we here, in this country, are really just an ootpost of tha British Empire. Mind ye, I'd rather be here than there." They both laughed and agreed on that point.

East and west Scottish accents are quite different. It is said one can always tell the difference, between a Glasgow accent and an Edinburgh accent, even though the two cities are only thirty seven miles (60 km) apart. The Edinburgh accent is perhaps more refined, whereas the Glasgow accent clips many last letters off words. For example, that, becomes tha', myself, becomes masel' and words like, to and do, are pronounced more like tae and dae, albeit pronounced very short. The Glaswegian is more likely to use, aye instead of yes, where the Ediburghers or 'Toonies' as they are sometimes called, will use either, depending on the usage.

The last two days of Bob's stay at the Chappells, started with the surprise that, not only were Robert and Jack at work already but so was Jean. Being the eldest of the girls, she was expected to put time into the bakery as well, and she would spend some mornings helping out. Robert would head off for the Carr St bakery at 1 am. Because the bread takes 3-4 hours to produce, it needs to be started early in the morning, so that it is ready for the customers when the shops open in the morning. The dough would need to be mixed and kneaded first of all, then left to prove (rise) for about an hour, when it would be kneaded down again. It would then stand to be proved again and then finally into the oven to cook. In between the provings, he would work on the other bakery products, the pastries, rolls, currant loaves, lamingtons, pies and pasties. By the time all this was done he would need extra help in the bakery preparing for the day's trade. That is when the girls would help out in the mornings.

As disappointed as he was, Bob settled down to breakfast with Mimey and the two remaining girls. "Good morning, Mimey," he said as he walked into the kitchen.

"Oh, good morning, Bob," she replied. "How did ye sleep?"

"I slept the sleep o' the dead," came the reply. "I cannae sleep well, on the beds at camp. Tha' bed oot there, is like sleepin' in heaven." He drew an imaginary line through the air with his hand and tucked it under his left ear, so as to make a pillow. The two girls laughed. "Och, how I needed that. Good morning girls. An' how are ye today?"

"All the better for seeing ye, Bob," Jessie giggled.

"Very well, thank ye. Jean's off at the shop with father this morning," said Berta.

"Och aye. Her turn today, is it?" he responded, trying not to look too disappointed.

"Aye. That it is Bob, But I dinnae think Robert will keep her all morning. Just 'til the rush is over," Mimey answered his question with a smile.

He need not have been too worried or disappointed, as not long after 10 am Jean returned. Her father was not going to keep her too long, only long enough to get him going through the early morning rush. He was only too aware, how little time she would have with Bob, even though he did not let on to her that he knew very well what was happening. He and Mimey had discussed the matter and were in agreement that Bob was indeed a suitable partner for their daughter, if that situation arose down the track.

Today Bob, Jean, Jessie and Berta, decided that a trip to the theatre was in order. The newly opened Grand Theatre in Murray St was showing a Charlie Chaplin double feature, 'The Champion' and 'The Tramp'. Jean had already seen 'The Tramp', but was not going to let on to Bob that she had. She was simply happy to be going anywhere with him, even if it was with her sisters as well. After lunch they took the all too familiar walk down to the train station and caught the next steam train, to Perth Central. A slow walk up through Forrest Place, to Murray St and along to the theatre, gave them a chance for some window shopping. The name "The Grand Theatre" was in this case, completely appropriate. It was indeed a modern and grand structure, with its tall arch like façade and grand entrance. It had been fitted out with all manner of plush fittings and furniture and was the pride of the Perth populous.

Bob felt that it was entirely appropriate that he was taking Jean to the most beautiful of theatres in the city. They arrived and Bob purchased tickets for them all and they took up their seats in the stalls, chuckling at the luxury of sitting back, in the comfort of these new, plush, velvet seats. The piano was, of course, already in action, serenading all the patrons as they arrived and eagerly waiting for the programme to begin. They sat, with Bob in between the girls. Jessie was still totally enamoured with Bob, so was extremely happy to be sitting next to him, even though by now she was not in with a chance.

Soon the lights dimmed, and the piano struck up with greater vigour and the movie commenced. 'The Champion' was a movie about a boxer, so Jean was not overly taken by the storyline, but the others enjoyed that movie. Charlie Chaplin was his usual, shy, hero type figure, waddling through the script. Of course, being silent movies, there was no spoken script, but words are not always essential, in getting a message across to the audience. Chaplin was, of course, a master, at the art of the silent movie. His ability to impart a story to the audience, without words, was unequalled at that time. He was able to hold a complete audience, in the palm of his hand and have them laughing, crying, scared, or any other emotion he wanted within seconds, simply with his gestures and facial expressions. Intermission followed and the three of them headed for the foyer to enjoy a penny ice cream.

The second film, for the afternoon was Charlie Chaplin's master film, 'The Tramp'. In this one, Charlie is, as the name suggests a tramp, or wanderer, who happens upon a farm where he gets work. At the farm is a young girl, the girl of his dreams he thinks, who he quickly falls in love with. The part of the girl is played by Edna Purviance, with whom Charlie has made several movies over the last few years. He ends up defending the farm and her honour, against a band of criminals and he looks set to win the young lady, when he discovers she already has a boyfriend. The tramp, being a man of honour and chivalry, does not wish to be a hinderance, to her romance, so heads off on the road again, where he is more comfortable anyway. The movie closes with Charlie waddling off down the road, swinging his cane in his usual manner, indicating his joy at being back where he belongs, on the road.

The film finishes with the sounds of sniffles all around the theatre. Handkerchiefs are all a flutter, when the lights come up and everyone makes for the door. Jessie and Berta are in tears, but Jean is not. Having seen the movie before she already knows the ending, but she is also the more sensible of the two older girls, and it takes a little more than that, to bring her to tears. She takes Bob's arm and exits the theatre, matter-of-factly but is really ecstatic that they are all there together and she can walk along holding his arm. Jean does not show a lot of emotion. It is difficult for anyone to work out what she is thinking, just by looking at her face and mannerisms. But she does feel the emotion. She has just become good at not being demonstrative about that stuff. However, Bob knows what is going on. The subtle squeeze of his arm and the gentle pulling in a bit closer at times, tells him she is incredibly happy, to be on his arm. He is pretty happy about that too.

"How aboot we tek the tram home today," suggested Jean. "It's a lot less smoky and it will be a wee bit different."

"That sounds like a grand idea," Bob replied, and the other girls agreed.

The four walked along Murray St, to Barrack St and down to the Tram stop. Instead of boarding immediately, they all settled in at the little café near the stop and ordered tea for four. Bob had purchased the afternoon paper and on page 7 of "The Daily News", was a photo of a horse and cart loaded up with Red Cross parcels. They all laughed, as this was part of the cargo from the 'Ulysses' that was bound for England and got water spoiled when the ship hit the rocks, in Fremantle harbour. It said that the ladies of the Red Cross had spent a whole day unpacking the boxes, drying and repacking them ready for their journey to England, in two days' time. They wondered, *what was the rush to get them done so quickly as they had already spent three weeks waiting for the ship to be ready?* This was however, followed by unanimous admiration for the people of the Red Cross, as they had done so much to coordinate the production and distribution of aid packs to the soldiers overseas. News was already filtering back home of the value of these packs to our troops.

They spent about half an hour there, chatting and drinking tea, until they realised they had better get home for tea. Mimey would be wondering where they were soon, so they headed out for the No 12 Tram. It took them over the Barrack Street bridge, over the train line that Bob travelled on to Blackboy Hill. The tram then travelled along Beaufort Street up to, and along Newcastle St. They arrived home in time for dinner and spent the rest of the evening, as usual, quietly. Robert headed off to bed early again, ready to rise at 1 am for the bakery morning shift. Jessie was to help out tomorrow morning but would not be needed in the shop until 7am.

For Bob's final full day with the Chappells, it was decided that they would just spend it at home, taking it easy. After breakfast, for something to do, Bob and Jean wandered down to the bakery, to say good morning to Robert and Jessie. They spent a few minutes chatting through the customer interruptions and then headed off back home, although perhaps not by the most direct route. That way, they could be on their own a little longer. Bob could not help but wonder, if this would be the last, he would see of Jean. After all, he was going off to war tomorrow. Just what, he thought, would that hold for him?

Back at Florence St, the ladies took up with their sewing, knitting, and crocheting that they were working on. Mimey was a dab hand at all those ladies crafts, throughout her whole life. Bob just read the newspaper and his book and chatted with the girls. The Day just drifted on slowly, with everyone just enjoying each other's company. Jessie arrived home late morning as well and joined in the day's activity. She had a preference for needlework, cross stitch, embroidery, tapestry and other similar crafts.

Robert arrived home mid-afternoon, a little earlier than usual, just to make sure he had some time to chat with Bob. No one really wanted the day to end. But before too long, end it did and they all headed off to sleep. Bob's mind was racing. What is coming? What am I leaving? Will I come back? If I come back, what will I do? Sleep was a long time coming but it eventually did.

Thursday morning, and all were awake a little earlier. No one wanted to waste any time. Bob bid Jack farewell, as he headed to the law office.

"Well Bob," said Jack, "I'll be seein' ye. I tell ye, if this war keeps goin', an' I can get oot of ma work, I'll meet ye in France. I promise ye."

"Jack, I hope it's all over befoor then, bu' somehow I think we might meet over there," Bob said extending his hand to shake. "Hope I'm wrong mind ye."

"I'll probably end up at Blackboy Hill masel' ye knaw. How funny would that be noo?" Jack smiled and warmly grasped Bob's hand. "Best o' luck to ye man."

Their handshake lingered, a little longer than would be normal protocol. This was different. Neither man knew if they would ever lay eyes on each other again, but of course, that, was never spoken. The respect each had for the other was encapsulated in that lingering handshake. Hugging was not a thing men did with each other in 1916, but if it had been, that hug would have been just as long as their handshake. Nothing else was said, nor needed to be said.

One down 5 to go. "Dear me, this is going to be harder than I expected," Bob thought.

He had to be back at Blackboy Hill Camp by 5pm. That meant he had to be on the train by 1pm, to be safely back in time, so there were only a few hours, to get used to this farewell business. In a way he wished for it to be over, but then that would mean not being with Jean.

Together, the rest of the family, except, of course, for Robert, had breakfast. The conversation went round and round, completely avoiding the obvious, as no one wanted to go there, at least not yet. After breakfast Bob packed all his gear ready to leave. Then he and the three girls went for one last walk. For one last time, they strolled up to Hyde Park, around the lake and back again. Bob was unable to get Jean on her own this time, as the other two were hanging on just as close, knowing this may be the last time they ever got to do that. He did not mind, in fact, because he too wished to be close to them all, for the same reason. Jessie was particularly upset to see him leaving, although she tried hard not to show it, she was not all that successful at hiding it.

Robert had decided, to come home for lunch today, which was something he did not normally do. He too, wanted to be there, as Bob finished his time with the Chappells. Mimey put on a feast for them all, as they recalled their time together, Bob's stories of his training exploits, and talk of what was to come. He knew they were heading to France but not what route they would be taking. That, of course, was hush hush. It was known the Germans had naval vessels in the Indian Ocean, hunting for troopships like the 'Useless'. HMAS Sydney had already sunk the German Battle cruiser 'Emden' off the Cocos Islands in the first few months of the war. In reality, the Emden was so severely damaged after the battle, she was going to sink, so she was run aground on the Cocos Islands before she could go down.

All too soon lunch was over, and Robert bid Bob, a fond farewell, saying he wished him all the Scots luck and a timely return. Robert headed back to the bakery and Bob and the girls and Mimey commenced their walk to the railway station. Not a lot was spoken on the walk to the station, but a lot was thought. All parties were, of course, wondering if this would indeed be the last time, they would see each other. This was not an option for Bob, but it was an obvious possibility. Jean too, was thinking similar thoughts. She had fallen rather fond of this older Scot. Fond was all she would admit to at this stage, she was, of course, the cautious one. Jessie was most disconsolate. She thought the sun moon and stars shone from Bob, and the thought of him not coming back, was just the last. That would be the end of the earth. She was holding back the tears all the way.

Bob had timed the walk to the station so that there would be little time on the platform before his train arrived. He did not want this farewell to be one of copious tears. They only had about five minutes on the platform, during which they all said their goodbyes and Bob gave each of them a peck on the cheek. That was all that was seemly in 1916. He wished that he could linger longer, in his kiss to Jean, but with all the girls there, that was going to be somewhat difficult.

Soon the good old G class loco steamed into sight with its all too familiar 4-6-0 configuration. The train would only have a minute in the station in which the passengers had to alight at the end of their journey and the others to board, for their onward journey. So it was that Bob climbed aboard and lingered at the door to say goodbye.

"Well Bob," Mimey spoke. "We'll all see ye at the ship on Saturday. We're coming tae see ye off."

"Och tha'll be wonderful, if ye can manage tha'," Bob was cheered by that remark. They would all travel down to Fremantle and wave him farewell. This news lifted his spirits no end, as it meant one more time, he would get to see Jean, in particular.

All too soon, the train whistle shattered the relative silence, followed by the hissing and all too familiar chuff, chuff, chuff, and the train slowly pulled away.

Bob leaned out the window waving madly and yelled, "I'll see ye all on Saturday then," he paused. "an' when I get back from France."

The stoicism finally broke and the platform was awash with tears. There were other people on the platform at that time and normally that sort of thing would be considered a public spectacle, but they all understood. Roughly 10% of the entire Australian population would eventually enlist in the AIF, so everyone had some connection with the war in those days. Yes, they all understood.

The 4 women all turned and walked that long, five minute walk home. Today, it seemed awfully long.

Chapter 7
Departure

Bob did not have time to settle, because he had to change trains in Perth only 5 minutes later. The station was full of troops again, all trying to get back to camp by the allotted time. At this time of the day, there was no trouble meeting the deadline, so Bob was not the least bit worried. Whilst they waited for the train to Midland and beyond, the men formed the usual groups and traded stories of their exploits, on this their last Australian leave. Bob found a few of the men from his section and together, they took up a part of the carriage together. Spirits were high. Tomorrow begins this big adventure. Again. Hopefully tomorrow would not be another false start.

They had all seen the article in the newspaper showing the mountain of supplies on the Red Cross cart. These relief packages had been damaged when the 'Ulysses' was holed and the local Red Cross, had retrieved these supplies and dried them out and repacked them ready to be sent on with the boys when they left tomorrow. Already the ship was being commonly referred to as the 'Useless' by the Aussie contingent. Rarely did any of the troops call her the 'Ulysses' anymore. It looked like this name was going to stick.

The train ride back to camp was fairly noisy, as the excitement grew. Most of the discussion centred around the current news from the Western Front and how it may affect their deployment. At this stage none of them had any idea, where they were going or what they were going to be doing. Of course, there were those who knew what they were heading for. That ranged from digging underground bunkers for the officer's protection, to miles and miles of trenches. The idea of bunkers for the officers was not all that popular with the miners of the group.

"That'd be bloody right!" they would say. "Trust the bloody officers, to have us lowly miners digging holes to protect them. We'll be stuck up above ground, taking it all, while they are protected down below." These statements would be greeted with rounds of agreement from the miners in the carriages. It would go against their grain to have to work for the ruling classes (officers). This kind of elitism, would not be tolerated. Many of these fellows, had been active in years gone by, in actions designed to break the bosses in the mines, where they had worked. They felt the hard work they were doing was just so the bosses could line their pockets, with profits generated by the miner's hard work, whilst they just got the crumbs. Resentment! That is what was being perpetrated here. Fairly normal behaviour for miners. in those days. Needless to say, none of the knowledge alluded to, had any basis on factual information. Then again why let the truth get in the way of a good story?

They arrived back in camp around 3pm so had a couple of hours to kill, until the curfew hour of 6pm. Bob spent the time checking his gear and catching up with Bill. He had had a grand time with the people he had been billeted with. They had been down to the baths at Crawley, a couple of times. Bill liked swimming, so the baths in Matilda Bay on the Swan River were just the ticket.

*

The Crawley baths were a public swimming facility only opened 2 years before and were a favourite haunt of anyone on the north side of the river. The baths were built by the State Government after the Perth Baths, at the foot of Barrack St, were deemed no longer suitable, as they were too shallow and too muddy for continued use. The Crawley Baths consisted of a jetty out into the river, with changing rooms, café and grandstand for spectators. Off this jetty ran two more minor jetties that could be used as start and finish lines for any 50 Yard (45 m) events. Later improvements, included a diving tower and a water slide. Many school swimming carnivals were held in this facility until its closure.

The baths were situated along Mounts Bay Rd about two thirds of the way from the city to the university, nestled in close to the southern face of Mount Eliza, below Kings Park. They remained Perth's public swimming facility of choice, until Beatty Park Aquatic Centre, opened for the British Empire and Commonwealth Games in 1962. Interestingly, Beatty Park is located at the top end of Florence St, where the Chappell's lived. The baths were demolished in 1964, and all that remains today is "Eliza", a statue of a swimmer about 15m out into the river on the site of the baths.

The troops continued to stream into camp up until 6pm, when they reported for evening meal. One of the big complaints our soldiers at Blackboy Hill had, was that the food was, shall we say, less than edible. The camp was quite notorious for the standard of the food. It was better than nothing, although some were not so sure. As the evening meal ended, the RSM gave instructions as to what was going to happen tomorrow and Saturday. After Reveille and morning muster, everyone was to pack his kit, except for what was needed for that day and the following morning. All washing was to be done and prepared for travel.

Different sections were then detailed for packing and preparing equipment, for transport to Fremantle that afternoon. The QM and his section would oversee this operation and loading onto GS wagons, for transport to the railway station. Everything must be ready to be loaded and moved the following morning, as soon as muster was completed. The logistics of moving 1300 plus men from Helena Vale to Fremantle, were quite something, so everyone must be ready to roll. It would take all day to move the men and remaining equipment to Fremantle, load the ship with them and depart port.

It is not recorded what the boys did in particular that day, but one can be assured they were kept busy all day.

0600 Saturday, 1 April 1916, and the camp is awakened by reveille as usual, but a buzz is about today. They are finally on their way. There is no early morning parade today and the morning is spent cleaning lines cleaning up their area, striking any tents and packing away. Lunch is held early, at 11am and as soon as this is over, troops gather their gear and fall in, for the COs parade at 12.30. As soon as the Parade is over, the troops are marched to Helena Vale station. It is only a short ten minute march from the camp to the station, but the train ride will be a long one. It will take them over an hour to travel the twenty miles (32km) to Fremantle station followed by a short 10 min march to the wharf. The trains were long, in order to load to the maximum, so were slow. No1 coy were the first to entrain at 1.30 and headed off leaving the others to follow in short order.

Despite it being a large undertaking, it speaks volumes for the organisation of this mass movement that according to (then) Lt O H Woodward, "All members of the Mining Corps were embarked on the Ulysses by 5pm." (Personal Diary of O H Woodward)

At the port of Fremantle, the HMAT A38 Ulysses lay at the wharf, ready to accept her passengers for the voyage, with a large plug of concrete, filling the hole that had been ripped in her side some twenty four days ago. There would have been a great deal of discussion, on the suitability of this repair in war time, as it would no doubt have negatively impacted on the ships' manoeuvrability, something that would have been rather undesirable, if you are trying to evade enemy submarines. Especially now they were setting sail on April Fool's Day. But Fremantle at that time was still a small port and lacked the drydock facilities, for large scale repair, so the best was done with what they had, and the ship would undergo full scale repairs, on her return from France.

The 1309 Mining corps troops were on board and about 800 infantry as well and, of course, they all crowded on the one side of the ship, to wave off their families and new friends. Bob scanned the crowds for any sign of the Chappells. It was difficult trying to find familiar faces amongst the hundreds of faces lining the dock, all looking similar. The men in their Fedora or straw boater hats, the women covered by wide brimmed straw or fabric hats adorned with many flowers or fruit. It took him a few minutes but eventually he found them. All of them. Robert, Mimey, Jean, Jessie, Jack and Roberta. Oh, how that made him feel good.

He waved madly, pointing them out to Bill. Jean had already picked him out, so as soon as he started waving, she returned the greeting enthusiastically. The boys moved along the railing to be opposite the Chappells and started calling back and forward. Jessie was, of course, the loudest and waved the hardest and fastest, but it was Jean, of course, that Bob really wanted to see. She had kept her promise. They were there. He was overjoyed. He tried to soak up the picture for memories sake. Jean was dressed in a full length white dress, tied at the waist, with some kind of blue pattern on it. He could not make it out from that distance. He had not seen this dress before. On her head was a white, wide brimmed hat, with a small bunch of flowers of blue.

He thought to himself, "That is just so tasteful. Understated and beautiful, not like some of the other women whose hats were bigger and were adorned with copious quantities of flowers. Yes Jean, you have dressed very well. You look beautiful of course." Mimey was in her usual Sunday best. A full length brown skirt and white blouse complemented with a broad brimmed straw hat, with brown band. Robert was in his suit and Fedora, Jack with his straw boater.

Then the air was rent, with the sound of the ship's horn and the tug horns. Lines started to be cast off. The bow started to peel away from the wharf. It was 6.15pm. Jessie could bear it no longer and took off around the corner of the shed. Bob did not see her leave but soon realised, she was not there. She was sitting, hiding around the corner of the shed, bawling her eyes out. Whether it was because she was worried about the possibility that she might not see him again or that she realised he wanted Jean we never found out. I like to think it was probably a little of both.

The ship pulled away from the wharf and the tugs guided her to mid channel, with lots of belching of smoke and horn blowing. Everyone was still waving, blowing kisses and screaming out. Bob found himself making a promise he would return to Jean. He would do whatever it takes to return.

Then with one final long horn blow and a churn of the water, 38 000 tons of ship, plus a few tons of concrete and her precious cargo of troops and Red Cross parcels, made way under her own steam, this time up the middle of the channel and out into gage roads.

Jean let out one final sigh, at the now deserted wharf, glanced back at the 'Ulysses', then took her mother's arm and turned and walked back towards the car. Jessie had by now, regained her composure and had re-joined the family. Tears however, were not far away from the surface for all of them. It was a quiet walk back to the car and an even quieter drive back to Florence St.

A38 'Ulysses' made her way through the heads, past the lighthouses standing guard over Fremantle harbour and out to sea. All the troops remained at the railings throughout the manoeuvring and well past the point of recognising anyone on land. Once they were well clear the men broke up and went about their business. The mood was distinctly quiet, contemplative. Most of them remained on deck but now spread out and the smokes were lit in abundance. Some broke out the cards but most just milled around and talked. Someone cranked up the Harmonica. It was a soulful tune, albeit and unfamiliar tune, but it just suited the mood. No one was in the mood for frivolity.

Many good friendships had been made over this last three weeks and no one knew if they would return to pick them up again. 'Ulysses' worked her way out into Gage roads and dropped anchor, roughly halfway between the coast and Rottnest Island for the night. They would stay there overnight and be under way, past the coastal reefs at first light tomorrow morning. The sun was well down now and gave the boys one of the west's famous sunsets, over a barmy warm, calm sea, with Rottnest in the background with her dual winking lighthouses. It certainly was a beautiful sight. When the call to dinner came, no one wanted to leave that magnificent vista, but someone mentioned that at last we might get some decent food, being out of Blackboy camp. So off they went and sure enough, he was right. The food was finally good, and plentiful what is more.

First light broke with the sound of the 'Ulysses' engines firing up and the anchor clanking its way onto the foredeck. She pointed her nose northwest and with a brief pause headed out to sea at 6am. The day was calm, and the sea smooth. A perfect day on the water. This would be the norm for the crossing of the Indian Ocean this trip, in stark contrast to Robert's previous crossing from west to east 4 years prior.

The next 10 days became a blur of parades, drill practice, lectures, guard duty, sporting events, different training exercises and lifeboat drills and boredom. Each day would see between 290 and 320 miles (460 and 510 km) covered, as the sea remained millpond like for that duration. As they got further to the north, more and more of the men slept on deck at night. Those cabins below deck, with too many men in them and the not so gradual heating up as they sailed into more equatorial waters, meant that staying below deck became unbearable for some.

Although none of the men knew which route, they would be taking, they hoped that it would be via the Cocos Islands. Others had reported going that way and seeing the 'Emden' beached on one of the islands. She was famously driven there to prevent sinking after being damaged, in a duel with HMAS SYDNEY, some one year five months previous. 'Sydney' was on escort duty with the first convoy of Australian troops heading to Egypt prior to Gallipoli, when on November 9 1914, officers received a signal saying the 'Emden' was attacking the communications station at Home Island in the Cocos Islands. 'Sydney' was dispatched to intercept and deal with 'Emden'.

They surprised 'Emden', but she had a surprise of her own. Her guns far outreached any distance, British intelligence believed she was capable of and as such was able to open fire first scoring a direct hit on 'Sydney', although it caused little damage or injury. By the end of the battle Captain Karl von Muller ordered the 'Emden', beached on North Keeling Island to prevent her sinking. 'Sydney' took off in pursuit of the German collier, 'Buresk' which, when 'Sydney' closed in on her, her crew, scuttled her to avoid battle. 'Sydney' returned to North Keeling Island to find 'Emden' still flying battle ensign.

'Sydney' called for the ensign to be lowered but when there was no reply and the colours remained flying, she again opened up with her greatly much more powerful armoury and pumped two more salvos into 'Emden', before she lowered her colours.

At that time, 134 were dead on board 'Emden' and 69 wounded, whilst 4 died and 16 were wounded, on board 'Sydney'. 'Sydney' set off for Home Island, to check on the condition of the personnel at the radio station, but then returned and collected the casualties, from 'Emden'.

The men had heard that if they were going by the Cocos Islands, it would be somewhere around day six or seven. By day nine, they knew they were approaching the Equator so would not be seeing the 'Emden'. There was great disappointment amongst the officers and men when they realised, they would not see the results of this famous battle.

The 12th day however saw a deal of frivolity as the crossing the line ceremony, took place as the equator was crossed at 2.30pm. This involved the Neptune Sports and the traditional dousing of those who had not crossed the equator, at any time in their life. The weather now was starting to get a lot warmer and definitely a lot muggier. The men enjoyed the afternoon as something was organised for them to have some fun together. All too soon though, the boredom returned as with the festivities over the usual routine fell back into place.

It was not until the 17th that the routine was broken, by the sighting of land as the men rose. The coast of the horn of Africa, Cape Gwardafuy, was barren, rugged and lifeless, but it was land. It was Africa. The first sighting of this continent for many of the men, who had never even left their hometown before, let alone the country. By lunchtime, the 'Ulysses' and her compliment of men, were into the Gulf of Aden and again out of the sight of land. In the run up to the entrance to the Red Sea they saw many Dhows, with their occupants in white robes and turbans or head wrappings, to protect from the incessant sun, and steamers. It was comforting to know that once again they were not alone on the high seas. It was unusual for a troopship to cross the ocean unescorted, but the 'Ulysses' was, on this voyage, alone because of the circumstances which delayed her. She just had to catch up as best she could. One advantage of a lone crossing is that the speed of the ship can be whatever the ship's master wants, as fast as he wants. Whereas in a convoy, the speed is restricted by the maximum speed of the slowest ship.

Tuesday 18th again saw the sight of land off the starboard bow. Aden was within range although they could not see the town, being hidden by the capes around it. The Arabian Peninsula coastline was extremely steep and rugged and the men could not understand how anyone could live in such a barren land. By 4 pm the 'Ulysses' passed Perrim Island and entered the Red Sea. For the next three days they were again out of sight of land and ironically in the most protected seas they had travelled on, it was also the roughest. More drills, lectures, parades were the order of the day, but now the urgency of proficiency was closer at hand. The realisation that they were nearly there had hit.

Saturday 22nd April has 'Ulysses' arriving at Suez around 6pm and dropping anchor. They remained at anchor awaiting orders until 2pm the following day. The first half of the Canal transit was protected by the British Battalions of Essex Field artillery, Essex Infantry and The Herts Yeomanry. Once through the Bitter Lakes, the canal was all narrow man-made passage, protected by the Australian 11th, 16th, and 28th Battalions as well as the 8th and 14th Field Coy Engineers. The troops were constantly amazed at the intensity of agriculture hugging the canal edges, and the barrenness of the land beyond. Water. That is the answer they said. Water makes all the difference. They lost the light around Ismailia just after the Bitter Lakes, but mostly woke at around 4 am as the ship cleared the canal at Port Said.

Due to the fact that the enemy had bombed Port Said and the canal the day before, the ship lay at anchor until 9pm, when they could depart for Alexandria 130 miles (215km) away, under the cover of darkness, arriving at 10am the following morning. The Australian Infantry Reinforcements taken on in Perth, now disembarked and were marched off for Tel El Kabir.

The captain of 'A38 Ulysses' said he was reluctant to take her out into the Mediterranean due to the repairs completed in Fremantle. With the hole plugged by many tons of concrete he had found that manoeuvrability had been severely compromised. With the likelihood of encountering German submarines being quite high, his reservations were entirely justified. He did not feel he could chance all these lives, in a ship with limited manoeuvrability. As was normal practice when travelling through enemy occupied water, the ships did not take a direct route, rather a somewhat circuitous, zigzag course, in order to reduce the vulnerability to submarine attack.

Submarine warfare was one of the many advances in this era of the modern war. Little had been worked out on how to combat the undersea menace at this stage, however the concept of not travelling in straight lines had definitely been decided upon. Millions of tons of shipping were already lying on the bottom of the Atlantic Ocean and Mediterranean Sea. The Captain of the 'Ulysses' was not going to add to that tonnage. A replacement was hastily organised, and the men disembarked and headed for the 8600 ton Cunard liner 'B1 ANSONIA' and boarded for the ongoing trip.

Now, one can imagine that a collection of miners, as the Mining Corps basically was, would be expected to be perhaps a little lacking in the discipline area. It was made up from men from all kinds of trades, but there was a significant proportion of miners. This had certainly been an issue in the past. The Corps had been thrown together in short time order and the training had been minimal, with a group of men who normally are not subject to strict control, so their adherence to military discipline was also in question. These 1300 or so men had now been cooped up, on board the ship for nearly a month and were told that they would not be allowed any shore leave.

Well, what would you do if you managed to get off the ship, onto dry land, the first dry land in four weeks, having been told you are not going to get shore leave? Yes, that's right, make a break for it and hang the consequences. So, a group of about 120 miners legged it, as fast as they could go, to get a look around Alexandria. In doing so, they managed to create quite a bit of havoc, both for the locals and the military. It is not actually recorded what, in particular, they did to upset the locals, but upset them they did. One can only assume there was a lot of drinking, fighting, stealing, and… well… let us just say, entertainment.

On the morning of the 26th of April, Robert was summoned to report with arms to Lt Woodward, to form a Picquet, to retrieve a group of prisoners, the local police had arrested. Robert found he was with a group of about 80 men, most who had been a part of the Guard, formed whist they were in Perth. The men headed off through the streets of Alexandria, to find the Provost Marshall's enclosure. The sights they saw impressed and surprised the men. Progress was so slow through the streets. Everything was so close together, crowded, cramped and tight. The shops spilled out onto the streets with people of all sorts rushing out to them, in an attempt to sell their wares to the unsuspecting soldiers.

When I say rushing, the streets were so narrow and busy that no one could actually rush anywhere. It was just a melee. All the antiques were, of course, genuine antiques. The girls were all quite clean. The art was all original. And of course, the flies were just so friendly. There were people going about their daily ablutions right there on the streets, right next to someone else selling their dates, who were right next to their friend with slabs of meat of whatever animal they used to be. The smells were... well, according to the men, ranging from amazing through to revolting, or at times, both. From the fragrance of incense, sandalwood, frankincense and myrrh, through to rotting flesh. There were chickens, goats, some little animals the troops thought could have been rats, fish, crabs and sundry other things they could not identify. It was sensory overload and some of the men found it fascinating whilst some found it revolting.

Eventually, they made it through to the enclosure, where the escapees were being held. The authorities, were by this time, becoming very anxious that their captives should be returned to the ship they came from. Discussions were very animated between Lt Woodward and these authorities. Lots of yelling, gesturing and what appeared to be pleading from some, and accusations from others. In good time the men were marched out to the guard who surrounded their compatriots as ordered and the men were marched onto the lorries under guard.

A description made at the time by Maj. Edgeworth David, Corps Commander, perhaps beautifully describes the men's brief period of freedom and their overnight incarceration. (His date in the recollection differs quite a deal from the diary of Lt Woodward. As Woodward's daily diary was written at the time, the author has used his dates.)

On the arrival of our troop ship in Alexandria, a party of some 120 of our 1200 miners, with the wanderlust strong upon them, broke loose suddenly from our Troop ship as she lay at the wharf, rushed the sentries, and went careering like a lot of released schoolboys up the main street of Alexandria, making for the heart of the city.

Some bad sport, one could rather say, one sound disciplinarian, telephoned the military police. And in due course the sappers were met by some charabancs driven by genial gentlemen, who offered them a lift.

The offer was, of course, accepted, and presently the vehicle swung into a courtyard, the gates of which were promptly closed, and the sappers then realised that they were prisoners. One hundred and twenty of them were locked up in a building designed for a maximum of 60. The sappers called it 'the boob'. The night was very hot and the 'boob' threatened to become a veritable black hole of Calcutta.

In the early dawn, an agonising SOS came from the military police to our ship to say that the sappers were tunnelling under the walls of the 'boob' and it was tottering on its foundations, and would we send a strong-armed party at once to hold and remove the prisoners.

Once the men were returned to their ship, the guard was reduced in size and posted to ensure no one else departed company with the ship. The guard split into shifts and patrolled the land side of the ship with orders to arrest anyone attempting to depart.

If ever there was a chance any of the men would get shore leave, it was surely gone now. Officers and men were all confined to the ship. There was now quite a lot of officers on board. 'Ansonia' took on a further 192 men, returning to their units in France following leave or recuperation, as well.

Chapter 8
The Mediterranean

7am on the 27th B1 Ansonia weighed anchor and put to sea. She headed north from Alexandria with a destroyer escort. This escort darted back and forth at great speed compared to theirs. It felt a lot more comforting knowing for this part of the trip they were not going to be on their own on the ocean. Ironically, the mere presence of the destroyer signalled greater danger than they had previously been in, as a result all men were to stay alert, life jacket at hand and ready to move to the lifeboats at a moment's notice. It seemed to the men incongruous that such a beautiful sight of these ships gliding through calm and reflective seas, could have been in so much danger. The following morning around 10am the destroyer slipped away from them and was replaced by another. Still the seas were mirror calm and no sightings of any enemy shipping were made, even as they zigzagged their way through the Cretian Archipelago.

It was not until Sunday afternoon that Malta came into sight and by 4pm they were at anchor in Valletta harbour. Robert had heard so much over the years, about Malta and the Knights Hospitaller. He desperately wanted shore leave, to explore and see the things he had read about. But alas, no leave was granted to the men. The officers all got leave from 6 until 10 pm, but the troops had to remain onboard. On his return Lt Woodward was telling the men that only yesterday a British ship, HMS Russell and two trawlers, had struck a mine in the outer harbour area. The trawlers sank, but the Russell was able to limp in for repairs. That was where the 'Ansonia' had just come through. A minefield. This war business was beginning to sound a little more real, every day.

Monday, the men were told they were going ashore and momentarily the men's hopes were high, only to be dashed when they were told it was for a route march. At least they would get off the ship and feel solid land under their feet for a few hours. Even on a march, they would get to see a few of the historic buildings and places, surely? For five hours, the poor sods got marched around, with a short break every half hour and longer break for a lunch stop. One of the boys in Bob's area of the march had been to Malta before, so was able to point out some of the structures and recount the stories of the Knights of nearly 400 years ago.

*

In 1565, the Ottoman leader Suleiman, sent a force of 40 000 to Malta to rest the island from the 700 Knights of St John and their 8000 soldiers. The Ottomans tried again and again to take the island, but eventually their forces were so depleted, and, along with a belief that the Sicilians were about to reinforce the knights, they gave up and withdrew. Little did they know, the relieving force was surprisingly small and there were only around 600 left on the island capable of fighting, but Suleiman had lost over 25 000 men, in his attempt to take Malta. The Knights had been led throughout this six month defence, by Grand Master Jean Parisot de Vallette and as a new city had to be built after the siege, it was decided to name it after him, hence the city of Valletta. The capital of Malta, and the port they were currently anchored in.

*

Robert had read so much about the battles and of Malta itself that he just wanted to get out and about. A route march was not the greatest way to see it all, but a route march he would have to settle for.

One thing Malta is not, is flat. For the men of the 1st Australian Mining Corps, marching was not what they got into this army for. But this was the first route march they had done since Blackboy Hill in Perth, so they were not so disgruntled at this one. At least not initially. Once they got going the hills started to take their toll. These poor soldiers had been cooped up on board ship now, for nearly two months and had not needed to climb anything steeper than a ladder onboard the ship. It was not long, before the grizzles and grumps started up all over again. Not only were the hills an issue but the whole place was, well…very white. Malta being made almost entirely of limestone, albeit different types of limestone, tended to make the scenery way too similar, no matter which direction one marched. The only things to break the monotony for most of the men, were the running commentary of what fort that was, what tower that was, and what happened here hundreds of years ago.

Bob was not like your average miner, so he found the whole thing fascinating and beautiful. He really was in his element here. He just wished he could break away from everyone and go exploring on his own. However, that was never going to happen. Not with him. Bob was not one for disobeying orders or breaking rules. He just hoped against hope that the opportunity may still arise where he could go exploring. He really wished he could bring Jean here and go exploring with her. They had not been told how long they would be in Malta harbour. The guys suspected only a day or two but hoped maybe longer. "To think that we are here, nearly 900 years of history right in front of us and we are not able to explore." How frustrating, thought some of the men.

The march ended up back at the ship at around 4pm. The sun was still quite high in the sky and the day warm and still. One of those barmy spring days where it would be nice to just go wandering and lie down on the grass soaking up the sun, but no; they reboarded the ship and made for their bunks for a clean-up, to be ready for dinner. The story is that they will be on their way overnight. Robert and his mates were a little wary of such rumours, as they were almost invariably wrong. This soon proved to be no exception.

The night passed uneventfully as did the following day, all aboard ship. Around 9pm the corps noticed 'Ansonia' making more smoke and ships moving around the harbour, so they guessed they were on their way soon. 10pm came and the ship weighed anchor yet again and made for the open sea, but this time in the company of nine warships. This was getting dinkum now. "Nine escort ships. Looks like someone is expecting trouble," the men thought. Once all ships had cleared the port, they all set a westerly course heading for the North African coast, zig zagging as they went.

Sometime during the night, they had a change, of course, because when the men rose and looked out, they were headed north. Must be heading for France now they thought. An air of excitement came over them now. Soon they would be in France, heading for the "Big Adventure."

2.30 on the afternoon of the 4th of May, the French coast came into view and the convoy now turned to run parallel to it. Night fell and the lights of Marseilles slowly came into view and by 9.30, the convoy was at anchor just out of the port. They had made it all the way from Australia in four weeks and five days, all without incident. Well, without any incident of a warlike nature anyway. Not much sleep was had by the troops that night. Even if they had wanted to, there was so much noise from those who just wanted to party, even though partying was not as such possible in those confines and without the necessary supplies to do so. Much singing and music seemed to be the order of the day, or night actually. Bluey and his harmonica were much in demand tonight.

Morning came, and the ship slowly moved into the Marseilles harbour and eventually pulled up at the wharf. All morning the men were champing at the bit to get going but nothing seemed to be happening. More Army "Hurry Up and Wait". It was not until afternoon that any movement started. Given the display at Alexandria, men were chosen to guard the exit from the docks, before anyone else had the opportunity to disembark. With exits sealed, a working party was chosen to unload kit bags, equipment and men.

So it was that 1305 men of the First Australian Mining corps paraded on French soil for the first time, at the docks of Marseille port, in the evening of Friday 5th of May 1916. No sooner had the men assembled and been checked, they were marched off for the nearest railway station, the Paris Lyons and Mediterranean Station. On arrival at the station the men were all issued with rations and a blanket for the journey. Once they had all entrained, it was again Hurry up and wait, as they sat in the station going nowhere, again. At 11.30pm the whistle blew loud and strong and with a distinct French accent and the train, slowly pulled out of the station and headed North, all 34 carriages of men and equipment, headed to, who knows where and who knows what. Much of the anxiety amongst the men revolved around the not knowing. They were basically told nothing, security of course, but it did play on their minds.

The best way of dealing with this was to indulge in some mind occupying activities. Many of the men gambled with each other, two up, cards, next to see a good looking girl, etc. Others just read or chatted whilst watching the scenery go by. All these were interspersed with the occasional fight. Usually prompted by an accusation of cheating. Miners cheating? Never. They all took the opportunity to get in as much sleep as possible though. Who knew how much they were going to get in the coming few days?

As morning broke, the men looked out on spectacular countryside. Rolling hills, covered in patchwork paddocks. Farms of green, orange and brown stretching as far as the eye could see. The air too was something different. After 6 weeks of sea air laden with salt, the freshness of this air was a godsend. So, this was a country at war? These scenes certainly did not portray any signs of that. Some of the men questioned if this was truly happening.

The convoy headed north up the Rhone valley through the 6th of May, for the city of Lyon. They followed the Rhone River for miles and miles, at times so close to the water, it felt like they were going for a swim in the train. They knew when they were getting close to Lyon, as there was much less agriculture and much more urban spread. Marshalling yard after marshalling yard, and then just city. After what seemed like an age, the train curved to the west and crossed the Rhone River and just a minute later the Saone River. Almost immediately, things went dark, as they entered a long tunnel. The irony was not lost on the men, tunnellers travelling by train through a tunnel. Not long after emerging from the tunnel they were back in the countryside.

Soon, they were travelling northwest for Orleans and north to Versailles on the outskirts of Paris. There was much excitement as most of the men had never seen Paris. Of course, they had all heard of it, but never really expected to really see it. Their wish was granted late in the day of the 7th, as they passed through Versailles and skirted Paris to the west. As the train passed by, they could see in the distance the Eifel Tower, Sacre Coeur, Arc de Triumph and a few other landmarks the men pointed out to each other.

The train then took a turn to the west as they headed for Rouen, and by the following morning they awoke on the coast at Boulogne sur Mer, and by 8am were at their first destination of Calais. Here they waited on the train for a short stay before moving off without warning, heading for their final destination. This time, there was ample evidence of the war going on, as they passed field hospitals, massed troops, trains loaded with artillery awaiting delivery to the front line, troops encamped along with hundreds of horses. By 11am they arrived at their destination of Hazebrouck and detrained. Once the troops had gathered all the supplies and loaded them onto the wagons, they were marched through town to the HQ, 10th Corps, at 80 Rue de Merville, a distance of about one mile (1.6Km) and divided up into their billets.

Hazebrouck was only sixteen miles (23 Km) from the front and it was showing signs of having been part of the war. The 1914 advance of the German Army came through this area before it was driven back to its current position. Whilst the town was predominantly intact, there were several buildings showing signs of artillery bombardment, and gunshot holes. It would fare a lot worse in the German's 'Operation George' two years later. The arrival of over 1300 troops certainly put a strain on the accommodation. Whilst may of the men were billeted in houses now abandoned by their owners, who had fled to safer southern family and friends, many also ended up in Tent city around the corner on the football ground. Bob and Bill were set up in a house around the corner from the HQ, on the Rue de L'Industrie, with 23 other members of the 1st Mining corps.

The house was large, with two stories and multiple rooms that could be used to house soldiers on a short term basis. There was also a lounging area, for when the troops had time off, a kitchen for snacking and tea making. The meals the men ate together in the corps mess. Most importantly though was, there was a bath, although the only way to get hot water was to boil multiple kettles on the stove in the kitchen. Sleeping was on the floor and the lucky fast ones got an old mattress, and the rest got an army issue palliasse. The afternoon was spent exploring the town.

*

Hazebrouck is a small regional market town about twenty five miles (40 Km) from the coast and one hundred and twenty miles (200km) north of Paris, in the Nord department, Hauts-du-France. It is a service town for the rural region that surrounds it, and it has been chosen as a base for the Australians to work from, as it is also a major railway junction. The architecture is a mix of Flemish and French, which is only natural as Hazebrouck was originally Flemish (Belgian), until it was incorporated into France in 1678. The men saw many fine looking churches and other important looking buildings, including the oldest building in the town, the St Elois church. A fine example of 15th century architecture, its classic Flemish red brick construction and its spire climbing possibly 100' (30m) over their heads. Yes, this was a town with a lot of pride in its appearance. "Now it has to endure war and how much will be left when it's all over?" they wondered.

*

Some of the establishments were still open. Some of the locals had remained behind to make sure that their homes and shops were not destroyed by the army and looters. Either that, or they saw an opportunity to make a bit of money from the soldiers, whilst the place still stood. Bob and several of the men found a little café, up past the St Elois church and indulged themselves on a spot of afternoon tea. All the while, far off in the distance, they could hear a low crump, crump, the indistinct sounds of artillery. It seemed to be coming from two directions, some from the northeast and some from the southeast. They were not sure which one. In fact, it was both, as Hazebrouck was only thirteen miles (21km) southwest the Ypres salient, and fourteen miles (23km) northwest the Armentieres front.

Early on, in their conversation, as they both sat there quietly chatting, they would pause briefly at each crump they heard, and making a silent sideways glance in the direction of the noise. Words were completely redundant. After a while, it became completely normal, and rated barely a skip in the conversation. This was to be the new normal.

Many of the other men were out looking for a public house to quench their thirst. Unfortunately for them, they were out of luck. The only establishments still operating were reserved 'Officers Only'. That did not half get the miners tongues raging. More ammunition to deride officers with. They would have to wait until they got leave to head to towns further from the front, to indulge that desire.

Australian troops had only been on the western front for two months, having been moved there from the disastrous Dardanelles campaign. They had been involved in so little action to this point, as the numbers were still being built up. Members of the first and second division had arrived and were in the sector to the north of Hazebrouck, but only to learn the methods of warfare in this new and modern type of war. They were then moved to the Armentieres sector to their west to put that learning into practice. As a result, not too many Frenchmen had come across the Australians yet. But that was to change. They were quizzical of the different hats they wore, and the lapel badge was different to anything else they had seen.

The uniform looked the same as the British, but they were definitely something different. "Tu n'es pas Anglais?" they would say as a question. "You are not English?"

"Nup. We're Australian."

They would get back. "Aussies." From then on, around the streets they would hear, "L'Australien?" or "L'Aussies?"

"Yep mate. You bet," they would hear in reply, and everyone would laugh and smile, even though they probably had no idea what that soldier had said.

"So, this is France eh? Not bad, not bad. Nice people, nice houses and not bad food either. Yep, a bloke could get used to this," Bluey had caught them up and added his tuppence worth to their thoughts.

"Aye indeed," Bob replied. "This would be a nice place in peacetime, dae ye noe think Bill?"

"Aye, I dae. Very different from Scotland or Australia," Bill answered. "Mind ye, it could dae with a bit o' fixing up noo."

They all laughed. "Yeah," said Bluey, "I don't go much for their open air look on some of their buildings. Could do with a bit of attention I think," Bluey sarcastically commented.

The following morning, when everyone was on parade, Major David addressed the men. "We may be here for a couple of days, before moving to our work. It appears that our Corps structure, doesn't seem to fit that of the British."

Did we just denote a tone of frustration in the Major's voice? they thought.

He went on, "The structure of the Mining Corps will have to be rearranged, before we head to our areas, and this may take a day or two. Then we will divide up, into 4 sectors, and move up the line and work with some of the other tunnelling companies, in some of those adjacent sectors. We will be joining the English and the Canadians, to be shown how they have been working."

In the meantime, it meant more training, more parades, more lectures, but at least now it would seem to have a little more significance, as they were already in France. And so it was. They got updated on the current standings. What had been happening, who was doing what to whom, and who was winning, if that could even be determined. And of course, route marches and drill.

When the reorganisation had been completed, the 1st Australian Mining Corps, ceased to exist and was replace by 1st, 2nd and 3rd Australian Tunnelling Companies, each of about 350 men and a 4th company, to be known as the Australian Electrical Mechanical Mining and Boring Company (AEMM&BC), consisting of about 250. The men thought this name was hilarious, as it had so many letters in it, they dubbed it the 'Alphabet Company'. The AEMM&BC would ultimately never serve together as a whole unit, but because of their specialist skills, would be divided over the whole front, as their expertise was required, assisting companies of differing nationalities, anywhere. Anything to do with tunnelling, whether it be pumping of water, wiring for electrical lighting or machinery, or boring for any number of reasons, the Alphabet company, were the men for the job. Each of the three Tunnelling Companies was further divided into four sections, each of about eighty five plus officers.

Both Bob and Bill found themselves in No 4 Section, 1st Australian Tunnelling Company. At least they were still together. In fact, not a great deal had changed except for a few officers being reassigned, some to infantry, some to HQ, and some of the men being separated from original friendships. From now on, it would be rare that the three tunnelling companies would see each other, being posted to different areas along the front line.

Part 2

Chapter 9
A Guided Tour

By mid-May, the reorganisation was complete. A couple of the officers were found to be surplus to the new arrangements, so were reassigned to Infantry units, whilst Major David was attached to Headquarters RE. As the British army did not consider the Australian miners as a corps, they also lost their CO, Lt Col Fewtrell. He was reassigned to a pioneer battalion. The CO of 1ATC became Major J. D. Henry. The company was called to parade to be told that the reorganisation was now complete. 1st ATC was to remain here, in Hazebrouck, 2nd ATC was to move south east, to an area south of Armentieres in France, and 3rd ATC was to move east, to an area west of Wytschaete, Belgium (the men called it white sheet).

At each of the new areas, the men would be taught the way of mining in wartime. 1ATC was to be further split along section lines, and taken to different units along the line, to be shown how things worked in reality. They would have on the job learning, until such times as they had picked up the system of tunnelling that has been used, all along the western front. It was expected that this would take at least a month, to fully absorb this new way of mining. It was no longer just a matter of digging holes. Silence was of paramount importance, so as not to indicate to the enemy that they were working in that area.

Numbers 1 and 2 Section were to be allocated to the area just to the north of Armentieres, on both the Belgian and French sides of the border. They would be allocated to Le Bizet (Bel), Houplines (Fr) and Touquet (Bel), under the tutorship of 1st Canadian Tunnelling Co. No 3 Section was allocated to the 181st British Tunnelling Co Royal Engineers (RE) at St Elois, three miles (5 Km) south of Ypres. No 4 Section was to head off to join the 3rd Canadian tunnelling Co, at Hill 60, with their HQ to be at Poperinge. When the men of 4 Section heard they were to go to Hill 60, there was an audible groan.

Hill 60 already had a big reputation, as hell on earth. At least they would be with the Canadians, they thought, not the stuffy Brits. Canadians and Australian were a kind of kindred spirit. Born of the same British stock but tempered by colonial attitudes and innovation, in order to survive the 'New World' that they had created. They had evolved from the stuffiness of the upper-class British system and had done away with that restrictive practice. All men were equal and had equal opportunity. It did not matter if you were an officer or an OR, you were all the same. Which was all very good until the time came that you must take an order from an officer you did not like.

Some blokes, especially the Miners, were more likely to tell the officer just to "get stuffed" or worse. It would not make any difference if that officer, was British, Canadian, or Australian. The British however, had not come to terms with this kind of talk back, so it was certainly safer if the company was posted to a Canadian unit than a British unit.

"Hell's bells," muttered Bill. "Hill... Bloody... 60. Wha' a way tae start." There were murmurings all along the ranks.

"This looks like a baptism o' fire," added Bob. 1ATC, and for the boys particularly, No 4 Section, was to move camp in two days. 4 Section was to set up their camp at Poperinge, about seven miles (11km) to the north east, about two thirds of the way towards Ypres. There they would start their intensive introduction, to Western Front "Mining." Not the usual sort of mining, the men had been involved with, up to this point in their lives for sure. If they were successful in this sort of mining, then many men were going to die, preferably on the other side.

The men had already heard a lot about Hill 60, in the time they had been in Hazebrouck. Not a great deal of if it was particularly complimentary. They had heard about all the mines that had been blown in the last two years. Both the Allies and the central powers had been involved in mining in the area for over 12 months, and the ground had been churned to the extent that it was unrecognisable. They wondered how they would be able to dig more mines in that kind of dirt. It simply would not be able to hold up. The front line had moved a lot during the last two years, but only backwards and forwards, neither side being able to get a permanent foothold. Each of them, setting and blowing mines under the other, every couple of months. Many men from both sides had already lost their lives in this hell on earth.

"And now we're going there," thought Bob. "We really have drawn the short straw wi' this one, Bill," he muttered, adding, "We have heard a lot aboot it, but I wonder wha' it is really like?"

"Well, I guess we're aboot to find oot, aren't we, Bob. I'm pretty sure it's noe goin' tae be like back in the Terries," Bill mused. This was a reference to their time back in the Territorial Army back in Scotland.

"Aye," continued Bob, "I dinnae think we're goin' tae see too much o' the old muzzle loaded artillery here. Definitely moved on from tha' era." This was a comment in reference to his time with the Ardrossan volunteers. A time when they had practiced on muzzle loaded artillery. "By the soonds o' things in the distance, there's also an awful lot more o' it than I've ever seen," he added.

The company had a day to rest, whilst the second and third Tunnellers headed off to their respective areas. The 2ATC were the first to set foot in Belgium. Some were glad to wait the extra day, others wish they could get it over and done with. The day of waiting was just annoying. As transport was at a premium, not all men could be moved at the same time, hence the company had to wait that extra day. Most of the men used it wisely to catch up on some much needed rest, and letters home, but to many of the mining men it was just another opportunity for a game of two up.

*

Two up! A quintessentially Australian gambling game. This was a strange gambling game using two pennies, one side having a head of the king, the other side some other pattern, either concentric rings if it was an Australian penny, or Britannia, if it was a British penny, known as tails. (Australia had only started minting their own coins in 1911, so much of the Australian currency was still British.) The two pennies were placed on a kip, which is just a flat piece of wood. The spinner stands in the middle of the circle of men, whilst the men around the circle bet on what the pennies were going come up as, when they land on the ground. Would it be two heads, two tails, or one of each.

This kind of gambling had been illegal in Australia, for many years, but around the goldfields, it was common practice, and played regularly in schools outside of the mining towns, away from the prying eyes of the coppers. Being played predominantly around mining towns, the Miners of the Tunnelling companies, brought the game of two up with them, to Belgium and France. To start the game, the 'Spinner', the one holding the Kip, lays a bet, usually on heads, which must be 'covered' by someone around the circle, i.e., one player bets against the Spinner.

All the other men around the circle bet against each other, a process known as side betting. Here, one man might tap his head with, say 10 shillings ($1), which indicates that he is prepared to back 10 shillings on two heads coming up, and asking you if there is anyone who is willing to bet against him. When that bet is taken up, the money is placed on the ground in front of the two men. When all bets are laid, and this usually takes about one minute, the ringer calls come in Spinner. That is the signal for the man with the kip, to toss the pennies high into the air. They must go over head height and they must Spin. If the coins land on heads, the Spinner wins, and he takes the money from the person that he bet with. The remaining men around the circle then settle their debts with each other.

If the Spinner tosses one head and one tail, it is usually called odds or a split, and the Spinner must re-toss the pennies. If the Spinner tosses three odds in a row, he loses completely and loses the kip, which is then passed on to the next player around the ring. He also loses the kip if he tosses two tails. It is a game of even odds. 25% of the time it should come up two tails, 25% of the time two heads, and 50% of the time odds or a split. But gamblers, work on it not being as he even as that, at least for them anyway.

Neither Bill nor Bob, being good Presbyterian boys, were into gambling in any way, so the two up game had no interest for them. So, they headed back to their billets to get their gear in order, and to get a few letters home written. Bob still had had sisters in Saltcoats, so he sat and penned off a letter to one of them, and one to Jean back in Perth. Mary was Bob's older sister. She was six years older than him, but she was his favourite sister. He had named her as Next-of-Kin in his enlistment papers, his parents both being dead. Of course, he told neither Mary nor Jean where he was going next, in these letters, he could not even tell them where he was now, just "somewhere in France."

There was no point mentioning place names, because they would all be removed by the censor anyway. All he could really tell them was that he was well, the countryside was beautiful, and he looked forward to seeing them all again someday soon. He promised Mary that if he got leave for long enough, he would come and see her in Scotland, not that he really expected to get that kind of leave, at least, not anytime soon.

Later that afternoon the two of them sat around talking with a couple of the others billeted in the same house. One of the others was also an expat Scotsman so they got talking about the old country as three ex-Scotsmen would invariably do.

*

Robert Lawsen (Bert) Carr was another carpenter in No 4 Section. He had billeted down in the same building with Bob and Bill. He was from Kinfauns, between Perth and Dundee, on the east coast, about thirty five miles (60km) north of Edinburgh. He had migrated to Australia in 1900 and settled in Perth WA. He was six years younger than Bob and four years younger than Bill. Being three Scotsmen together, in a strange environment, they gravitated towards each other and they sat there talking that afternoon.

*

Bert mentioned that he lived in Queen's Park in Perth. Bob mentioned that he had been billeted with a with a family in North Perth, during their enforced stayover.

"I spent some time wi' a family in Florence St, called the Chappells. Robert and Mimey Chappell. D' ye ken them Bert?" Bob asked.

"Know them? Why ma family's good friends with them. Robert is a braw Baker."

"So, ye'd know Jean then would ye?" Bob asked.

"Aye, sure dae. She's a bonnie wee lassie that one is" Bert came back with. "A right bonnie one. Mind ye, Jessie's noe too bad on the eye either." He added. Bob laughed.

"Aye, that she is. I think I broke her heart the dae we left Fremantle. She seemed tae tek a shine tae me. But I only had eyes for Jean by then. I think Bert, when I get back tae Australia, I'm going tae marry that girl, if I get back tae Australia, tha' is."

"Ye've got good taste there, Bob. Jean is one wonderful young lady." Bert added.

"Aye laddie, tha's very true. I have tae admit, I first though Jessie was the one, bu' after a while I realised Jean was really the special one. Quiet and

101

reserved mebee, but behind that reserve is a bonnie lassie. A right bonnie lassie." Bob was thinking back to Perth now and smiling to himself.

"So, all we have tae dae noo, is tae mek it home in one piece, eh?" Bill chipped in.

They all turned and looked at Bill in silence. After a short pause Bob spoke up. "Ye really have a way with words, dinnae ye noe Bill?"

"Sorry boys, bu' it is the reality of the place. We've only just started here, and we have go' a long, long way tae goe yet." He was correct in his summation, but the med really did not need that right now. He would not say anything like that again.

You would think a day of rest was just that, a day of rest. Oh no! Not in the army. It was still an early morning muster, a roll call to make sure nobody had scarpered, followed by breakfast and an early morning PT session. You cannot let the troops think they are going to have a day off. After lunch they formed up again and this time, they were off for a route march. The boys figured that if the officers did not know what to do with them, then a route march would sort things out. They headed east, on the back roads to the village of Pradelle, about three miles away (5 Km), then south to Sec Bois, and then returned to Hazebrouck via a zigzag route. Not a long route march, only about nine miles (14 Km), but long enough to stop the men getting into too much trouble. The rest of the day, what was left of it, they had to themselves. Bob, Bill and a couple of the other fellows, headed down the road, around the corner to a favourite little café, near the big Catholic church. The boys called it, "The Cathedral." Here they were able to take in some of the local cuisine, which was not a lot, but it was certainly better than army tucker.

The following morning after breakfast, they packed their gear into the trucks and carts, and loaded all the equipment they had with them, and then they were moved up the road to Poperinge. There they set up camp on the eastern outskirts of the town. They were now only six miles (10 Km) from Ypres. The very first thing they noticed was how much louder the noises coming from the front were. Every now and then, they could even feel the ground shake beneath their feet. That area to the east of them, was known as the Ypres salient, and it was already well known to the men.

A salient is a bulge in an otherwise straight line and as it had been heavily defended by the Allied troops, the Germans had pushed around basically three sides of the town. This meant that any of the troops in the town itself, could be fired on from three directions, from the north, east and south. As a result, Ypres had suffered an incredible pasting of artillery and small arms fire. It was indeed a siege town, although not a great deal of the town itself was left operational. Ypres had been the block in the execution of the Germans' Schlieffen plan. There had already been two major battles over the town of Ypres, one in late 1914 the other in mid-1915.

This second battle had seen the introduction of poison gas. The German army had released chlorine gas, on the French, British and Canadian armies. The effect was devastating, not just in terms of the injuries that it caused, but in its morale destroying effects as well. Gas had introduced a whole new perspective into warfare, as both sides now used chlorine gas, against each other. If you heard the gas bell ring or someone shouted 'GAS', there would be a flurry of activity, as everyone scrambled to get their gas mask out. Generally, they only had a few seconds to get it on, before the green haze of the gas could be smelt, and by then it would be too late. Chlorine gas attacks your lungs, and they would be eaten away. A painful, choking death would follow.

Many of the men who had less exposure to the gas would end up with lifelong breathing problems. Inhalation of the gas in any sort of quantity, usually meant you were finished with the army and you ended up being repatriated, back home to your country of origin. The men had all heard stories of soldiers who had been exposed to the chlorine gas. It was terrifying. The early defence mechanism, when gas was called, was to get a cloth soaked in water and place it over your mouth, nose and eyes. When water was not available, the men pissed on a cloth instead. Well, it was better than inhaling the gas, wasn't it?

Poperinge was a town about the same size as Hazebrouck, but even more of the people had left, moving to safer areas with friends and relatives or to one of the many refugee camps throughout France and even Britain. This time, the men were camped in tents though, on the eastern outskirts of town. This was to be their base for the next month or so, whilst they underwent induction and training with the 1st Canadians. They would move up and back, on a four day rotation, learning everything the Canadians had learned in their time at Hill 60.

On their first day with the Canadians, they had learned that Hill 60, was not really a hill in the normal, geographical sense of the word, but really just a scrap heap from the digging of the railway cutting. The Ypres to Commines railway passed through this area, and as the area was slightly raised over the rest of the land around, they had made a railway cutting about 20 feet deep (6m), at its deepest point, and about half a mile (800m) long, when they built the railway. At its deepest point, the railway was crossed by a road bridge on the Zwarteleen road.

The small village of Zwarteleen was only about 300 m further east of the bridge. A village in name only, as there was nothing left of it, except rubble. The dirt that had been dug out of the cutting, had been dumped in three heaps, one each side of the railway on the south side of the Zwarteleen road and one to the northwest of the bridge. The pile of dirt to the northwest of the bridge was called 'The Dump' and that was in British hands. The one to the south west of the bridge, was called the 'Caterpillar' as it kind of snaked its way across the countryside looking like a caterpillar, and one to the north east of the bridge was called Hill 60, because the top of that was 60 m above sea level. The German army was entrenched on both Caterpillar and Hill 60.

At various times, occupation of both these features had alternated between the British and Germans, and because the area was so flat, any sort of elevation of the landform, made it particularly desirable, for observation purposes, for any army. With elevation on your side, it was easier to see the disposition of the enemy armies and therefore easier, to direct artillery and machine gun fire on to your opposition.

Ypres itself is about twenty five miles (40 km) from the coast, so for this feature, 60m above sea level to be notable, it means the land around is particularly low, and particularly flat. Therein lay the problem, with mining in this area. As the land was extremely low and flat, it was also incredibly wet. One did not have to dig particularly far, before one was already having problems with water inundation. The clay layer was not all that far down, hence everything above that was wet. This meant that any mines the men dug, had to be shallow otherwise they encountered water. As a result, all the mines that had been dug and blown before this, were no more than about twenty feet below ground level. Naturally, this problem affected both the allied digging, and the German digging.

On their first day working with the Canadians, the issue of digging mines in that area that had already been blown, was answered, and the answer was top secret. These mines being dug at Hill 60, went down to 100 feet below ground level. They went through the water layer and the soft Kemmel sand and went down into the clay that underpinned this whole area. This was a particularly sticky clay, a type of blue clay, known as Ypresian clay. Obviously if they dug out the blue clay underground, they had to dump it somewhere.

As a result, they had to go to extreme lengths, to make sure that the Germans could not see that the clay there were digging, was the blue clay. If the Germans discovered they were digging in blue clay, they would know the depth they were digging at. At this point in the war, no one had tried digging mines that deep, and because it took so long to dig those mines, many months, they would have to keep it secret for a long time. If the Germans discovered that they were digging at that depth, German countermeasures could be employed to destroy those mines. At this point in time the Germans had not considered deep mining was possible, due to water inundation, so had neither attempted it, nor developed countermeasures against it, because no one could do it, or so they thought.

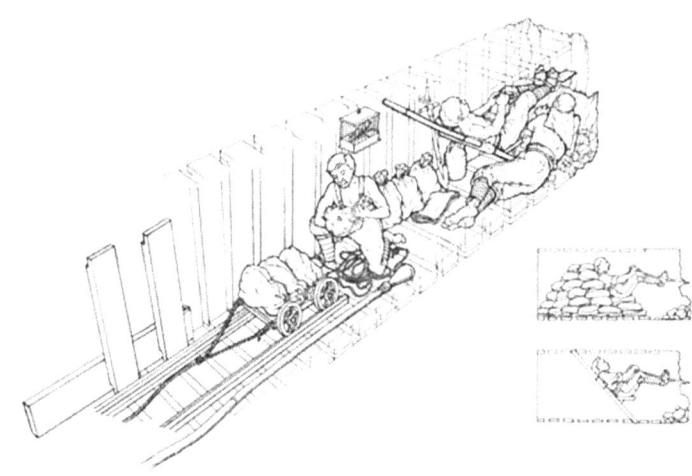

Fig 1
Clay Kicking, removal and transport of spoil. Note the Canary in the cage.
(Courtesy Tunnellers.net)

If you have ever tried digging in the clay, you will know how difficult it is. The clay sticks to the pick, the shovel, your feet, and digging becomes extremely slow. As speed is of the essence in digging these mines, a faster method than pick and shovel needs to be used. When digging underground in London, John Norton-Griffiths found the same problem in the clay beneath that city. A new method of digging the clay out, became necessary and the process of clay kicking was born. Clay kicking, is a process that uses a timber, wedged between the floor and the roof of the tunnel, and inclined at about 60° backwards of the face. A small seat is attached to that timber, and the kicker sits on that seat, facing the face of the tunnel. He has a small, narrow, spade or shovel, with a foot peg on it. The kicker places his foot on the peg, and pushes it into the clay, then levers the spade down, and a second man catches the sod of clay. The Sod is passed backwards to a third man, who bags it, places it on a trolley and sends it backwards for removal.

It is a quiet process, and this is essential if they are not to be discovered by the Germans, digging at that depth. You would think, digging underground, that you would not be able to be heard by anybody else. But this is not so. Each army had designed devices that would allow them to hear, what was going on underground, determine its direction and roughly how far away that sound was. For this purpose, the British army had designed a device called a geophone. A simple device, it consisted of a stethoscope like head piece, connected by 2 lengths of rubber tubing, to two small metal cans a little like boiled sweet tins.

In these tins were a couple of discs of wood 3-4 inches (75-100 mm) in diameter, between which was a layer of mercury wedged between two mica sheets. This arrangement had the capability of magnifying any detected sound several times and could be used to detect sounds up to 100 yds or metres away in this earth. By placing these tins on the floor of the chamber and moving them left and right until the sound in the listeners the ears were the same, they were able to determine the direction that the sound was coming from. It would be at right angles to the line between the two tins.

By repeating that process on the walls of the tunnel, the listener could determine the angle of declination, i.e., is the sound above or below them. By then repeating the exercise from another LP, triangulation was used to determine the location of the detected noise. The Allied armies knew the Germans had a similar detection mechanism to themselves, so silence during digging was of paramount importance.

On this first day with the Canadians, they also discovered that there were the two types of mining going on here at Hill 60. Hill 60 was the name given to all of the workings, here along the Berlin sap, whether it be Hill 60 itself, Caterpillar, or the German frontline. There was the shallow defensive mining and a deeper offensive mining. The purpose of the defensive mining, was to determine what mining activity the Germans were using and to protect their own mining activities. They needed to know what depth the Germans were at, what direction they were heading and whether they were in danger of finding the deep mining shafts. Offensive mining was, as the name suggests, to attack the Germans.

These mines were much deeper, and as such the entrance was much further away from the front line, for 2 reasons. The first reason was for security. Situating the entrance well behind the line made its opening, easier to hide and defend. The second reason made it easier to have a long, slowly declining sap for access purposes. The entrances to the offensive mines were located about 500 yards (450m) away from Hill 60 itself, back along the rail line, in an area known as Larch Wood. Larch Wood also served as the headquarters or company HQ. The entrance to the defensive system was from the frontline trenches or communication trenches.

To access the defensive mines, they went down a shaft to the main sap, or in some cases down an inclined shaft, which lead straight towards the enemy front line. This was located just behind the front line. There were several shafts down to the main gallery spaced at about 100 feet (30m) to 150 feet (45m) apart. Once out under No-Man's Land, the entry sap intersected the main lateral gallery, which ran parallel to the front line. This gallery ran the whole length of this sector, at about 18 feet deep (5.5m), just above the water line. Every 50 feet (15m) or so, another shorter gallery continued towards the enemy front line, a distance of about 30 feet (10m). At the end of each of these short galleries, another short 20 foot (6m) Sap was cut parallel to the enemy line. These T shaped galleries, just go out, to form the listening posts along the front line and were used to determine what mining the Germans were doing.

Both Bob and Bill were amazed at how complicated this whole system was. Up until now, the most they knew about the system was on paper, and on paper it looked quite simple. The other thing that surprised them, was how little space there was in fact, underground. Bob was only 5 foot 9 tall (175cm), and Bill was 5 foot 8 (173cm), but when it came down to the listening posts both of them had to get down on hands and knees, as these were only between 3 and 4 feet high (1-1.2m). They were also incredibly stuffy, with not much air movement through them. Thankfully, the guys down at the listening posts only had to spend a couple of hours there each time, until they were relieved. Bob's purpose of being down there, was to check out the timbering system, for shoring up these drives and tunnels.

Bill, of course, was more interested in the water that was there, as even though they were above the water level, there was still a lot of water in these tunnels. Much of the timber for the tunnels had been sourced from local forests or woods, but there sure was a lot of timber in these tunnels. Some areas, where the ground had been softer, had a lot more timber in them, than others. Bob could not help but think that down the deeper tunnels, probably a lot less timber was required, as the tunnels were cut through the clay.

"If there's this much water in these tunnels," Bill commented, "hoo much is goin' tae be doon in the deeper mines?"

"You ain't seen nothing yet," replied the Canadian who was showing them around. "You just wait till you get down to the deep mine, then you'll see some water."

The men of 1ATC were in groups of about ten, which means there are about five groups touring around the area to a familiarise themselves with what had been going on in this area. This tour the men were on, would only last couple of hours. After that, they were all thrown in off the deep end, pitching in to complete this mine-system at Hill 60 and Caterpillar. The best kind of learning, would be on the job learning.

Back on the surface, the noise accosted the men's hearing. They had not realised just how quiet it was below ground. Sure, they could hear the Crump, Crump, Crump, of the artillery above, but they were basically the only sounds they could hear. They were met with gunfire, machine gun fire, and artillery fire, all around them, as this was one of the hottest sectors on the western front line. Some of the men yearned to go back underground, others were glad not to be underground any more, it just depended on your point of view. Some men, and it did not matter what you are in the tunnellers or in the infantry, just could not handle, being underground. Above-ground meant you could get shot or hit by an artillery shell or shrapnel but below ground, there was always the danger of cave-ins or camouflets, and being buried alive. That was the biggest fear the men had.

When your listening post, had determined that there was a mine being dug in your vicinity, a small hole could be bored through the wall about eight inches (200mm) in diameter, towards the sound of the digging. A long pipe loaded with a small explosive charge of about 200 pounds (90kg), could be pushed through this hole towards the sound of the opposition's mine and when exploded, would cause a cave-in to occur. If the explosion did not break through to the surface, these charges were known as camouflets. If the explosion did break through to the surface, then they were craters. The trick with a good camouflet, was to choose the right charge to explode the opposition's mine but leave yours undamaged. If it did cause any damage to your own mine, then the men were quick to redirect the drive around the damaged area and continue on their merry way.

Now being above ground, the men kept their heads down and headed north west, back up the communication trenches, parallel to the railway line, all the way back to Larchwood. The noises were a lot less back there. The rat-a-tat-tat of the machine guns was just the far off barking. Back at battalion HQ at Larch Wood, they immediately headed back underground. This time on a long, downward, sloping walk. This tunnel was known as the Berlin sap. So, called because it was so long, the men thought, it must be headed for Berlin. In fact, the sap was about 500 + yards (500m) down to the 100 foot (30m) level. Halfway along, they encountered a vertical shaft to get them down through the water saturated layer. This shaft was made of timber and pitch, in order to try and keep the water out. Once they were below the water level, they discovered that that system was only partially successful and as had previously been explained to them, this area was now exceedingly wet.

"Ok boys," their Canadian guide explained, "at this point in the Berlin sap, you are running parallel to the railway line above, and also, following directly below the trench that you have used, to get from Hill 60, back to Larchwood." They continued along until a short while later they came to a point where the sap split into 3 smaller galleries and he continued, "Here we are at the point where the bridge is directly above us. As you can see upfront, the Berlin sap splits into three separate tunnels, A, B and C galleries. "A" gallery, heads 45° to the left and we plan it to go a further 50 to 100 feet (15-30 m) further, until it is directly underneath Hill 60. "B" gallery goes straight ahead and is planned to go a further 300 feet (90 m), where it will end up directly under the Caterpillar. "C" gallery heads off to the right, and we plan that one to end up under the frontline of the Germans, on the north of the railway line, at a point about halfway between Caterpillar and the bridge. If we can get all this done, we'll give them Huns one helluva big shock, when they go off, them's as what lives anyway."

These three galleries were where the work was currently going on. He went on, "You may have noticed the canary in the cage at the work face. He's not a pet. Down here, you cannot guarantee the quality of the air. There are pockets of trapped bad air or gasses in some of this earth. Unfortunately, we can't smell them, so that's where this poor little sod comes in. If he keels over dead, get the hell outta here, coz the air is bad, and don't come back until the proto men have set up ventilation and given the all clear. No ifs, no buts, just get out." The men just turned and looked at each other in the half light. They of course, had heard about the canaries' role in the mines, and the miners amongst them knew their value, but the other tradesmen had not seen them before. It was a collective 'Poor little bugger' look.

"I see wha' ye mean aboot the water," Bob mentioned to their guide. "Will it noe be a problem when ye charge these mines? I mean, water with the explosives. Will it noe kill them by saturation?"

"That is a problem our engineers are working on at this very moment." He replied. The explosives will be packed in Kerosine tins and greased up to prevent any water getting into them. So, they think they have that part of it all under control. The bigger problem is going to be with the leads that come down here to the mines. They, of course, are electrically fired and water and electrics; well that's just not a good mix. So, the chances of short circuit in the leads it is quite high. At the moment, they're looking to have a series of leads coming down, so even if one does short circuit, the others should still be able to carry the load.

"With multiple sets of leads going to the surface, and with constant testing of those lines, the officers should be able to establish, whether those lines have either short circuited, or whether they have indeed been cut by the Germans. That last one is of course, what we're trying to avoid, with the listening posts all around the area, to determine whether the Germans have indeed worked out the depth we are mining at. If they do, we're sunk, 'cause there's 20 sometin' mines between here and Plug Street Wood."

After having been with the Canadian guide for about an hour, the men were starting to get a bit of an understanding of the Canadian drawl. Some were still having difficulties however, so a bit of translating was going on between some of the fellows in the group. Mind you, he was having trouble with their multitude of accents as well.

Plug Street Wood was the slang name, to a forest about 6 miles (10Km) south of them, called Ploegsteert Wood. They all reconned that the names around here were difficult to pronounce so Ypres became 'Wipers', Wytschate became White sheet and Ploegsteert, became Plug Street. Their Canadian friend continued, "At this point in time, it does not appear that they have worked out we are that deep, and we'd like to keep it that way. That's why we're asking you all to keep your voices down to whisper and keep your boots muffled. Old Blighty, he's been pretty good givin' us the boots with the metal underneath them to make 'em last a long time, but they sure as hell make a noise, when you're walking down here. Noise is as much your enemy, as those Huns, so for god's sake, keep it quiet."

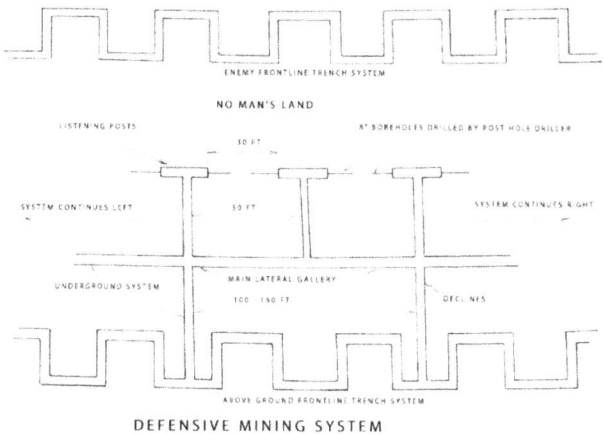

DEFENSIVE MINING SYSTEM

Fig 2
Diagrammatic layout of the defensive mining system and listening posts

From the 3-way junction, they headed down to the workings in A shaft. They had not gone too far down there yet, but the men were able to see how the clay kickers, were set up and working. Bob and the other carpenters, studied the clay kickers seat closely. It all made sense now. It was simple, and it was effective, and they could see just how easy it was, to pare that clay out of the wall in front of them. The Miners in their group, obviously concentrated on the way the clay was being kicked out of the wall in front, or more correctly, pushed, and levered, out of the wall in front of them. They were pretty chuffed to be able sit down on the job. But enough for the jokes right now, they were not going to make any excess noise, whilst they were underneath those Huns, who were now, directly the above them.

Now in a crouch walk, they went back to the three way junction and headed up gallery B to see how progress was going there. It was, of course, much the same as in drive A, but they still had a lot further to go than A. Drive C was like A, approaching its destination. The groups then turned tail and headed back along the Berlin sap, up the shaft and back out to Larch Wood HQ. By the time they made it to the surface, dawn was starting to break, and the early indications of the day were starting to be felt. Much of the movement around the frontline area, had to be conducted during the hours of darkness, and, as with the Hun having possession of Hill 60, the highest point in the area, he could direct artillery fire down on to any movement between Ypres and Larch Wood.

Tomorrow night, when they came back out, they would be attached to a similar tradesman as themselves and start on the actual work itself. Bob noted that all the timber they were using was Oregon pine, which has one of the highest strength to weight ratios of any timber. It is reasonably light and exceptionally strong. It is also an easy timber to work with. If, as they had explained to them by their Canadian guide, there were twenty something mines being dug down the Messines ridge to Plug Street Wood, then an awful lot of Timber was going to be needed, by the time all these mines have been dug. That seemed like a supply nightmare to him.

Chapter 10
Baptism of Fire

The feelings amongst the men as they made their way back towards Ypres, past the rows of crosses to their right, were a mixture of excitement, anticipation, fear, and doubt. It was only two miles (3 km) back to Ypres, and much of that was through trenches or saps that the British Sappers had cut in the year prior to this. There were miles and miles of them. All these trenches had been given road names that were familiar to them, so the main trench system they use to get back to a Ypres was called Bensham Road. Once through Bensham Road, they would go right to enter Ypres through the Lille gate, but first they had to pass through 'Shrapnel Corner'.

Now, to say that the men were displeased at having to pass through an area called Shrapnel Corner could be considered somewhat of an understatement. This intersection, which had gained the name Shrapnel Corner, was at the intersection of the Commines road, Kemmels road, and Rijselse road. At the same time the railway line crosses through at this intersection as well. It got the name shrapnel corner because it was such an obvious intersection, the German artillery were able to zero in on it, with months of practice to get their range and bearings correct.

As a result, any movement that was seen at this intersection, was easily blasted by the artillery and shrapnel went in all directions: hence the name, Shrapnel Corner. It was for this reason that any movement through that area, should be made during the hours of darkness, or very quickly. Any movement during daylight hours was hazardous to say the least.

Back in Ypres, before the sun came up, the men settled into their prearranged "accommodation/" Ypres had been abandoned by the locals. No one was left in the town. Many of the town's houses and buildings, had been bombed either by the artillery or the Huns' aircraft. Everyone wanted possession of Ypres, but the

Allies held it throughout the war, but that did not stop the Hun from trying to winkle them out. By the end of the war virtually nothing would be left standing in the town. It would take many years to rebuild all the bombed out structures.

*

Ypres had been a major trading centre in Belgium for hundreds of years. The most common commodity traded through this area was textiles, high quality textiles. Ypres is known to have existed about 2,000 years prior to this war that these men were fighting. It first came to prominence at around 1000 to 1200 AD as a textile trader, then trading linen with London. It was the centre of textile trade for all of Europe. The now famous, Cloth Hall, was built sometime during the 13th century and St Martin's church was built just behind the Cloth Hall and became a cathedral during the 16th century. St Martins would become significant for the men, in the months to come. Ypres had a long history of conflict, having been subject to a multitude of rulers. At various times in its life, it had been under French, Austrian-Netherlands, and Spanish rule, and finally under the sovereign state of Belgium. Now it was subject to an attempt at German rule.

*

The weary men were now directed towards a selection of least damaged houses, and advised to get a good sleep, preferably in the cellars of these houses. Bert joined them as they sat around their little stoves. He had been in a separate group being shown around the workings but had come to much the same conclusions as the rest of the blokes. This was going to be one hell of a job, they had in front of them. They sat around discussing what they had seen today, and some of them even had ideas, on how they were going to tackle, their part of the job. Tomorrow would see if those ideas came to fruition, or was that later today? Already time seemed to be distorted. This, distortion of time, was soon to be their new normal.

Later that afternoon, after a sleep of sorts, the men roused, cleaned and ate their small evening meal on their own little Kerosine stove. At least the tea was hot, and sweet and black. There being no refrigeration, milk was a scarce commodity, so black tea it was. They would get used to it; they had no choice. As soon as it was dark enough, they made their way up through the Lille gate, through Shrapnel Corner and then up the railway line, this time all the way to Larch Wood. As soon as they arrived at the HQ, the other half of this section, headed back towards Ypres. The remaining half section was then divided up, with about thirty going down Berlin sap, the other fifteen or so, heading along the trench line, to the defensive mining system. There was less work going on in the defensive system.

Once down the Berlin sap, the men were allocated to Canadians in their own trades. Bob and Bert, set about shaping timbers to shore up the work that had been going on, in the last hour or so. The Timbers had to.be measured up and worked out at the face, but any shaping work on the timber, had to be carried out way back at the trench entrance. Certainly not at any depth, where the Germans could determine that they were working deep. Some of the timbers needed 2 men to carry others only the one. Needless to say, the carpenters attempted to keep the shoring timber identical, all the way through the tunnel system. That way there would be much less need for timbers going backwards and forwards, as it was a long hike and would take a lot of time. The main problem for the carriers was the wet. It was not unusual to come upon one of your mates lying flat on his back with a timber or two on top of him. You always helped him if you could, as quietly as you could. The procession of timber carriers was relentless, back and forward, back and forward.

Bob's estimation of the amount of timber required at these depths proved correct though. This blue clay did stick together rather well, so did require less timber than the shallower run. There being 3 sub-galleries, working off the end of Berlin sap, the need was relentless, regardless of the firmer clay.

So it was, on that first day that Bob and Bert, spent their time shaping and cutting timbers, mostly back at the tunnel entrance. In that area, all the accommodation, offices and workshops, were underground. Anything above ground was subject to artillery fire, so would not last particularly long. There was a carpenters' workshop there, so any of the shaping could be done either outside for the larger timbers or underground for anything smaller. In this area, being 500 yards or more from the front line, they could make as much noise as they liked, shaping their timbers, cutting their timbers and talking to each other. It was only once they were down the vertical shaft, part way along the Berlin sap, that they had to quieten everything.

Bob was doing some thinking as they were going along the early part of the tunnel, "I tell ye wha', Bert, I don't think I learnt any o' this in ma apprenticeship.

And I'll tell ye what else, no one's life, ever depended on wha' I was doin' in ma apprenticeship either. It never prepared me for this."

"Aye! I'll agree with ye on that one Bob. Hardly what one would call precision joinery though, is it?" Bert returned.

Bob giggled and added, "That's for sure. That's for sure. All the same, I dinnae wannae ge' it wrong though. It's a sod o' a walk all the way back here."

"Aye it is that," replied Bert. "I'm very glad we've go' this electric light doon here though, would be a bugger tae get it right by kerosene lamp."

"Aye, sometimes I think it mebee easier tae do it ootside an' brave the whizz-bangs. They're noe very accurate so far." Bob said this more in hope than observation. They had not been there long enough yet, to experience the full force of an artillery barrage.

Over the next week, the new norm became, shaping timbers, ducking for cover as the Minenwerfers dropped in, dodging whizz-bangs, carting timber, erecting supports, building new clay kicking seats, moving the kickers forever forward and anything else to do with wood that the command wanted them to do. All the time in the mines, was spent wet. Exceedingly wet. The water was an ever-present problem. It seeped through the ceiling, it wept from the walls, it ran along the floor. The rats did not seem to mind though. The men on the pumps had a constant job, keeping the water out. These pumps were a two man affair. One on each side, working the handles backwards and forwards. And the mud! Oh, the mud. It stuck to everything. Boots became 3 times as heavy and never dried out. Thick, sticky gluey mud. Blue mud underground and orange mud up top. It stunk as well, although after a while you became used to it and did not notice the smell.

"Surely there has to be a better way," Bob thought. There were so many of these pumps, attempting to keep up with the seepage. It took lots of manpower. Manpower that could have been put to better use. All the time the mines kept getting closer to their final objective. All the men involved from 1ATC learned their jobs quickly and efficiently, even the miners, eventually, whose complaints about slave labour, seem to disappear the longer time went on. In fact, not only did their complaints disappear, but they seem to excel in the work they were doing. The Canadian engineers marvelled at how quickly 1ATC miners could get the clay out of that wall and down the gallery. Early in the piece, progress by the miners of 1ATC, tended to be too slow, due to their ignorance of the clay kicking techniques. Major Hill, CRE, was constantly on at the miners to increase their work output.

Now, back in the early 20th century, miners were not exactly renowned for their love of bosses, rules or authority. Whilst this may well have been the army they were in, it did not stop them from complaining about the work they had to do, their bosses, the officers or the pressures they were being put under. GHQ did not quite see it that way, they put it down to typical miner dissatisfaction, their tendency to strikes for no reason and general lack of discipline. Once they got the hang of the clay kicking process though, they were hard to stop, and progress was swift.

To the men's surprise, after a period of only twelve days, they received word they would be moving on. The training was complete, and they would be moving to the other end of the Messines ridge, to Plug Street Wood. Whilst the men had certainly become accustomed to the life at Hill 60, they were glad to hear they were moving out of this hell hole. Mind you, there were those who believed in "better the devil you know, than the devil you don't". Still, they had been told that Hill 60 was an exceptionally hot part of the line, so anywhere else should be a little safer. By now it was almost the end of May, and galleries were approaching their final point. It would not be long now, until the Canadians started charging those mines. The sizes of the chambers they were to build, indicated that there was an awful lot of explosives to go down there, and they would be glad to be out of it.

That evening, the men loaded up their equipment, trudged their way back to Ypres, and settled down in their billets for the night, in the knowledge that tomorrow, they would be out of this sector. Tonight, in between whizz-bangs, their entertainment would come from a newspaper that had been started up in Ypres, by some of the British officers, several months prior. It was a somewhat tongue in cheek newspaper that delighted in taking the mickey out of British authority. It was full of humorous stories, poetry, tongue in cheek advertisements, and some parts of it were obviously deliberately aimed at certain officers.

The newspaper they were reading was called 'The New Church' times. Apparently, it had been started right here in Ypres, some four months or so ago. The name of the newspaper when it was printed here in Ypres, had been a play on the word Ypres and the British difficulty in pronouncing it. It had therefore been called the "Wipers Times." Each time the publishers of the paper were moved, they took their presses with them and renamed the paper with wherever they were at the time, but they were all incarnations of the 'Wipers Times'. The men had lots of laughs at the expense of certain officers and lots of the articles in the newspaper. This included a singsong of a couple of verses of one of the parody songs, to a well-known tune.

With the help of Bluey on the mouth organ, they all chimed in at one time or another. They only had one copy of the Wipers Times (New Church Times), so not everyone can sing at the one time because they could not all get around the one sheet at once. But they all knew the line "never mind" and it was assumed that even the Germans, who were over three miles away, could probably hear them all scream that line out.

If the Hun lets off some gas—never mind.
If the Hun attacks in mass—never mind.
If you're dugout's blown to bits,
Or the COs throwing fits,
Or a Crump your rum jar hits—never mind.
If your trench is mud knee-high—never mind.
You can't find a spot that's dry—never mind.
If a sniper has you set,
Through dents in your parapet,
And your troubles fiercer get—never mind.

During their choral exploits, they were aware that they were not alone. It was evident that other basements in their near area were chiming in with "never mind/" At least they had something to laugh about, for a change. The nearly two weeks they had spent there at Hill 60, they had lost three of their mates carted off to hospital, wounded. Whilst working at Larch Wood, they were far enough from the frontline that they did not have to worry about rifle fire. What they did have to worry about however, was the incoming artillery that had been labelled whizz-bangs. This term came about, as there was no warning of these artillery shells coming in, so the first you knew of it, was as the shell whizzed by, before it landed and went bang.

As the shells were travelling faster than the speed of sound, they arrived before the sound did. Up at the frontline, they also had to contend with whizz-bangs, but they had the added pleasure of having to deal with Minenwerfers, or

Minnies, as the men used to call them. This was German for mine launchers. They were a sort of trench mortar, with rather large shells fired from a particularly short-barrelled artillery piece, generally fired quite high, to come down and land in the trenches. The German army employed 3 Minenwerfers, a 7.58 cm (3 inch), which could be moved around by one person, a 17 cm (6 ½ inch) and a 25 cm (10 inch). Both latter two, required at least one horse to tow it around. The 17 and 25 cm versions could pack quite a punch and cause an awful lot of damage.

They were, however, not particularly accurate, and were somewhat indiscriminate in the choice of their landing site, so you never knew quite where they were going to land, but at least with these, being of low muzzle velocity, you did get some prior warning of their arrival. The three men they had lost wounded, were all results of Minnies that had hit on the frontline, where the men were working on the defensive mining system. At this point, they had no information on how any of the other three sections had fared, but they would find out within the next day or two.

After the levity had died down, the men settled into their tea and rations, in their snug little basements in Ypres. At least being late May the nights were not too cold.

"Imagine what this would be like down here in the basement in midwinter," Bob commented.

"Oh, my Lord! It would be worse than Dundee," said Bert, "and that is really bad."

"I hope we're nowhere near here in winter. I left Scotland tae get away from the cold. Sydney's winters are more like Scotland summers, and I miss them already. But Belgium in winter, can get very, very, cold," Bob added.

"Aye!" was the consensus amongst all the men there.

"Brrrrr. Just imagine being huddled around your little stoves trying tae get some warmth oot o' that. Noe much chance o' heat there," Bill postured. He went on, "Mind ye, I dinnae see this lot being over by Christmas, at the current rate, so I guess we can expect tae spend the winter over here somewhere and I don't think it's going tae matter, whether we're here in Ypres or down on the Somme or up the coast, it's still going tae be dashed cold."

General agreement followed this statement, with a few nods and a few shakes of the head, and things went rather quiet. "Eh Bluey, 'ows about strikin' up a tune on that mouth blower thing o' yours. I think we can do with a bit of cheering up again, after all, we are out of 'ere tomorra." This was Davo. There is always a Davo in an Australian unit. It is, of course, short for David, which does not really need any shortening, but Australians can shorten anything, even if they make it longer.

Over the next hour, they had choruses of "It's a long way to Tipperary. Pack up your troubles in your old kit bag, Danny boy, Waltzing Matilda, Loch Lomond," and anything else Bluey could come up with, plus a few nobody knew.

When all went quiet again, apart from the distant artillery, or occasionally not so distant, one by one they all turned in, each wondering where they would be this time tomorrow. One thing about army life, you never get told what is coming up next, it is always a surprise, one way or the other. Sometimes it is really good not knowing what is coming up. Other times it just plain frustrating, is just like they do not trust you. Bob settled down on his bed and his thoughts wandered 9000 miles (14500 km), to a little house, on a little street, in a little city, in a big country. He wondered how Jean was going. Yes, he did think about the others as well. He wondered what they were all doing.

It would be the middle of the day in Perth, so Robert would be in the shop, and yes with the lunchtime rush, Jean would probably be there helping him too. Yes, she would be there helping him. That's what she will be doing. He smiled, pretended to sniff the air, and imagine the aromas coming out of that bakery. All her could smell though was mud, filth and explosives. Oh, how he missed them all, but most of all, of course, he missed Jean.

When will I get to see you again? he thought. *Will I get to see you again? Will she say yes? Will Robert allow it? Will Mimey allow it? Would she move to Sydney? Would I have to move to Perth?* All these thoughts were running through his head.

He leaned over and gave Bluey a shove. "Wheesht man! Stop yer snoring. Ye'll bring the whizz-bangs doon on us wi' tha' racket." He gave a laugh, rolled over, pulled the blanket up around his neck and went to sleep.

3 am came around quickly and the boys were slow to rouse. They pulled their kit together, climbed out of their cellar and made their way down to the main square. On one side of the square, was the imposing structure of the Cloth Hall, a building dating back to the 13th century. Formerly a beautiful example of the type of architecture of its time, it no longer looked as pristine as it used to, having been subjected to artillery fire from the German army. There were significant signs of damage to this beautiful building, and to St Martin's Cathedral behind

it. The spire in Cloth Hall, climbed way above the rest of the building and would have been a perfect observation point, which undoubtedly is why it had been so relentlessly subjected to artillery fire. The spire had been significantly damaged and was no doubt useless as an observation point now. Bob hoped they would spare the remains of that building, but this was not to be, as they would find out in the months to come.

The men all headed out through the ruins in the west of the town, across the moat, as the men called it and down the road a mile or so, to the lorries waiting for them. This was the side of town that was the most protected from enemy fire. Once they were all loaded up, their convoy commenced its journey towards Poperinge. There they joined up with the rest of the company staff and headed south towards the border with France. The ride in these lorries was particularly hard. They had heavy springs and solid rubber tyres. The advantage of the solid rubber tyres of course, was that they never went flat, so unless they were significantly damaged, there was no need to stop and change tyres.

This was a significant advantage in a war zone, where any stationary vehicle, soon became a stationary target. They travelled about 12 miles (20 km) south to the border then crossed over into France and continued to Bailleul. Here they were to set up camp again the same as they had in Poperinge. This was to be their base whilst they were off the frontline. It was about 6 miles (10 km) from their eventual worksite. This site was at the southern end of the Messines Ridge, at a place known as Hill 63. Hill 63 was a headquarters area, on the north side Ploegsteert Wood. Finally, the men would get to see this Plug Street Wood.

Chapter 11
Wallangarra Dugouts

They arrived at Bailleul, at around 5 am. It was, by now, already light enough for them to set up camp, which they did in fairly quick time, as by now they were getting well practised at it. First item on the agenda, a nice hot cup of tea. It really is amazing, how in English-descended countries that a nice hot cup of tea, cures all ills. Even weary bones that have been subjected to a pounding for the last hour or so. One cup of tea, and all is forgiven and forgotten. After their cuppa, the men paraded for instructions for the day, and then headed off to breakfast. They felt they had deserved it by now. As both halves of the company were now back together, they sat around chatting about their experiences, through breakfast.

Unsurprisingly, everyone had similar stories to tell. Trying to understand the Canadians, was almost universal, as most of them had never come across anyone with that accent before. They agreed that it did not take them too long to realise that they are not actually that much different from themselves. Really, the only difference was in how they sounded and how they dressed. They had the same complaints, the same issues with authority, the same issues with food and the work they were trying to accomplish.

Secondly, the work was tough and fast paced, which gave little room for rest or breaks of any kind. Third, working underground to many of the men was creepy, and incredibly difficult, none the least because at any moment the Hun could break through the wall of your tunnel and start shooting.

Also, they could have found us by now and be setting a camouflet, which could blow us in and that, would be the end of that. The men universally agreed that to be blown in and to be stuck on the other side of a blow, little oxygen, and little chance of rescue, would be about the worst way to go.

"Hell's bells! You could be stuck on the other side of a blow, with no light, no food, nothing. Just you and the inevitable death," one of the other boys commented.

"Can you imagine just how panicked you would be? If you had your rifle with you, which you probably wouldn't, you could shoot yourself. That would be preferable to dying down there slowly," said another.

"All right boys, how about we talk about something else. We don't need to dwell on that one," one of the other fellows chimed in. "At least it sounds like we're going somewhere a little safer than where we've been. I sure as hell hope so anyway," he added.

After breakfast, they were given time to sort their kit out, and then once again loaded onto the lorries, where they were taken a few miles to the north east, through Nieuwkerke, and then down to an area, just west of what they were told, was Plug Street Wood. They were dropped off on the road about a mile (1.6 km) short of the wood.

"Where the 'ell is this wood?" called out one of the boys.

One of the drivers pointed to an area to their east and said, "See that bunch of sticks standing up over there, well that's your Plug Street, Wood. Well, what's left of it anyway. It's had the shit bombed out of it for the last two years, by both sides actually, as they both had it at one time or another. The frontline is just on the other side of that patch of sticks, and that's where we plan to give 'em hell. Good luck boys! See you in a couple of days."

"See you later, Jack, thanks for the ride," they chorused back.

"Strewth! That's what they call Plug Street Wood? Some bloody forest! Looks like it was a reasonable size once, but she sure as hell ain't now." Bluey echoed the feelings of all the men, when they saw those bunches of sticks, they called Plug Street Wood.

The sergeant, another Scot, came forward to where the men were gathering, and pointed to a clearing, to the left of the timber, where there was a slight rise. "That rise ye can see there, tha's Hill 63 and tha's where we're headed. That's where we're going tae be building the headquarters, undergroond. It's aboot a mile (1.6 km) behind the frontline, so given that ye will be undergroond most of the time, ye should be quite safe there. At least ye won't have tae worry aboot counter mining on the part of the Germans, it's way too far behind the frontline for them to reach underground. We'll have the whole company together again doon there, within the next couple o' weeks. Come on then, form up."

Off they marched, well sort of ambled anyway, in the general direction of Hill 63. It took them about 25 minutes to make their way across the open ground, to the area known as Hill 63. They could see the drive being made in through an opening in the side of the hill. They were on the leeward side of the hill, so the enemy were unable to see them, or what they were doing, so they are able to move around with impunity.

They were met at the workings by Captain McBride. "You're going to be working here, at Hill 63 building this headquarters and accommodation for about 1200 men," the captain explained. "Not only that but you'll be working on several trench projects in this sector, and a few other bits and pieces as well, which will be explained to you along the way. Today, you get to have a look at what's been going on, which is not greatly different from what you've already seen, however, in this case there will be a lot more for you to do within the caverns that you dig. You will be erecting accommodation within these catacombs, offices, messing areas as well as defensive gun emplacements, in order to protect the people housed below."

"From what I've heard of your progress at Hill 60, this job should be a piece of cake for you. We need to have it finished by November, so you will need to put your backs into it, but I am confident you will achieve this target. Section commanders, carry on."

The men broke up and had a look through the catacombs, as they were now calling it. They were shown the plans detailing what was required and they agreed that it was straightforward enough but a huge task all the same.

"Right boys, let's show 'em what we can do," somebody yelled. They separated into their trade sections, took their instructions, and got straight down to work.

For days they toiled away in their catacombs, extending galleries, digging rooms, digging offices and all the passageways to join all these together. In the accommodation area there were beds to for the carpenters to build as well as installing supports, tables, seating and all the other items required for accommodation area. All the passageways needed shoring up, doorways to be installed, gas doors to put in place. The offices needed their tables and chairs and workspaces to be built as well. In this respect, Bob, Bert and the other carpenters, had plenty of work to do. At least this time, there was a bit of variety to their work, unlike there had been back at Hill 60. One of the first things they did though, was to build themselves a couple of decent workshops, and install some decent workbenches and equipment; amongst the mud as usual.

Whilst the men of No 4 Section toiled away at Hill 63, the remainder of the company was working to their south, between Ploegsteert and Houplines, on the outskirts of Armentieres. During late May and early June, they were working down on trench 88, and trenches 95-101. By the end of June, they included in their tasks, diggings in trench 123, which was only a mile (1.6 km) east of where the men were at Hill 63. So it was that the 1st Australian Tunnelling Co had taken over full responsibility of all the diggings between Plug St Wood and Armentieres. Word also made its way through to the men at Hill 63 that the other sections had lost three men killed, including Lt Smith, and seven men wounded.

The evening of the 10th of June was a fairly quiet affair with only the occasional sound of distant machine gun fire. This sound was always around. It was common practice for both sides to randomly fire off at the opposition trenches just to make sure everyone kept their heads down. At around 2 AM the men were roused by a large explosion to their south east, not that far away.

Bob said to Bert, "Soonds like someone's getting' a bit o' a touch up tonight."

Bert replied, "Aye. That one's a wee bit oot of place. Only the one explosion. Mebee someone's blown a small mine."

"I hope not," answered Bob. "Tha's doon towards the diggings at birdcage. Hope they're ok. Oor boys are doon there."

They need not have worried that night. As they were to find out in the coming days, Lt Woodward had been given the task by command to take out a suspected German mine entrance at a place called "Red House." It was well out in no man's land, right next to the German front line, about 180 m (200 yds) from allied front lines. He had been chosen as it was known he had explosives experience, and this, Red House, was causing much consternation amongst allied command. Woodward, Sgt Fraser and Spr Morris, crept out and set a 65 lb (30 kg) charge of ammonal in the cellar of this house. They discovered once they got there that it was not an entrance to a mining system but a heavily armed machine gun post that had been pouring constant, copious fire down on the allied trenches.

Lt Woodward fired the charge, from about 20 yds (18m) in front of their own trench, as the leads they had were not long enough to make it back to their own trench. Once the explosion subsided, they all bolted for their own lines before the German front line could open up on them. They just made it back, before the air became hot with machine gun fire. For his efforts that night, Lt Woodward would be awarded the Military Medal (MM). Sgt Fraser would eventually receive a promotion to Lieutenant and transfer to the 3rd Field Co Engineers. He would be awarded the DCM and was KIA 31st of May 1918. Spr Morris would receive a promotion to Sergeant and be awarded the MSM. He would be WIA late in the war and RTA 21 December 1918. Red House was no longer a problem after that. It no longer existed.

By the time August came around, the men of No 4 Section were becoming concerned about their progress. They knew what the plans were, and they were achieving anywhere between twenty and fifty feet (6 to 15 m) per day, depending on the width of the cut, but they could see at the present rate they were not going to hit the November target. They needed more men, and they voiced their concerns. In turn, they were informed that men from the rest of the company would be coming to join them before too long, as they completed projects they were on. True to their word at the end of August, more men started filtering back to the Hill 63 dugouts, from outlying jobs. They were really glad to see their mates again, but just as glad to see more men working on the job with them. It gave them hope. Hope that they would get it done in time.

By now, the catacombs were being known by an alternative name. That of the 'Wallangarra Dugouts'. The men figured that Lt Woodward, who was now with them on the job, was from Tenterfield, NSW, just south of the border with Queensland and Wallangarra was only ten miles (16 km) north, on the Queensland side of the border. Something about their diggings must have reminded him of the Wallangarra area.

Every now and then, Fritz tried dropping artillery over on the backside of the slope that was the entrance to Hill 63 dugouts. Despite occasionally destroying a few more trees and giving the boys a bit more work to do cleaning up, their efforts were largely ineffective. That was, until 8 September, when they managed to drop their artillery, right on top of the Ellen sap head, one of their entrances. It caused quite a bit of damage and necessitated the release of a lot of men from other jobs to repair that damage. Thankfully, there were no injuries from that artillery explosion, so the men just repaired it all and moved back to what they were doing before.

By the beginning of October, the rate of work in the dugouts had increased substantially. They were now hitting over 60 feet (19 m) per day. At this rate, the men could see that they would indeed hit their target of being, completed by

November. At about this time Nos 1 and 2 Section had completed their work on trench 123, so some of them joined the group at Hill 63, and others of them returned to Ypres to work on the Lille gate dugouts, a similar, but smaller system to that being dug at Hill 63. Once again 1ATC was spread around Belgium.

Now that the workforce was substantially bigger, there were times when Bob was able to take a break from the carpentry work, so he would head outside and up the Hill, to the lookouts. He scrambled up the hill, dodging the shell holes as he went, and settled into one of the observation trenches, at the top. The Hill was not particularly high, but in flat ground any extra height made a good look out. To his left could see the town of Messines, about two miles (3 km) away. The town after which the ridge they were mining, was named. To his right, only 1 mile hence, was a small village of Ploegsteert, and two miles beyond that over the border in France, Armentieres. In between, was a scene of utter devastation. Not a tree was left with any foliage, not a blade of grass left unturned. You could still see the roads, or what was left of them, sort of. They had become somewhat indistinct, due to bombardment, but you could still make out that they were, at least at one time, a road.

Even from his distance, he could see the edges of the roads littered with wreckage and dead horses. Plug Street Wood, in which he was situated, offered no barrier to the views other than the occasional stick, which used to be a trunk of a tree. The bulk of the trees had been destroyed, by artillery fire. He could clearly see the frontline, as it was only one and a half miles (2 ½ km) away, zigzagging in an arc from directly in front of him to 45° to his left. He could see, hear, and feel the effects of the artillery, as they exploded on each side of the frontline in an attempt to dig out the opposition. Because by now, he knew where to look, he could see the workings of the mines down at the Birdcage, Factory farm, Trench 127, up to Petite Douve farm. He could not work out whether to smile, laugh, shake his head or cry at the name Petite Douve farm. Not so much the Little Dove part of the name, but the farm.

That was a farm? he thought. *There sure is not anything left of the farm now, and if there is, when our guys are finished with it, there won't be anything left at all. All the work that family have put into that farm, destroyed. If they ever get back to it how are they going to start again? How are any of these poor farmers, ever going to start all over again?* He just sat and stared, thinking about it all. Sometimes one can have too much time to think.

He went back down to the dugouts and into the workshop, where he found Bert. He sat down on one of the benches, and just stared into nothing, totally embroiled in his own thoughts. "Hey Bob!" He snapped out of his dreamland to see Bert standing right in front of him. "Are you okay, Bob?" Bert asked.

"Aye, thanks Bert. Have just been up top. Had a look aroond a' what is going on oot there, and I just got tae thinking about all those poor farmers, who are going tae have tae come back to wha's left whenever this lot is over. Those poor bastards."

"Aye Bob, I ken what ye mean. Perhaps it's just as well they cannae see what's going on tae their places. But I guess ye could say, we are helping tae see that they do have a place tae come back tae."

"Aye Bert, I guess so. But do we have tae destroy it first?"

"Come on, Bob," said Bert. "I need a hand with this frame. Can ye help me noo please?" The two of them then set to work, setting up one of the bunkbeds, in one of the new accommodation dugouts. All the while though, Bob was unable to get the sights out of his mind. Not just the farmers, and the damage to their prized farms and their animals, now long gone, but the bombarding of all those poor blokes, down there in the trenches. He had seen the results of that, at Hill 60, and he did not like it.

The work at Hill 63 dugouts, continued apace, almost hitting 100 feet (32 m) a day. As fast as men dug the tunnels and rooms the carpenters filled them up with whatever furniture they needed. Comfort was not a priority though, and the beds for example were two and three decks high bunkbeds. This meant you could fit more men into a smaller space, as space was at an absolute premium.

Working outside was still dangerous however, and for the month of October, a further twelve men were wounded. By 26 October, the catacombs had been completed, albeit with a little bit of tidying up and general work to do. This went on over the next four days. When finally, the work was over, company officers called all the men together, and congratulated them on the standard of workmanship in these catacombs. The men were presented with a summary of what they had achieved in the last 63 days since the entire company was working together. They had removed 192,000 ft³ (5437 m³) of dirt, which is the equivalent of 15 ft³ (0.424 m³) per man per day. They had created 2722 feet (830 m) of galleries, and they had used 520,000 super feet (1248 m³) of timber. Additionally, the men of 1ATC had constructed a steel framed officers dug out, which had accommodation for fifty officers and 150 ORs. This was done outside of the catacombs and was buried under 12 feet (4 m) of spoil taken from the dugouts.

1 November was set down as the day for the official opening, of the dugouts at Hill 63. The men worked feverishly all morning, to tidy everything up and make sure everything was spick-and-span. The official opening was at 3 PM and was being opened by none other than the commander of the 2nd Army, General Plumer. This was one officer, the men had a lot of respect for, so they were really pleased to be able to say they had seen him, in the flesh. They were also able to count five corps commanders and thirteen or fourteen divisional commanders. General Plumer inspected the works and was astounded at the amount of work they had done, the standard of the work they had done and the fact that they had finished ahead of schedule.

He addressed the men, "I have today inspected the workings of this fine dugout system. I have to say that the scale of these dugouts is huge and the workmanship that has gone into them, first class. I can assure you all that everyone will be told who built these dugouts. You should all be incredibly proud of your efforts," he told them. "You have certainly picked up the necessary skills very quickly, since you arrived in Europe and I am sure you will be very successful wherever you go after this. Congratulations to the 1st Australian Tunnelling company and thank you." The men applauded him, and they did indeed feel proud of the work they had done.

After the opening was over, the troops of 1ATC packed their gear up, loaded it onto the lorries, and headed back to Bailleul. Once back at camp they thought they were settling in for a reasonable stay, away from the action. But this is the army, and good work is rewarded by more work. The company would move back to Poperinge base and set up camp there again. "Poperinge again? I hope tha' doesn't mean wha' I think it means," Bill thought out loud.

"I ken wha' you're thinking Bill, and I dinnae like what ye're thinking," replied Bob. "Surely they're noe sendin' us back there."

"I was jus' doin' some calculatin' and those Canadians have been at the hill for six months noo. Time for them tae change oot," Bill remarked.

"Och God noe," answered Bob. "I dinnae wannae goe back there. two weeks was enough. Six months would kill us."

Sure enough, the men's worst fears were realised only a few minutes later, when they were informed that they were heading back to Hill 60. This time, to take over from the Canadians. It was felt, by the higher authorities, that 6 months in any one tunnelling system was enough for anybody. The 3rd Canadian tunnellers, had been at Hill 60 now for six months and it was time for them to take a break. 1ATC would have Hill 60 underground to themselves: and the Germans.

"That explains why we had to leave our gear on the lorries Bill," Bob laughed. "Not much point unloading them and then reloading them, even if this is the army." The men had a good old laugh at that comment, all the while agreeing 100%. They all headed off to the mess tent to enjoy a hot meal and a nice hot cup of tea, or two. The mood over the evening meal table, was a mixture of emotions. Those that were talking about the job they just been on were congratulating themselves on the job and reliving some of the escapades along the way. Those that were looking ahead, were a little more sombre. Only number 4 Section had seen what Hill 60 was like, so they were mostly the ones in the sombre mood, but they had certainly passed on their feelings about it to the men of the other three sections.

The others had certainly been on the frontline especially in trench 123, but that, was not Hill 60. Hill 60 had by now, gained notoriety, amongst all the Allied troops on the Western front. The mere mention of the words "Hill 60", was enough to send chills down your spine, and instil fear and dread into anyone. They were not looking forward to this return. Sections 1-3 were about to find out that the men of 4 Section, had not exaggerated the danger of the hill.

Once it was almost dark, the men loaded into the waiting lorries, and started on their trip back up the road to Poperinge. It was certainly not a long distance between the two towns, but when you are travelling in the dark, unable to use full lighting, due to turning the trucks into targets, you can only drive at little more than jogging pace. 1ATC arrived at Poppo, as they all now called it, at about 10 PM. They unloaded, set up camp and turned in for the night. At least being in familiar surroundings, was comforting for some of them, for those who had already been to Hill 60, it was not quite so comforting.

What would tomorrow bring? Was it still as bad as it was? All these, and plenty more, thoughts raced round and round in Bob's head. Eventually, sleep came. Blessed sleep! At least here, one could escape from the horrors, most nights.

Chapter 12
Hell on Earth

The following day, the company was allowed to rest through the daylight hours. They had earned a rest, and they were not going to be made to try and travel during daylight. As evening arrived, they had their last hot meal in camp, boarded the lorries again and headed for Ypres. From Poperinge, the lorries could enter Ypres fairly safely, still they were not going to try it in daylight hours. They were taken through the town and dropped off by what was left of the railway station. From here they moved down to the Lille Gate, where they would exit Ypres for the workings. Here they got to see a little of the work that a few of the men of 1ATC had been working on, in the month previously. It was dark enough now, so once more they headed out through Shrapnel Corner, and up the railway line to Larch Wood.

This time however the lack of activity at headquarters was evident, as the Canadians had left the previous night. Handover had occurred the previous day, so the Canadians left for a well-earned rest. The section learned that the Canadians had completed the tunnels, built the chambers and charged them all. The job of 1ATC, was now to maintain the mines, defend them and ensure that the Germans did not detect their presence. Both mines, Hill 60 and Caterpillar, had been laid, detonators inserted and wired back to HQ. It had been decided that the third mine under the Hun front line was not to be charged, as it was no longer deemed necessary. The Hill 60 mine had been laid with 45,700 lbs (20,411 kg) of ammonal and 7800 lbs (3538 kg) of guncotton, giving a total 53,500 Lbs or 24,267 kg of explosive. The mine had been set at a depth of 90 feet (27 m) below the surface. Caterpillar mine was 10 feet (3m) deeper, at 100ft (30.5 m) feet and had been charged with 70,000 lbs (31,750 kg) of ammonal.

Initially, the company were confused. Why were we, an efficient Tunnelling Co, being used as a bunch of babysitters, just to look after a mine that had been completed? All was revealed in quick time. First of all, Lt Woodward was a mining engineer of some renown. He had worked on many mines where water was a problem. Their first task was to deal with this water. The second task was to extend the mine system as quickly as possible to include further mines under the German frontline.

That's a relief, thought Bob. He then spoke out aloud, "I'd hate tae think we were here for nothin'. At least this way we'll be kept busy. Looks like ye're going tae be busy Bill, if ye will be dealing wi' all this water noo."

"That looks tae me like a bit o' an understatement," he replied. He went on, "It's going to require some amount of pumping tae get this amount o' water oot of here. Plus, it's also going tae require a bit moor diggin' I would suggest, because ye would need tae build a sump, tae collect the water in first, and that is one big system tae try and drain. It'd require one hellava system tae get that amount of water oot."

Bob was not far off the mark, it turns out, but a major part of this technique he had never seen before. Lt Woodward had the men dig sideways a short distance, next to where the vertical shaft dropped down to the 100 foot level. The next task was to get a large screw jack down the tunnel to the new digging. Bob, and a couple of his fellow chippies, were tasked to supply a couple of heavy timbers at least 6 foot long (2 m). During the night, carts delivered what appeared to be large metal tubes, about 4 foot in diameter and 5 feet high (1.2 m x 1.5 m). It looked like it would be the devil's own job, to get those tubes down Berlin sap, but Lt Woodward was once again, one step ahead of them. He had previously checked to see that the sap was big enough to fit these tubes through.

"Just turn them sideways, and roll them down the sap," he said. "Your only problem is going to be stopping them, because the sap is inclined downwards, so make sure you've got more men on the bottom side of the tube than the top. Once you get to the junction, we'll set up a block and tackle and lower them down to the lower level." And it was as simple as that, in the end.

Bill's idea of the sump was indeed correct, but he had never seen it done like this before. Lt Woodward, or Woody, as the men were now calling him, not to his face of course, had the men place the tube on end, in the middle of the newly dug area. The large timber, was then placed across the top of the tube, ensuring it was horizontal and then the screw jack was used to force this tube down into the soft dirt. Once the tube was forced completely into the dirt, he then directed a couple of the diggers, to dig the dirt out of the tube, one at a time, because it was only 4 feet in diameter. When all the dirt had been removed, the next ring was bolted to the 1st, and then the process was repeated until that ring was level with the ground. The diggers then dug the dirt out of the ring again and then the process was repeated yet again. Eventually, with 4 tubes in place, they had their sump 20 feet deep (6 m).

Woodward had also prearranged with the alphabet company, to deliver a new type of electric pump. Once delivered, the pump was set up in situ and extensive piping was then connected to join the pump all the way out to the drainage along the railway line. Needless to say, this was not an overnight event, it took several days of planning, all down to Lt Woodward, and several days of installation. The wait, however, was worth it.

Immediately, any water above the line of the sump, ceased to flow down the rest of the mine and was taken to the outside, which then drained down the railway line back towards Ypres. It just then remained that the rest of the mining system needed to be drained back towards the sump, as it was deep enough to drain the entire system. This new vertical shaft was christened 'Sydney' shaft. Melbourne sap, would be constructed alongside the Berlin sap but at a slightly lower level and inclined back to the sump, in order to drain the water from both mine charges.

The entire company of 1ATC was not yet working at Hill 60, but those that were, were treated to an afternoon of levity, on November 3rd. Observation of German activity was difficult, without having any high ground to look down from. As a result, the British utilised observation balloons, which were large, torpedo like, hydrogen filled balloons. Underneath the balloons was usually strung a wicker basket, with an observer, equipped with binoculars, to watch and semaphore back to the ground any activity. Late that afternoon, one of the captured Hun balloons, which was being used by the British Observer Corps, broke free from its ground anchor.

Unfortunately for the Observer, the wind direction meant he started drifting towards the German frontline. There was nothing left for him to do but to jump. Fortunately for him, he was equipped with a parachute, which he deployed and safely floated to the ground on the British side of the line. This brought a rousing round of cheers and applause from the British side of the line, which intensified once he reached the ground. There was little in their lives at this point, to cheer them up, but this event most certainly did that. It is assumed the Germans got their balloon back, but just how they got it down is not recorded.

Whilst working at Hill 60 the men of 1ATC, worked on a 4 days on, 4 days off roster, working 12 hours each day. The mining activity continued, 24 hours a day with the two shifts operating, twelve hours each, every day. During this time both shifts remained at Larch Wood, spending their time off in the on-site accommodation. This option was not available to them, 6 months ago, when they were here with the Canadians, as the full Canadian compliment occupied the accommodation. Now having completed their 1st four days, and getting everything underway, Bob, Bill and Bert headed back towards Ypres. Just as they were leaving Larch Wood, they passed the other section coming to relieve them, and this was to be the way of things for the next seven months. Once back in Ypres they were loaded onto the lorries and headed back towards Poperinge. They were most certainly looking forward to their break. It had been a hectic four days.

Whilst on the job, Bob and Bill saw little of each other because they were both working in different areas, different trades. They caught up on their lorry.

"So, Bill, what did you think about the pumping idea?" Asked Bob.

"Bloomin' marvellous was it noe?" Bill was clearly impressed. "Those metal liners that went doon through the clay, 'twas like a hot knife carving through butter. Doin' it that way, made sure they were sealed agin' the wet layer beautifully, so it just cut its way through the water layer an' sealed it off. I'm awfully glad I didn't have tae dig that last bit oot though, because most of that was underwater. Necessary, but bloody cold!"

"Aye," replied Bob, "I were there when he came up to be relieved, and I'll tell ye man, he was nearly blue. He would have needed a good few tot' of rum, to warm him up after that, I can tell ye noo."

Bill continued, "I'll tell ye man, this Woodward guy's all right. He knows wha' he's talking aboot. Ye can tell he's been aroond the mining game, for quite some time. Befoor this job is finished wi', I think we're going tae see a few interesting things happenin'. He hasnae been given a date when the mines are tae be blown, and he's been given the go-ahead tae set a couple of more mines under those damned Huns. So, it looks like it's gonnae be quite some time befoor they goe sky high. We could be here for some time yet."

"That's just what I was afraid of," Bert broke in. "I have a horrible feelin' in ma bones that we could be in for the long haul here, and I dinnae like it, I dinnae like it at all." There was general agreement around the lorry, for that last comment.

"It's a bit too hot for my liking," chimed in one of the other guys. "I mean, this time it wasn't too bad, the last four days, but when we were here last time it was bloody horrible. I guess it will hot up again, and it's times like that I'm glad we are working underground. I think the chances of getting hit by one of the Minnies or a whizz-bang, are much higher than getting blown by a Hun camouflet." By now, the men were getting quite used to working underground, the temperature was more even, there was certainly no bullets flying around and no Minnie or whizz-bang was going to get them there.

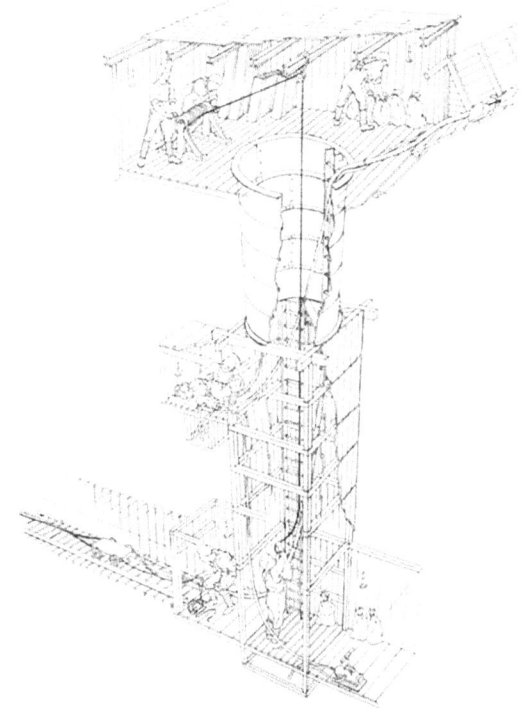

Fig 3
Sydney shaft. Detail of the steel liners used to get through the wet sand layer. The spoil from the clay kickers comes along the lower Berlin sap on the trolley and is then winched to the upper sap for removal back to Larch Wood. (courtesyTunnellers.net)

Now that they were getting the underground water under control as well, things were not quite as unpleasant underground as they were before. They all agreed that the Canadians would be a bit jealous if they could see the Berlin sap now.

By the time they made it back to Poperinge, the sun was up. Mostly, the men just wanted to sleep but before that, breakfast, a hot breakfast was the order of the day. A bath would be pretty good too, but that would have to wait. After breakfast, they hit their bunks, and slept the sleep of the dead.

In Poperinge, a bath house had been set up for the troops. That afternoon the men headed straight for it and indulged in some good hot water and soap. Oh, how nice to feel clean again. After the bath, it was time to try and wash one's clothing. They also had a laundry set up next to the bath house, so that was the next stop. This uniform of theirs was made from wool, so whilst durable and warm in winter, it also took a long time to dry. They were able to leave them hung in the drying house overnight and by morning it still was not dry, so camp was occupied by a mass of scantily clad men. Thank heavens there is no women around they thought.

By midday they were dry, so the next step was the delousing powder, unceremoniously thrown over all the men's clothing, in a somewhat vain attempt to keep the men lice free. It was ok around the camp, but the trenches, well that was another story. They had a choice of lice, rats or whizz-bangs. Generally, there was no chance of avoiding any of them. At least the rats did serve a small purpose, in some areas, helping to dispose of decaying bodies in no man's land, but they could bring their diseases back to the trenches if the men were not careful.

By their next shift at Hill 60, the whole of the company was finally back together headquartered in the same camp at Poperinge. November 10th was the first full complement day at the hill, and someone must have told the Hun, because that afternoon they sent over their biggest barrage since the return to Hill 60. A direct hit crumped the dugouts and killed two, and three were slightly gassed. The men took it as a "Welcome to Hill 60" barrage. It continued right the way through to the 14th. It took until the 13th, for British artillery to answer theirs, which they did with a vengeance, giving them the pasting, they deserved. It did not stop them though, as on the 14th, their trench mortars joined the fray scoring a direct hit on the cookhouse. That incurred the loss of Sgt William Ruddick and Cpl "Jock" Mudie, along with two injured, Sgt Thompson who lost a hand, and Spr Smith.

The loss of Jock Mudie affected Bert greatly. They had both grown up with each other in Dundee, Scotland and although Jock was a few years older than Bert, their families were friends, and they knew each other well, even though they had not seen each other for sixteen years. Mates are always mates. Now things were heating up for 1ATC, and the mood changed yet again. Before they were just 'doing a job', as they saw it. This action turned their efforts to a fierce determination. A determination to see this enemy were stopped in their tracks and turned around, and sent back to their home, from whence they came. They had no right to be here. No damned right at all. They also had no right to be killing our mates, damn them.

Whilst all the work was going on in the deep mining system, there was still shallow work as well. If all that work had stopped, to concentrate on the deeps, the enemy would get somewhat suspicious. Some upper level blows needed to continue, and they might as well be useful at the same time. The miners had been digging an intermediate depth tunnel, "D" left, and it was started off the Berlin sap, at a point just short of the road bridge over the rail line. It ran left and up to the German front line. Lt Woodward received word during an intense HE and shrapnel barrage that the mine they had been working on, was to be charged and fired. The barrage continued from 10pm to 11pm and there would be no carrying of explosives during a barrage.

At midnight, the charging of the mine with 3000lbs (1360Kg) of ammonal commenced and was completed by 4am. The men doing the charging had to be extra quiet when stacking the tins of ammonal. Lt Woodward had been listening in the chamber when he indicated to the men to freeze. He thought he heard something, so stopped to check. Sure enough, with only his ear pressed to the wall he could hear the shuffling of feet and talking. He could even feel the vibrations of their movement, only a few feet away. They needed to blow this mine as soon as possible. The detonators were inserted, and the leads were run and tested as ok. Testing of the leads was a touchy operation. The detonators used to set the explosives off were electrically fired, and the only way to test the conductivity and continuity of those leads, was electrically.

The process involved sending a small current down the leads, small enough that it would not excite the detonators, and reading its return current. One had to be careful, not to send too big of a current down or the detonators would fire. It was always a breath holding exercise, the first time the leads were tested.

With everything testing correct, orders were given at 6 pm to 'Tamp' the mine. Tamping is a process of re blocking the gallery with sandbags. If a mine was detonated without the gallery being blocked off first, the explosion would just blow back along the least path of resistance, back along the tunnel and would do more damage to the attacker that the attacked. Tamping meant filling the tunnel with hundreds of sandbags until the least resistance was calculated to blow where you wanted it to. That would be either to the surface, or into the enemy's workings. In this case tamping went on until 1.30am. All men were withdrawn from the system as a safety measure when this tamping was complete.

When a large charge is fired, the damage is caused by an extremely rapid expansion of gasses in the explosive reaction. When this occurs underground, the explosion is not the only killer. The gasses remaining can kill, in whichever system they get into. This is why, all men are withdrawn from the system prior to any large blow. The gasses produced, largely carbon monoxide and carbon dioxide, are both deadly and odourless.

Once everyone was back at Larch Wood, around 2am, the mine was detonated. Even at that time of the day they could see the smoke and dust emanating from behind the enemy lines. Their placement and timing of the blow had been spot on and resulted in the destruction of a significant sector of enemy mining. An hour later, men were sent down to check the saps, and no gas was detected. Mining was then allowed to recommence.

Chapter 13
Christmas

Late in November during one of Bob's shifts in the mining system, Woody turned up at the dugouts, with three pips on his shoulder.

Bob immediately noticed and said, "A captain now, sir? Congratulations."

"Thank you, sapper," came the reply and the men gathered around to all congratulate him. Such was the reputation of this man that the men were genuinely pleased for him. Not the least of reasons being that now he was the CO of 4 Section, 1ATC. That pleased the men no end. Apparently, his promotion had been backdated to 23rd October.

"This is why he's been acting like our CO recently," one of the men chirped in. "Coz he has been!" The men laughed and set about their duties once more. Capt. Woodward set off to inspect the works. The following day, Bob and Bert were asked by Sgt Hood (no relation) to accompany him, with weapons, down one of the galleries to LP 25 (Listening post 25). Capt. Woodward was already down at their destination.

"Sappers Hood and Carr, sir," the Sergeant whispered.

"Yes, thankyou Alex," Woodward replied. "Can you two, remove these two timbers from the supports please. There have been reports of some air movement around here and I think we may have found the point of entry. We will have to be as careful as possible, as it may be an incursion by Fritz, so keep your weapons handy."

"Yes, sir," Bob replied. They examined the timbers to ensure they were not likely to cause an earth fall, and then set about gently prising them from their position. As they did so, a piece of the wall fell at their feet. Each man reached for their weapons immediately, and covered the hole from different angles, as instructed previously, so that any intruder would not have an easy time shooting in 4 directions at once. They stood there silently, waiting, illuminated only by the glow of a single candle flame. Silence. No one moved, no one spoke.

Slowly, Sgt Hood took the torch from his tunic and shone it into the void. Nothing. He could see nothing but a vacant space. They all then moved quietly and slowly, towards the hole and scraped a little more dirt away from the hole. The captain put his head through, only to find a whole gallery beyond. It was at a slightly lower level than the one they were in. The 4 of them dropped through the hole into the gallery, weapons at the ready. There was no one there. They let out a collective sigh of relief. Upon investigation, they found that the gallery ran out under no man's land. It appeared to be a gallery previously dug by either the British or Canadians, and then closed off, probably because Fritz had crumped it at some time. It did not however, appear on any of the maps of the mining systems, which is not surprising really, as in the early days of the tunnellers, much of what was dug and blown, was random.

Bob and Bert headed back to the workshop and left Capt. Woodward and Sgt Hood to investigate the tunnel. They had only been back at the workshop for half an hour, when one of their mates came rushing in and called to them, "Come outside boys. There's an aeroplane fight going on outside." They all dashed outside, to see two aircraft dodging and weaving and circling overhead. They could hear the machine guns rattling away at each other. All the boys on the ground, were ducking and weaving with their every move. There was also plenty of advice for both pilots. Most of the advice for the Hun plane, was to stay in a straight line and be shot down. This went on for about five minutes, before the British pilot correctly predicted the Hun's next move and did in fact shoot him down.

The Hun craft went into a spin and crashed behind the German trenches. Yet again, they all let out a cheer, as the enemy went into a spin and went down. There was lots of slapping on the back and handshakes after that bit of entertainment. Once everything had settled down, they all went back to their work, albeit with a smile on their faces. There were lots of recounted stories, to those who had not seen the spectacle, for the rest of the day.

Work continued as normal over the next two months with the only item of note being the first attempt to bomb them from the air. A Hun bomber flew over them at a few thousand feet and let his payload go, only to land a quarter of a mile away (400m). Of course, it did no damage to their workings and only encouraged the men. If that was the best they could do, then they felt safe from aerial attack.

"You'll have to do better than that if you want to win this war Fritz!" one of the lads called out to the aircraft, not that he would be able to hear, but it brought a nervous laugh from those around.

It was a cold winter, but then again, all winters in Belgium are cold. Snow lay all over the area and for those who had never seen snow before, the novelty soon wore off. On warmer days, the snow melted and turned to slush. Mud! Mud everywhere. All through the trenches, all around headquarters, all through your clothing. Ankle deep mud. It made walking difficult, as the mud caked on your boots. There were places along the frontline and communication trenches that the mud was knee deep. It was not safe to venture off the duckboard in some places. There were rumours, of fellows disappearing in the shell holes, if they stepped off the duckboard. Not that anyone believed these rumours, but just to be on the safe side, stay on the boards. The only respite from the mud, and that was brief, was on those cold, cold mornings when everything froze. Then it was walkable, without sinking, at least for a short while.

Christmas passed, with barely a recognition. Not like the Christmas of 1914. Bob thought back to his time at Hill 63. On one occasion, he went up to the top of the hill to look around and was talking to a British soldier on lookout. In an area directly in front of him, between the Birdcage mines and Trench 127 mines, had been the place where men from both sides, from both lots of trenches, had laid down their weapons and gone out into no man's land and played a game of football. This story had done the rounds of the men, on numerous occasions, but they were not sure whether to believe it or not. The Brit who pointed this out to Bob, swore that it was in fact true, as he knew someone who had taken part in that football match.

"For an hour or two, these men were not adversaries, just men from two different countries playing football. Just like in peacetime," he commented, with a sad face. "You see, that man was my friend, my neighbour, but not anymore. He copped it down the Somme a couple of months later." There was a long pause of silence. Neither man spoke for some minutes. They just stood there, looking at that piece of open ground, that piece of ground where the war stopped, and those soldiers became just people. After a while he continued.

"The Germans started singing their favourite Christmas carol, Silent Night, in German, of course, *Stille Nacht*. Our boys joined in, in English of course, and together they all sang. At the end of the singing, one of the Hun, stood up on the top of his trench, with his hands in the air, not as in surrender, but just to say, 'Look, I'm unarmed.' Then one of our boys did the same, and slowly men from both sides, emerged from the trenches unarmed, and cautiously walk towards each other, where they met in the middle of no man's land. Very few of the men could speak each other's language, but that was not really an issue, as they shook hands and smiled at each other."

"Apparently, he swapped a tin of Bully Beef for a medallion that his German opposite had with him. It was Christmas, so all the men were standing around, chattering, when one of the Germans came out with a football. Well, that was it, wasn't it? Show a football to an Englishman, and you have a football game on your hands. I do not know which team won the football match, but all the men involved that day were victors, winners in my opinion. When it was over, they all went back to their trenches. That afternoon, civilisation was the loser. They all went back to shooting each other. The authorities found out about it, and they were not pleased. All our boys were transferred to the Somme within days and an attempt was made to hush the whole thing up. But it was too late. Word had gone out."

Again, the Englishman went silent, this time, for a few seconds. He cleared his throat and then added, "Makes you wonder what it's all about a doesn't it, my friend?" And he left it there.

Bob really could not think of anything to say in response, so he just nodded, and repeated the man's words, "It does, just make you wonder what it's all about."

No, this Christmas, would be a Christmas, like no other he had ever experienced. Cold, wet, muddy, and where everyone was trying to kill everyone else. There would be no smiling faces, no children laughing, no gifts to exchange. Just thoughts. Thoughts to escape this world. Thoughts of sitting in front of the fire, in Saltcoats, with the family all around, and Christmas pudding and warming up with a nice tot of the fine scotch whisky, the finest whisky in the world. Then his thoughts moved to Australia, where Christmas was altogether different. For a start, it was hot, sometimes blazingly hot. That certainly takes a bit of getting used to, he thought.

His thoughts then went to Jean, Robert, Mimey and the rest of the family in Perth. What would they be doing for Christmas? There would probably be a nice roast lamb, with roast vegetables and gravy, followed by, well of course, a fine

Scots Christmas pudding, and even though Robert was the Baker, Mimey would have made the Christmas pudding, as was the tradition in any fine Scottish household. Oh, how he longed to be there and away from this wretched war.

Whilst the first half of January was relatively quiet, the same cannot be said for the second half. On the 15th of January, it had been snowing hard for days, and the temperature was 16°F (-9°C). The Hun took this opportunity to start an artillery barrage. It was an intense barrage for hours, and ended with three more of the crew dead, and 8 wounded. The following day, the British artillery opened up with a 48 hour bombardment of the Hun lines. That bombardment included, half an hour of rapid fire, the sound which has to be heard to be believed. It was intense. The noise just went on and on. There was no respite for the ears. There would not have been a Hun left above ground level, during that period. Not to be outdone, their artillery replied in like manner, however this time, 1ATC received no casualties. The dugouts and mines were deep enough that it offered full protection, from artillery fire, especially as they were forewarned of likely artillery retaliation, so were well prepared.

Later that month, the further intense bombardment of the German Lines, was a little bit different, in that it seemed to be targeted, at only one part of the line. From Larch Wood, it was clear that there was an edge, to this bombardment. The following day the men found out why this was. The brigade to their northeast, had used the bombardment as cover, to conduct a raid on the German Lines. It appears that this ploy worked particularly well, as they were able to eliminate, many of the enemy during a that raid, as well as taking several prisoners, including some officers. Before leaving the German trench line, they were able to inflict a significant amount of damage, in that sector.

Only one week later, the Germans tried a similar technique and attempted to raid the British frontline in that same area but were completely repulsed and no British injuries were reported, nor were any captured by the Germans.

Mid-February saw another great aerial battle overhead. This time they seemed to be fighting around 2 to 3000 feet (6-900m) above them, and several aircraft were involved. There was one fight going on between one of each side's aircraft, and it was obvious that the British plane had the upper hand. The German aircraft was trying everything in his power to get out of the way but was unable to do so. The inevitable happened, and the Hun aircraft caught fire and went into an almost vertical nose down spin, until he crashed and exploded.

That was the first time Bob had seen an aircraft crash and explode. Even though he was an enemy pilot, he still hoped to see a parachute floating down, but alas, no such parachute was seen. Before he went down though, the German must have inflicted some damage on the British aircraft, as it was last seen losing height, heading towards Poperinge. He apparently made a forced landing in a field just outside Poperinge. A further two Hun aircraft were downed during that encounter. Once again, the men cheered and clapped as the German Aircraft succumbed to their fate. This time though, Bob found he could not celebrate.

A few days later, the men near the frontline, were all told to keep their heads down. Between 1.30 and 3.30 that afternoon, the British artillery laid down a combined HE and shrapnel artillery barrage, in front of the German trenches, in order to cut the barbed wire. This was a usual practice, just before raid, so that the raiding troops did not have to contend with all that barbed wire. It would make their attack much swifter, reducing the time where the troops were susceptible to enfilading fire. This artillery barrage had a two-fold purpose. Not only was it to well prepare the ground, for a coming raid but it also kept the Hun focused above ground.

Belowground, a lot was happening. At LP 5 and LP 8 sounds had been detected in recent days that indicated the Hun Miners were getting way too close to the upper workings. Consequently, Captains Woodward and Tandy, were given the job of charging these two sites, LP 5 with 300 pound (136kg) and LP 8 with 1800 pound (816kg) of ammonal. The charge at LP 5 was to blow in the German underground work and the LP 8 charge was directly under the Hun frontline and was aimed at blowing their trench in. The charging and the tamping were completed by midday the following day, and once again all men were withdrawn from the workings, both shallow and deep. At 4.55 that afternoon, the charge at LP 8 was blown. Even from a distance at Larch Wood, one could see the effect that had on the Hun. A huge plume of smoke, dust, mud and fire, erupted from the German's frontline.

This time, there was silence at the HQ. Amongst the dirt and fire dome, you could see solid objects. It was impossible to tell what they were, but many of the men had a pretty good idea. three minutes later, the mine that LP 5 was detonated. This time, all that was seen, was a small puff of dust and smoke, emanating from what must have been an entrance to the German Mining System. They did feel the explosion. It was not a particularly big explosion, so it was not a huge tremor, but they did feel it. As soon as the two blows had occurred, the artillery opened up for about ten minutes on the site of the LP 8 explosion, timed no doubt, to coincide with German rescue efforts on their exploded frontline.

"Christ almighty!" someone whispered. "Don't you think they've had enough?"

Someone else added, "They deserve every bloody thing they get, and then some. They've had it coming for a bloody long time."

"All right boys, enough's enough," Bob found himself saying. He was not sure who to agree with. Yes, they were an aggressor, and should be sent packing, but they are still human beings. He knew they had a job to do, and would do it, but at the same time, he wished there was another way.

As soon as the artillery barrage was finished, flares and rockets were fired off, which would normally indicate the commencement of a raid. In this case, it was nothing of the sort. It was just bait. As soon as the enemy saw the rocket fire, they automatically assumed a raid was imminent and they immediately started strafing the British frontline at Hill 60. The only problem was, there was no one there. They had all been withdrawn in anticipation of the strafe. At the same time, a battalion of the 140th infantry brigade, raided the German frontline a few hundred yards away, at the place known as "the Ravine." Once again, this proved a successful ploy, as it resulted in 15 casualties, the capture of 114 enemy, two officers and four machine guns. At the same time, the British suffered 10 KIA and 60 WIA. On the balance of things, a particularly successful raid. In turn it also showed how an integrated approach to offence, could be used to great effect.

Chapter 14
Stepping Up

Time may well have been marching on, and they were starting to head out of winter, but it was still bitterly cold. The men were unable to light fires up in the trenches or the shallow mines, to heat food, due to the danger of being observed by either those up on the hill or the constantly circling aircraft. Those up on the frontline or in the shallows, relied upon warm food coming up from the kitchens, back at headquarters. While every attempt was made to get hot food to the men, at this time of year, by the time it made it to the frontline, it was already frozen.

Oft times, men would have to chip tea out of the pannikin and suck on it or with the bully beef, try and chip a piece off with their bayonet, and hold it in their mouths long enough for it to thaw out, so they could actually eat it. Many a time, the men figured they were using more energy to eat the food, than they were getting, from the food. If the men were able to get undercover anywhere, and they had or could find a candle, they would use that candle in an attempt, to thaw the tea and get some warmth into it. If they managed to get any heat into that tea, it was sheer luxury.

One big advantage of the cold weather was the absence of mud. It had frozen. At least it no longer stuck to their boots. It was not a particularly exciting existence. They were indeed thankful that their time at the front was only four days at a time. They would yearn for their time back at base camp, at Poperinge, just so they could get some warm food. Even there, it was rare to get hot food, at this time of year. In the freezing temperatures it cooled down exceptionally quickly. Bob and Bert did not enjoy their time working in the shallows, for this reason. Generally, if they had work to do up there it was only on a maintenance basis, as most efforts were targeted at the deep Mining System.

From the day they arrived at Hill 60, back in November, Lt, now Capt. Woodward, had plans to extend the underground system of mines. Initially they started on Sydney shaft, which was the name given to the shaft to drain the mines to enabled water to be pumped out. As mentioned before, this was situated at the point with the Berlin shaft dropped vertically about halfway along its length. The Melbourne shaft was to continue roughly parallel, with the Berlin shaft all way to the three-way junction leading to the Hill 60 and Caterpillar mines but was situated several feet lower. When it was joined at the junction, it therefore drained all water away from those mines back down its length to the Sump, where it was pumped out.

Several other galleries were dug leading off from this Melbourne shaft. Brisbane shaft left the Melbourne about fifty m from its commencement and headed in a west-south westerly direction. The Perth shaft left the Brisbane shaft after about 200 m and headed due north and split, with the Newcastle shaft heading to the right, intending to end underneath the German front trenches on the left slopes of Hill 60. The Adelaide gallery, left the Melbourne after about 150 m and headed north east, intending to end under the German front trenches to the east of the road bridge. The Ipswich shaft left the Melbourne gallery at a point below the road bridge, and headed south west, and the ANZAC shaft was situated just north of this. If all these mines and galleries had been completed, it would have totalled an additional 1500 yards (1400m) of underground tunnels.

As well as all these extra tunnels, more accommodation was dug for the Australian troops, and many hundreds of yards of infantry trenches were completed to allow the attacking troops to the frontline, whenever these mines were fired. Still no date had been set for this firing, but Capt. Woodward knew that it could not be too far away. As such, he had the men working around the clock feverishly digging, and setting new digging records, every week. The men relished this opportunity to show both the British and the Canadians just what they could do.

At one point, Capt. Woodward, dropped into the carpentry workshop, to check on progress. By now Bob and Capt. Woodward were well acquainted with each other and quite comfortable talking together. They were about the same age so were a little older than the rest of the men. "How's it going Bob?" the captain asked.

"Our biggest problem at the moment, sir, is timber. We simply dinnae have enough timber. It's just not getting here quick enough, for us tae keep up with the diggers," Bob replied.

The captain thought for a moment and then suggested, "I understand Bob. I was expecting this to be a problem, if we were to extend the mines as far as we're going. I think we're going to have to get the Quartermaster into Ypres, and salvage whatever timber he can find. Would you like to assist him with that task Bob? You know what you need for this job."

"Yes, sir. I can dae that. We will need something tae collect the timber in, like a cart or a lorry," Bob replied.

"Yes!" he agreed. "We will need something like that. I'll see what I can rustle up. I'll leave you to liaise with QM on the timing."

"Very good, sir. I will dae that," returned Bob.

So it was that a couple of days later, Bob and the QM, along with Bert for a little extra muscle, headed into Ypres to find timber. By this time, Ypres was starting to look more like a pile of rubble. The bombardment had been incessant, and there were not many buildings left in the town undamaged. The three of them, headed towards the main square of Ypres, as that area was at least navigable, and started to select timber, from the ruins of the Cloth Hall and the adjacent St Martin's cathedral. All that Capt. Woodward had been able to arrange for them, was a horse and cart, as all available lorries were being used for troop transport.

They loaded up the cart, at night time, and drove it out through the Lille Gate, through shrapnel corner and down the Commines Road, to a point level with Larch Wood. This was as far as they dare go. They unloaded there and headed back into town, where they loaded yet another cart load, and did likewise with that. Men were organised at the base, to collect these Timbers and take them back, to the preparation area, at Larch Wood. From here on in, each time they started to get low on timber, this process was repeated. This then allowed the carpenters to keep up with the demands of timber for the mines.

Of course, Bob recognised the timber he was using now, was oak, a much too fine a timber, to be using underground, but it was all they had, and time, was of the essence. He recognised the fine quality of this timber, as he had been used to working it when he worked as a carpenter in Ardrossan all those years ago. It certainly seemed like an absolute lifetime ago now. He managed to salvage a few pieces for himself as well. He figured that in his down time, he could work on a project or two for himself. He decided that he would build a jewellery box and send it home to Jean. What a grand idea that would be, if he could send her a gift made from the very timber he was working on there in Ypres, with his own hands. What better gift could a girl get but one made by the giver himself?

In his days off, he would prepare the timber, planing it down, piece by piece, until it was ¼ inch thick (6mm), then sanding all the imperfections out of the surface. In his time off at the hill, he would use the workshop and its tools to perfectly mark out each dovetail joint corner, each rebate and each chamfer. Bob was a patient man, he needed to be, to be a high class carpenter. Nothing was rushed. There were no machines to prepare the timber, so all of it was done by hand. Each piece lovingly prepared. Each piece as perfect as he could make it, knowing who it was going to. This would be a simple jewellery box, but that was no reason to not put the maximum effort into it. He made the two small hinges himself as well.

Once the box was completed, he thought it lacked something. He was pleased enough with the box itself, but the top was just a little too plain. On his next trip back into Ypres, whilst scavenging around St Martin's cathedral, he found some of the cathedral silverware that had been destroyed in the bombardment. He salvaged a few pieces of that, took it back to the workshop, flattened it out and polished it up. He then fashioned this piece of silver into a scroll shape onto which he then engraved the word 'Ypres'. This was then pinned to the top. Now, it looked complete.

Bob picked up the box and, with a smile on his face, gently kissed the box. He figured that would be like sending a real kiss to Jean. Not that he had asked her if he could. That would come later. He kept that box in his kit, so that on his next leave, he could package it and send it home to her. He wished he could take it home to her right now, but that too would have to wait.

If Hill 60 was a hot spot on the western front, then listening post five (LP 5) must surely have been by a hot spot at Hill 60. It had seen incredible amounts of action previously, but around the 4th of April Cpl Sneddon, reported noises of boring by the enemy, as well as sounds that appeared to be charging of a borehole. He immediately withdrew the crew from that vicinity, as was normal practice. After a period of three days, the CO, Major Henry suggested that some form of device be arranged, to give the false impression of work continuing in that area, so that the Hun would fire the mine, and achieve no casualties, and therefore would have been a somewhat pointless blow.

Unfortunately, whilst rigging this system up, Cpl Sneddon was killed when the mine was blown. LP 5 was in an area of instability, and the framework in this area was particularly unstable, so the Hun blow caused a lot of damage and Cpl Sneddon was buried.

On this same day, a small mine at LP 15, was charged and tamped. During this time, the artillery concentrated heavily on the Hun frontline in that area. At 7.55 Capt. Woodward fired the mine, and a dummy attack was made towards Hill 60. This was a dummy attack, to draw defenders across to this sector. At 8:00 PM the main attack commenced, once again, at the area known as the Ravine. The men of the 47th battalion, 1st AIF, were able to penetrate the German frontline to the third line of defence. Whilst they suffered no casualties themselves, they were only unable to capture eighteen of the enemy. The raid itself, was successful, but the outcome was somewhat disappointing.

Chapter 15
Friendly Fire

Two days later, as luck would have it, Bob, Bill and Bert, and the rest of the section, were granted four days leave. At this time, they were able to travel away from the front line, for four days rest and recreation. Hot food and sleep, were numbers one and two on their hit list, for their four days. Back at the hill, whilst efforts were still being made to dig Cpl Sneddon out of his entombment, the Germans raided in a similar fashion to the 47th Battalion raid of the 7th, on both sides of the cut. The cut was the name given to the railway cutting itself, between Hill 60 and the Caterpillar. They penetrated even further through the Allied Lines, about 200 yards (183m), causing untold damage to trench systems, dugouts and other installations.

A lot of planning had gone into this raid, and the timing was perfect. It occurred when the change-over of the 47th Battalion and its replacement occurred. The German raiding party of about 600 was able to spend around an hour creating havoc. The main purpose of the raid, was to attempt to find the entrance to the mining system. They were unable to locate that entrance, however. In their time in the Allied trenches, 33 British and 43 Germans were killed but there were 200 other casualties. One tunneller was killed, one was severely injured and five were taken prisoner. The five men, when interrogated, gave up no information at all, on the allied deep mining system.

However, the Germans did notice that their boots, were covered in blue clay, the clay from much deeper in the area, then they were digging currently. From this, they were able to deduce that the enemy was indeed working on a deeper Mining System. At this time, no date had yet been set, for the blowing of the mines on the Messines ridge however it is believed that this raid, may have at least been partly responsible, for the decision, on a date for the detonation, to be brought forward.

On the day of this raid, Nos 1 and 4 Section were both back at Poperinge, engaged in a football match, so were blissfully unaware of the drama unfolding back at Hill 60. Had they known what was going on, to their mates back at the front, they most certainly would not have had such an enjoyable game. No 1 Section had a better day than number four and ran out winners in that match. The following day, those that were leaving camp managed to board a lorry headed for Calais. The boys had three wonderful days off the frontline and spent most of the first day sleeping, catching up on as much as they possibly could. They manage to get out and do a little sightseeing, and down by the coast were able to gaze across the white cliffs of Dover. Whilst those cliffs are in England, not Scotland, it is part of their home island, and made all three of them somewhat nostalgic for their homeland.

"I guess we'll get tae go back home on one o' our leaves," Bob stated somewhat wishfully.

"I certainly hope so," Bill added.

"It's been five years, since I saw ma family," Bob went on, "and I have tae say, I would like tae catch up with my ma sisters again. Who knows if I'll ever get to see them again after this wee lot? I'd also like to tell them about Jean. Although I've written to them about her, I'd still like to tell them about her, and show them a photograph."

Silence for a while and then Bert joined in. "I've not been in Scotland for 17 years, I dinnae really remember much about it. I was only a bairn of seven, when I left. I still have lots of relatives there, aunties and uncles, but I dinnae really remember them, at least not what they look like anyway. I'd still like tae go there though. It would be good just tae make contact for ma mother and father. I could tell them, I had caught up with their brothers and sisters, and I would get to see ma Cousins."

They sat there for hours, just gazing across the water, talking old times, old yarns and the things they had seen and done in common. The war seemed a million miles away, they wished it could stay that way. War was no adventure; it was just plain dirty. All three of them agreed, they would rather be back in Sydney and Perth. It was, after all, their choice to move there.

"I wish this war would hurry up and be over," Bob remarked with a sigh. "Then I could get back to ma Jean and ma work and ma home." With the evening approaching, the three of them headed back into Calais, and searched for a café. It was not hard to find one and the boys settled down to a café meal of fish and various vegetables. Food like this, they had not had for over a year and they certainly enjoyed it to the fullest. They sat back after the meal enjoying a coffee. A coffee, because these frogs are not so good on tea, it is almost impossible to find. The coffee was, however, extremely good. It was hot and it was sweet.

The following morning, Bob and Bill, went walking and sightseeing again. Not far from their hotel, they happened upon a photographic studio, and decided to go and have the portraits done. They had not had this done and since they been in Europe, and it did become quite a fashion for the boys who were a long way from home, to have a portrait done and sent home as a postcard. Bob had his little soldier's camera, but he had to be careful not to be seen with it by any officers, because they were not supposed to have a camera on the frontline, so he kept it well in the bottom of his kit bag. Most of the time, he forgot it was there. Besides, it only took a small photograph, and these postcards were of a decent size, so we are much better anyway.

The three of them all made up for lunch again at yet another quaint little café, and then whiled away the afternoon doing, well, very little actually. Just more sightseeing, sitting, talking and generally just resting. The following day, they all headed down to the depot, to catch a lift back to Poperinge. Once back at camp they caught up with all the details of the last four days which was just more of the same. That, however, brought them all back down to earth again. For the next two weeks it was just much of the same until the second anniversary of ANZAC day.

On this day, Aril 25th, Capt. Avery and Lt Tandy were preparing the detonators, for a forthcoming camouflet in D gallery. They were setting up a 50 pound (23Kg) charge of Guncotton, a particularly touchy form of explosive, at the time, and organising the detonators and the Guncotton to be used to set off this camouflet. Guncotton, also known as cellulose nitrite, is a highly volatile fibre like explosive, extensively used in the mining industry, over the last 50 or so years. It had to be handled and stored carefully, as it was not stable if incorrectly handled. They were working in the forward officers' dugouts, getting everything ready when their charge exploded, killing both men instantly. Because of the instability of the ground in the area, it crumped a whole section in that frontline. This not only led to the deaths of Captain Avery and Lt Tandy, but also Lt Evans and eight others. Lts Clayton, Lindsay, Jones W, and Jones P, were wounded along with six other ranks as well.

When the men back at Larch Wood base, heard the explosion, they all looked up and saw that it was from their own frontline, they rushed the 500 or so yards (450m) to see if anything could be done to help. They were immediately held back, as there was a significant amount of toxic gas that one person had already succumbed to. Those that had survived the blast, but were injured, were quickly moved backwards to the dressing station, at Larch Wood. Some of those officers who had survived the blast, were resuscitated on site, and then spirited back to that dressing station as well, to be forwarded to the nearest casualty clearing post, and then hospital if necessary.

'Proto men' was the name given to rescuers who were equipped with the Proto breathing apparatus. This was an early form of breathing apparatus, which was made from canvas and rubber material that formed a hood in which there were eye pieces. The hood was connected via a tube, to a chest bag and oxygen cylinder. The Proto system recycled the carbon dioxide that the wearer breathed out and cycled it through a sodium carbonate container, then mixed the resulting gases, with oxygen from the cylinder. With skilful use, a wearer could get up to two hours working time out of one Proto set. Given that the use of the Proto, was often in a combat zone and under often extenuating circumstances, the wearer usually relied on there only being about one hour to one and a half hours use.

As the forward proto room itself had been collapsed, that needed to be cleared first, in order for the equipment to be freed, so it could be used to search for survivors, and any of those that did not survive. Once the Proto room was cleared, the searching began but no further survivors were found. The first Proto man to emerge from the carnage, reported "all bodies appear to be lifeless." Bob's heart sank. He had been one of the men who had rushed forward from Larch Wood and had been held back from going in any further because of the gas situation. He knew that Capt. Avery and Lt Tandy had been in there, as he knew they were getting the charge ready, because he had been working on the entrance prior to the blow.

He did not know Captain Avery particularly well, but he did know and like Lt Tandy. As he and the others waited backwards of the blown area, they just hoped, against hope that somehow, they may have survived. The Proto man's report however, put paid to any hope, the men had survived. They did not have a full list of all the officers in that forward dugout, but they knew there had to be other officers in there.

Bob 1912

Break time for the Mining Corps at Blackboy Hill

Blackboy Hill. Armoury right foreground and rail line to Kalgoorlie and eventually Sydney

Using Geophones to detect direction of noise underground

The Mining Corps marching through Perth 08-03-1916

Bob at work

Carpenters working on underground accommodation.

1ATC at work in Villers Bretonneux

Bill and Bob, 12th April 1917

The miners at work in the chalk country of the caves

Workers outside the Carpentry works of Henry Wallace, Barr St Ardrossan early 1900s (Henry 3rd from left). Photo Courtesy North Ayrshire Heritage Centre

For the Boys of our Pride.

Our illustration shows a consignment of Red Cross goods which was being conveyed from Melbourne to the headquarters of the British Red Cross Society in London by the steamer which was stranded at Fremantle on March 8. As a consequence of the mishap to the vessel the goods were very much damaged by sea water. The local Red Cross Society took the matter in hand, and had the goods unpacked and washed, a band of ladies re-packing the entire 40 cases in one day. Red Cross workers will know that this is not by any means a mean achievement.

Daily News article of March 29th 1916

The wounded await evacuation on the Menin Road outside Hooge after the advances of 20ᵗʰ September 1917

British 137ᵗʰ brigade after taking Riqueval Bridge, St Quentin Canal October 1918

Road up to the Hill 63, Wallangarra Dugouts

Entrance to Wallangarra Dugouts. Troops of the 2nd Division at rest. Probably 20th Battalion

Hill 60 viewed from 'The Dump' looking south. Railway cutting front right corner. Larch Wood behind and to the left

The Aftermath of the explosions at Hill 60. All that is left of most of the trench, foreground left photo, is the firing step. The rest of the trench is crushed.

The human toll.

Hill 60 crater July 1917
Note officer in crater for scale

18 September 1917. Underground Hooge Left to right: 3261 Spr E. J. Anderson; 3716
Spr J. Mullins; 174 Spr G. Mann; 3559 Spr J. G. Brindley; 3607 Sergeant A. Hood.
Only Sgt Hood did not survive

Hill 60 crater 2014 From same position as above

Memorial erected at Hill 60 for the men of 1 ATC. The holes are bullet holes from WW2

Caterpillar crater 2014

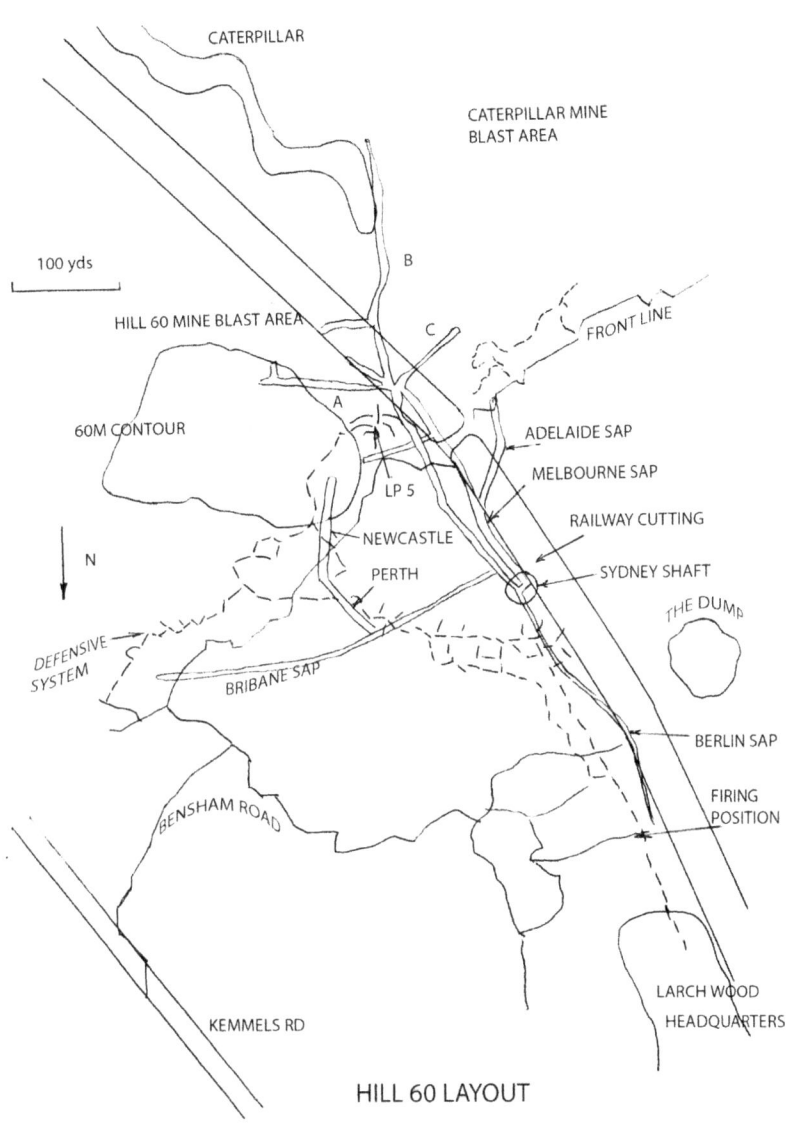

CATERPILLAR

CATERPILLAR MINE
BLAST AREA

100 yds

B

HILL 60 MINE BLAST AREA

C

FRONT LINE

60M CONTOUR

A

ADELAIDE SAP

MELBOURNE SAP

LP 5

RAILWAY CUTTING

N

NEWCASTLE

PERTH

SYDNEY SHAFT

THE DUMP

DEFENSIVE
SYSTEM

BRIBANE SAP

BERLIN SAP

FIRING
POSITION

BENSHAM ROAD

KEMMELS RD

LARCH WOOD
HEADQUARTERS

HILL 60 LAYOUT

As soon as the proto men gave the all clear, the air was tested and the men were given the go-ahead to start clearing the debris and pulling out any bodies. When he went in to assist with that clearance, Bob was astounded by the level of destruction. The entire officers' dugout and the rooms either side were totally demolished, along with Proto room, kitchen and sleeping quarters. The explosion not only destroyed this area, in the shallows, but as this had been directly above the Berlin sap, it also caved in a large section of that as well. As the men commenced digging, they knew there were going to find more bodies, than they perhaps had hoped.

It took them three days to clear out the debris and find all the bodies. 11 of them all told, including Avery's Batman, Sapper Charles Glew, who was in the room adjoining the officers' quarters. He took the full blast of the explosion and would have died instantly. (Author's note: further research turned up an interesting link with Charles Glew. It appears he is related to me, through my father's side of the family. One of my great grandmothers, was Dinah Glew)

A third officer had been in the dugout with Avery and Tandy but had run back to Larch Wood to acquire a tape measure. It was while he was away that the explosion occurred and from his testimony, the likely cause of the explosion was determined. Apparently, they were setting up the detonation for the later camouflet and were going to use the detonators in the Guncotton to set off the explosives. The usual practice was to run a small test current through the detonator to test continuity. This was usually done under a sandbag in case the detonator was supersensitive and exploded. It would cause no harm if it exploded under a sandbag. This officer indicated that they had no sandbags there at the time, and they had not tested the continuity of the detonators at the point at which he left the dugout. It is likely therefore that they in fact did have a supersensitive detonator and as there were no sandbags to test it under, it had gone off and ignited the Guncotton. The official version, however, was somewhat different. It stated in part:

...that a minenwerfer exploded during heavy enemy bombardment which pierced the Officers Dugout Quarters, exploding therein.

Probably for the families and friends, this was seen as a preferable way for their family member to have perished. And it was left at that.

Their time at the hill was not all death and seriousness. As anyone who has been involved with the armed forces or emergency services will know, you tend to develop a sort of black humour. You find the humour in the strangest of things, even tragedy at times. You might not display this however, away from your mates in the service. One such episode occurred late in April. To say the British officers were not overly popular, would be an understatement. The men believed them to be up themselves, too aloof and that they considered themselves better than the average trooper.

On this day, Bob and Bert were working forward in the shallow defensive system. It had been an unusually quiet day in the scheme of things. It was a beautiful spring day, cloudless and with a hint of warmth in the air. Fritz must have been busy on some other project as there had been unusually few visits from either whizz-bangs or Minnies. One of the British officers had come out of the dugouts and decided he was going to take this opportunity to give himself a shave. He set up his little mirror on the wall of the trench, took out his shaving brush and commenced to lather it up, with his tiny block of soap. He took a great deal of care, to ensure that his face was adequately covered with foam. Bob and Bert were both entranced by his detailed care in doing the job properly. Once he had foamed up, he drew out his razor and opened it carefully, raising it to his face. Before his first stroke, he stopped, frozen to the spot. He cocked his ear to the sky and then screamed out "Minnie incoming."

At that call everyone in the trench dove for the floor, covering their heads. The Minnie landed about 10 ft (3m) in front of the trench and exploded with a mighty roar. Not exactly the stuff that humour is made of, but if the Hun who fired the Minnie, could have seen the results, he too would have joined in the following frivolity. When the dust from the explosion had settled, everybody started to get back up. The last to rise was the officer, but when he arose, he was not covered with a nice white shaving foam, but a face full of mud and foam. He looked hilarious. It reminded Bob of the Vaudeville acts, where white actors painted their faces black to look Negro.

The officer just sat there and slowly wiped one section at a time away with his index finger, flicking it away down the trench. He said nothing throughout this procedure, but if looks could kill, that Hun would suffer a long and painful death. One could sense the stifled guffaws and sniggers at the time, from all those who witnessed the event. No one dared laugh though, at least, not until they got to a safe distance. The two boys took great delight in passing this story on to their mates, when they got back to the HQ at Larch Wood.

The war went on, of course, and the repair work went ahead at a frantic pace. Bob was redirected along with Bert and the other carpenters, down into the deep Berlin sap, to shore up the section that had collapsed, as the Miners dug the collapse section out. The officers up top, continued setting the charge of 600 lbs (273kg) of ammonal and 50 lbs (23kg) of Guncotton, as Avery and Tandy had started to do. They did it, with a great deal of care.

The month of May was much like any other at the hill, pressure to keep digging, to get those new mines organised in time for the big blow. Between Captains Woodward, McBride and Anderson, testing of the leads to the mines, under Hill 60 and Caterpillar, now became a daily occurrence. Resistance of the leads, had to be tested and measured and each day checked, to see that it had not altered. If everything remained the same each day, it would mean that the mine had not been tampered with, nor detected by the enemy.

When the boys arrived at the hill, at the end of the first week in May, they found that there had been a fire in the infantry dugouts, which had damaged a lot of the timber structure. Whilst this fire had been a really close call, the men there at the time had gotten on to it quickly, and had managed to get it under control, but not before a significant amount of damage had been done. It took a solid two day's work, to repair all the damage that had been done. Thankfully, no one had been injured during the fire, although some of the men did lose some of their equipment.

By mid-May, the pace of work had changed. Bob became suspicious that maybe a date for the blow had now been set. His suspicions were confirmed when Capt. Woodward turn up one day with a load of switchgear. Bob, and the other carpenters, were directed to build a platform, on which the firing mechanism, was to be set up, and thus, where it was intended for the detonation sequence take place. It was situated, about one hundred yards (90m) forward of the Larch Wood dugouts and within twenty yards (19m) of the entrance to Berlin sap. This position was chosen due to its ease of access from the dugouts and where there was a good view of Hill 60. It would need to be camouflaged above, as Hun aircraft were seen over head almost daily, and this would give away their intentions.

"I tek it a date for the detonation has been set, sir, has it?" Bob asked Capt. Woodward.

"It has indeed, Bob, although I can't tell you when that is, as I haven't even been told yet."

"I understand that, sir. Are we goin' tae get the other galleries finished in time though, sir?" inquired Bob.

"We're certainly going to give it a try, but I think your concerns may be well justified. It's going to take an herculean effort, to get them done in the time that I think we've got, but we've achieved a lot already, so we going to try." Woodward looked to his left and then his right, at the shelling that was going on up at the frontline and beyond. There was a mix of trench mortars and artillery dropping in that area, not particularly intense, but intensity did not matter if that one shell landed on your trench. It did not make any difference if it was one of one, or one of 1000. He then turned to Bob and said, "We'll have to keep this well covered Bob. We don't want any of that lot dropping on top of this, not at this late stage."

"The boys are currently preparing the coverings doon in the workshop as we speak, sir. We will have them up by midday. We're just going tae use some hessian loosely over the top and we'll make sure we muddy it up beforehand," Bob replied.

"That sounds grand. We do not want it to be too clean around here. It would stand out like a dunny in the desert if it was clean." Woodward smiled, clapped Bob on the back and started to move off. He'd only gone a few yards when he stopped, turned around and said, "By the way, at three this afternoon, we're having a demonstration, of the torpedo trenching for General Babington. I think it would be useful if you were there Bob. Do you think you'll be finished here by then?"

"I think so, sir, we should be finished well before then. There may be a little tidying up tae dae and a few little finishin' pieces, but any o' the boys can dae that," Bob replied.

"Good. We'll see you then." The captain turned on his heels and was gone. Bob smiled. He enjoyed talking with the captain. It was like he treated him as an equal, not as an underling. All the same, Bob was not quite sure why it would be useful for him to be there, at the demonstration. That puzzled him.

The men did indeed, finish the platform, with plenty of time to spare. There was a small, raised area on this platform, made to take the exploder mechanisms and the backups. Failure was not an option, so even the backups had backups. Multiple sets of leads had been run to both mines, so if one set failed through corrosion or being cut, there was always another set waiting to be used. The fate, of thousands of men, rested on the successful detonation of these two mines at the top end of the Messines ridge. It was not lost on Bob either that the fate of possibly thousands of Germans, also rested on this successful detonation.

That afternoon, Bob joined a group of about forty or fifty men and officers, to the demonstration area out along the Poperinge road. The demonstration this afternoon, was to show General Babington, the technique of digging long lengths of trench in a short period of time. This would be useful for setting up attacks and for situations where quick digging in was required. The technique utilised long lengths of threaded pipe, torpedoes they called them, filled with explosives. These pipes would be pushed horizontally through the soil using a press, at the required depth, for the purpose of this demonstration, about 5 ft (1.5m). The next pipe would then be screwed to the first, and once again pressed through the soil. The next pipe could then be connected to the first two and the process repeated over and over, until you had reached the desired length.

The first time this was ever tried, it resulted in a somewhat amusing outcome. It was assumed the pipes would keep going in a straight line, only they did not. After some distance, the lead pipe deviated and continued in a wide sweeping arc. It was only when the pipes were detonated that they discovered that they had curved right around almost back to the point of origin. Fortunately, no one was injured that day, but lessons were learned. Slow and steady gives you a straight line.

For the purpose of a demonstration this day, they were going to dig 250 ft (75m) of trench in as short a time as possible. The reason so many men had been brought along, was, as soon as the torpedoes had blown their trench, the diggers would race in and clear the way for a firm usable trench. The technique had been perfected over the previous year, but not all army groups had, as yet, been acquainted with the technique. Hence the demonstration for Gen. Babington.

*

Lt Gen James Melville Babington, KCB, KCMG, DL was a British army officer, who had given exemplary service during the Boer war and had been commander of the New Zealand defence force from 1902 to 1907. He was now in command of the 23rd Division. Babington, was yet another Scot, having been born in Corstorphine, Edinburgh, in 1854, so was now 62. Despite his age, he was renowned as a tough but fair commander, well liked, by his men and fearless in battle.

*

Today's demonstration was to show the general how a trench could be dug in quick time, to allow for a protected advance on an enemy position. A technique of advancing over open ground, to attack an enemy position, had been extensively used during this war, by both sides, but was incredibly wasteful of human life. Some commanders were now beginning to see that advancing troops needed more protection, so any method that can provide that protection required investigation. Captains Woodward and McBride were both there to guide the demonstration. They started off, by showing the General, the torpedoes, detonators and pressing mechanism. Bob watched on, as the torpedoes were then pressed through the soil, from the starting trench, one torpedo after the other. In this sandy clay soil, the torpedoes pressed fairly easily. Rocky soil made this process difficult, to near on impossible, due to either high resistance being encountered or significant deflection. As each pipe was pressed in, the men paused, only to reset the press and screw the next torpedo to the previous. Once all the torpedoes were in place, the detonator was inserted in the open end and run back to the firing device.

Once everyone was safely undercover, Capt. Woodward fired the torpedoes. A mass of dirt exploded into the air, along the entire length of the torpedoes, and then settled back to earth, on either side of, what was now, a trench of sorts. Bob had seen this technique on numerous occasions, but the rise and gentle fall of all the dirt, in a graceful arc, always enthralled him. Once the dust, smoke and any gases had cleared, the diggers were sent in with their shovels to clear the loose dirt out of the bottom of the trench, to enable a firm base to the trench. Where necessary, the next move would be installation of the duckboard, any shoring up of sides that was required and ladders for the advancing troops. "Maybe this is why I'm here," Bob wondered. "That's about the only area where a carpenter would be required, but we do all of that ahead of time." Bob was still thinking to himself. He was none the wiser as to his inclusion in this demonstration.

From start to finish, the whole process took forty five minutes, used forty men and produced a working trench 250 feet long (75m) and 6 feet deep (2m). General Babington and the GOC, were both hugely impressed. Both could see the advantages of having a trench that could be shot out towards an enemy line, in quick time. Back at the hill, work continued at a feverish pace. The captains still wanted to try and get the new galleries out under the German Lines, in time for the coming big blow. On the 23rd of May, the diggers broke their record by hitting 33'6" (10m) of 6' x 3' (2m x 1m) tunnel in the day. They beat that the next day by 3' (1m) and the following day by another 5 feet (1.5m). The men certainly were not slacking on the job through May. This also meant lots of timber was needed, so Bob and the boys were kept really busy sourcing and shaping timbers.

Chapter 16
The Big Boom

Throughout these months, the Germans continued to search for the deep mines. It seemed that while they had worked out there were deep mines, they were unable to accurately locate them, as their attempts at Crumping them, were somewhat random. However, on the 25th, they got much closer than they realised. A sizable charge was blown, in between the cutting and ANZAC shaft. It cratered and collapsed a significant section of the main gallery leading to the Hill 60 mine. It also damaged sections of B gallery, Beta gallery and C gallery. It also cut one of the sets of leads coming from the mine. The Australians were fortunate that there was no follow-up to this blow. The Hun did not appear to check to see if this Crump had opened up any Allied digging. Had there been a follow-up, it could well have led to the mine at Hill 60 being discovered.

A large section of tamping had to be removed to allow for the repair work to go ahead, and to check that no damage had been done to the charge, sitting, waiting, under that hill. The damage in beta shaft, trapped a listener there for two days. He was uninjured, but for that 48 hours, one can only but imagine, the thoughts going through his head. Many a tunneller, had been trapped underground permanently over the last two years. In fact, many of those tunnellers remained there, to this day. This listener was, of course, rescued and lived to fight another day.

In a way, the Crumping proved fortuitous. This section of A gallery had been unavailable to access, due to it having already been tamped. Now that it was open again it provided 1ATC with an advanced listening post. Almost immediately, Capt. Woodward was called forward to this area, to listen to an unidentified noise. It did not take him long to identify that noise, as the creaking of a windlass, as it raised and lowered the bucket from the diggings. It raised huge concerns, as their measurements indicated they were dangerously close to the main charge under Hill 60. By counting the creeks of the windlass, they could determine the progress of that shaft.

Each day, the creaks increased in number, meaning they were getting deeper. Each day, it meant they were getting closer to their own depth. Each day increased the concern. By the end of the month the creaks the men counted, remained the same each time. That meant that the Germans had reached their desired depth and were now digging horizontally. It seemed that they may be digging parallel to their own A gallery, only a handful of feet away. If they stayed on that line, it should mean that they were safe but if they deviated, the whole plan could be thwarted. Even though they knew the Germans were close, the mine had to be re-tamped and just trust that they kept going parallel. There was nothing else for it.

The next few days saw all almost constant testing of the leads' continuity and resistance, observing carefully for any change in either, which would indicate a breakthrough by the German army. Each day the testing came back with the same results.

Naturally, the information was reported back to divisional HQ. A discussion between the Brass hats, came to the conclusion that the mines had better be blown sooner rather than later. They would rather that the extra galleries that 1ATC was digging, would reach their target, and thus increase the damage on the German Lines, however, that was still, estimated at 4 to 5 weeks away. The Brass decided that they could not wait that long, so an earlier date was set for the firing along the entire Messines ridge. There was too much danger of discovery, so the mines would have to be blown. It would take at least two days to amass all the troops on the frontline that would be required for the ensuing attack. The result of course, was a flurry of activity behind the frontline from Ypres to Armentieres.

On 2 June 1917, Captain Oliver Woodward arrived at Larch Wood HQ, at around 10:00 pm. He called all the officers and NCOs together for a meeting.

"Well men, a date has now been set for the blow and we need to advise all those still digging, to cease and remove all their equipment. The mines will be blown at 3.10 am, on the 7th, five days hence. Unfortunately, the extra drives we are making won't make it in time, so we can pull out of all those now." There was a collective groan and many sighs from the group. He continued, "The rest of our time here will be getting ready for the advancing troops and setting up everything in readiness. We will remove most of our men, so the infantry can have somewhere to doss down, prior to the advance."

The switchgear bench had already been set up and Bob and the boys had installed the switchgear, as directed, although they had not connected them to the leads to the mines. The mines were still connected to the test bench and the final connection would be left to the captain himself.

The next three days were spent doing the final tamping on the two mines and shoring up the timbers that they still required, to ensure they would survive the blast. The tamping had never been fully completed, just in case they had to remove the tamp, to investigate any problem. The final part of the tamp could be completed in fairly quick time, but if the whole tamp had been in place and they had to investigate anything, it would have taken too long to remove the entire tamped section. Now with only a couple of days to go, it was fingers crossed and hope like heck that the Bosch did not find any of the mines. This would have been going on all way down the mines of the Messines ridge. Twenty five mines in all, had been dug and loaded with a total of 1,196,100 lbs (542,542 kg) of explosives. Due to a variety of reasons, only nineteen of these mines, totalling 934,000 lbs (423,655 kg) of explosives, would be fired on the morning of the 7th.

All this activity continued, throughout almost constant artillery bombardment. Whizz-bangs from long distance and trench mortars from the enemy front line. Occasionally, of course, they scored a hit, on the trenches that were to be used for the advancing troops, and the diggers of 1ATC were in constant demand to clear these crumps and obstructions. The day of the 5th was spent removing all unnecessary personnel from the HQ and underground. They were sent back to Ypres and Poperinge. Only a few listeners remained underground, to report any Hun activity. At about 6:00 PM, the infantry of the 69th Brigade, started to move into the dugouts, accumulating in the dugouts at Larch Wood and the forward infantry dugouts just behind the front line. Only about 40 men from 1ATC remained at the Bensham Road firing site.

Once again, Woodward asked Bob to remain on site, explaining he needed someone who knew the lay-out of this system, to remain in case assistance or repair was required. "Also, Bob, once it is light," he went on, "and the advance has pushed the enemy into retreat, those of us remaining, will need to check over the mine site, to measure it up, and to salvage whatever equipment we can from the German retreat. The lieutenant and sergeant here will be in charge of that, so take your directions from them. The few diggers we've hung onto here, will be used to break through the back walls of the craters so we don't have to climb over the top exposing ourselves."

"Of course, sir," Bob replied, "I'll stay oot of the way for the while. I'll be doon in the workshop, packing up the last of the equipment, for the move to wherever we goe next."

"Thanks Bob," returned the captain, "and by the way, job well done. Thank you to you and all of your men."

As Bob moved off to the workshops, the captain's words resonated in his head. "Your men?" thought Bob. "They're noe my men. I'm just a Sapper like the rest of them. Sure, I've teken some of them under ma wing, some of the younger ones, but I have noe rank, noe authority o'er them. I just tried tae help them. Woody must have noticed something. Maybe that's why he's included me in so much."

Hardly any activity took place on the 6th, other than constant testing of the leads. All the men were given the opportunity to spend the day resting, as the next couple of days were going to be extremely busy for them. Resting? Well, as much resting as one can do, when one is being attacked by artillery but, of course, by now, the men are well and truly used to it and just keep their heads down and stay underground. Captain Woodward connected the mines to the firing mechanism that afternoon but continued to test leads through the night. At 2:00 AM, everyone was cleared from the dugouts and the mines and the infantry took up position in the frontline trenches, in preparation for their advance, following the blowing of the mines.

Their advance would take place the moment the dirt had settled from the explosions, to maximise the confusion amongst the enemy. There were so many infantry on the frontline, at this moment, that some of them even crawled out of the trenches and lay prostrate, in no man's land, just to relieve the overcrowding in the trenches. Throughout this time, the British artillery continued to bombard the German frontline. This was more a ploy, to keep the German heads down, preferably underground, where the mine explosion effect would be maximised.

From 2:30 AM, on the 7th, the remaining men of 1ATC, gathered at the Bensham road firing platform. The air was thick with anticipation, as well as the dust from the artillery barrage. There was not much conversation, just everybody quietly waiting for the signal. The culmination of over one year of digging, had come down to this moment. Bob reflected on his time at Hill 60. They were told that no one should spend more than six months at Hill 60, but today marked 7 months and one week since they had arrived for this stretch and was a year and three weeks since his first introduction to the Hill and Caterpillar. A lot of water had travelled under the bridge in that time. Of all the men that came here, not all were going to leave. They were leaving some, in the cemetery here at Larch Wood, some in the Railway Dugouts cemetery and some at the Lille Gate cemetery. He guessed before this war was over, they would leave a few more, in a few more cemeteries around Flanders. He had seen a lot of things, a lot of horrible things and today, he guessed, he would see a lot more, horrible things.

The time of 3:10 AM, was chosen, because in Belgium, at this time, in summer, dawn is beginning to break. By the time the dust had settled, from the mine explosions, there would be enough light, for the advancing troops to see where they were going. The twilight would be long and allow for a good distance to advance, before the sun came up. For the infantry advancing at Hill 60 and St Elois, the next mine to the right, the rising sun would be on their left as they would be advancing to the south. For the troops advancing, from the remaining 17 mines, the rising sun would be in their faces, as they would be advancing to the east, so as much ground as possible needed to be covered before the sun came up, and made vision difficult for them, for a while.

As 3:10 AM approached, nearly all the officers were engaged in watch watching. Bob could see the nervous energy as each of them fiddled with their watch covers or fobs. The CO this morning, was Brigadier General Lambert of the 69th Brigade, 23rd Division. As the second hand on his watch hit the 12, he gave the command to fire. Captain Woodward pulled the firing arm down and the switchgear gave a spark. Nothing happened for what seemed like an age but was probably no more than 2 seconds. Then, only just perceptible at first, the ground started to tremble. The trembled grew to a rumble. The rumble grew to an earthquake.

As Bob looked towards the hill, it was silhouetted against the faint dawn. He could see the surface of the hill slowly rising, just like a balloon inflating. It seemed in slow motion, but that earth grew and grew in a huge arc, of dark grey dirt. As the arc got higher and higher it fractured into what reminded him of that tessellated pavement, in Ireland, at the Giant's Causeway. All of a sudden, up through the middle of this massive expansion, burst a ball of bright orange, red and white tongues of flame, as bright as the sun and the most incredible noise he had ever heard. It was deafening.

Bob thought, "*It was as if we had been responsible, for rending the earth wide open and allowing the flames of hell to reach through and drag Fritz back down below.*" Now silhouetted against this fire ball, even at this distance, they could see recognisable solid shapes flying through the air and landing hundreds of yards away. Still, no one spoke. Many of the men stood with their mouths agape. Some covered their ears. Some shook their heads. All just stared in amazement. The fire ball dissipated, but the smoke and dust rose higher and higher. Huge clumps of earth, equipment and men fell back to earth, a long distance from where they started. In fact, a lot of the dirt travelled as far as the men who had crawled into no man's land, waiting to advance and partially buried them.

The men at the Bensham Road station, were also conscious of other simultaneous explosions to their right, as similar fireballs erupted into the early morning sky. Whilst all the OCs down the line of the mines would have had their watches synchronised prior to the detonations, variations in individual time pieces accounted for the explosions not actually being simultaneous. However, all nineteen mines were detonated within a few seconds. Down the line of the Messines ridge, thousands of other men, were watching, as many thousands of other men died simultaneously.

The men at the detonation site, stood there for probably a minute, with no one speaking, until from the back of the group came a very quiet, "Jesus, fucking, Christ! Did we just do that?" It seemed to break the trance that everyone was in. They all started moving now and talking to each other. General Lambert, came forward to Captain Woodward and shook his hand. "Congratulations captain. That was just perfect. You can be so proud of your men. I am sorry you could not complete the extra tunnels that had been planned, but your men performed extraordinarily well, getting further than anyone ever expected in that time. You understand we had to blow them now though, before you could finish them."

"Yes general, I do understand. We really had no choice but to blow them now. 'Tis far better to blow them now, short of our target, than to risk being discovered," the captain replied.

"It must have been fairly close, by the sound of what you told us the other day," said the general.

"Yes, sir," Woodward replied. "I believe that Fritz was within a few feet of discovering our mine. It was certainly very close."

The general went on, "The attack should start any second now, and by the look of what we just saw, I don't think they're going to have too much resistance, at least, not for the first few hundred yards anyway."

That is exactly what happened. Crossing no man's land, the advancing troops encountered no resistance and once they entered the German frontline, all they found were bodies or bits of bodies and non-existent trenches. Any enemy soldiers they encountered that were still alive, were either sitting or lying there stunned or weeping. They offered no resistance whatsoever. Those men were quickly rounded up and sent behind Allied Lines, as prisoners of war. The troops did not encounter any resistance, until they were through Battle Wood, a distance of about three quarters mile (1.2km). Finally, after about two and a half years, the British had retaken Hill 60. Reports from along the entire Messines Ridge that came in over the next few days, all reported the same lack of activity for the first half mile (800m) at least. The plan had worked to perfection.

Back at Larch Wood, the activity for the first few hours after the explosion, revolved around clean-up and packing up equipment. Over the next few hours, prisoners of the German army trailed through the Larch Wood HQ. The expressions on their faces told the whole story. Not one of them look at any of the diggers, they just stared into space. Their hands were supposed to be raised as they marched through, but none of them was above head height. Mostly they were just turned to show open hands as they shuffled through. No one spoke. No one could speak. Their uniforms were torn, some had no boots, most had no helmets and there was certainly no light in their eyes. They had been stunned and their eyes showed that their heads were in no man's land. They had survived the blast but by the looks on their faces they probably wished they had not. They were the walking dead.

Once it was light enough, the officers and the men of 1ATC moved forward to examine their handiwork, to make appropriate measurements of the crater and to prepare it for defensive use. The diggers job was to break through the rear wall of the crater, to enable access without having to climb over that rear wall and expose themselves to enemy fire. That allowed for defensive troops to enter the crater and use the forward crater wall for protection. The officers and other men examined the German frontline and the crater itself. They similarly found German bodies, and parts of bodies, everywhere. The dirt blown out by the explosion covered hundreds of yards around the central point.

Hun trenches, within 100 yards of the crater, had been compressed, so that no trench now existed. The entire earth had been moved sideways. That meant that anybody who was in that trench, was still in there, but crushed. There was evidence of this with the occasional arm, leg or head poking through where the trench had been. The Germans had a habit of weaving branches as the walls of their trenches, like wicker baskets. Everywhere they looked, they could see parts of this weaving poking through from below. There was not a sign of life, anywhere to be seen. Anyone who had survived, had already passed by them, back at the Larch Wood HQ in that stream of prisoners.

Bob just stood there. He slowly surveyed the scene, scanning all around him. He slowly took in everything he saw, the bodies, the parts of bodies, equipment, dirt, concrete, clothing, animals, machine guns, trench mortars lying on their side or just poking their snout through the dirt, evidence of even more bodies trapped and timber, timber everywhere.

And how many are underground? he thought. He just stood and stared, over and over and over again. *How many have we killed here, in just a few seconds today?* he asked himself. *This was only one mine, of 19. Every one of them will probably show the same thing. That would make thousands of dead in those few seconds. Just how did we get here?* He just could not believe the scale of the devastation. *And we haven't even had a look at Caterpillar yet*, he thought. *Oh, my lord, what have we done?* he just kept repeating this to himself over and over again.

Eventually, he un-anchored his feet, and wandered around the site, collecting any useful equipment, as he had been instructed to do. No one said anything to those just standing looking, as everyone at some point, had done the same. No one there, that day, had ever seen anything on the scale of this before. Even those from the mining industry. They had seen explosions before, and plenty of them, but none of this scale, and none that cost human life like this one did. At this moment, they were not the enemy, they were just poor, unfortunate men, in the wrong place, at the wrong time. Just humans, like me. Some of the men went about their duties wiping tears from their eyes. This was 1917 and men did not cry. But this day, they did.

It had taken a while, but the Hun artillery started up on them midmorning, so they had to scurry back to the frontline, or what used to be their frontline and take shelter in the dugouts. There would be plenty more time tomorrow, to get the measurements they needed, and the photographs. Their job was done for the time being. Once the dust had settled from this little escapade, command would find new work for us to do they thought, but for their next couple of days, we will just do what we have to do around here.

It is believed, the explosions were felt as far away as London and Belfast in the British Isles. By the time, the war was over, the casualties from the explosion of the mines along the Messines ridge were listed as, 10,000 missing, presumed dead and 7000 captured or surrendered. Something like 20,000 men were engaged in digging those mines, over a period of about fifteen months. Recent research casts some doubt on the figure of 10 000 dead, as it has been discovered that there may have been some differences between the way the Germans reported and recorded their casualties, but one thing is for certain; many thousands of Germans lost their lives that day in horrific circumstances.

The detonation of these mines along the Messines ridge, effectively saw the end of offensive mining activities, as they had been here, for the rest of the war. Never again, would combatants use these techniques to counter a foe. Because of the time taken to dig these mines, it would only work in a static war and the Great War was the last static war.

Over the next two days, the remaining men took turns to go out and scavenge the remains of Hill 60 and the Caterpillar, to search for any remaining useful items. There were still plenty of armaments and ammunition to be collected, mining equipment and backwards of the enemy's former front, cooking equipment servicing equipment and all sorts of bits and pieces that they would be able to find useful, back at HQ. Of course, one of the most prized finds would have been documents, but most of them had been removed by the retreating troops. Anything of any value, would have been at their headquarters well behind the frontline and that was well beyond their area of searching. That was up to the advancing infantry to try and discover.

When Captain Woodward arrived back at the hill on the 10th, they conducted a survey of the two mine craters and came up with the following dimensions. Crater A, which was the former Hill 60, was 270 feet (83m) in diameter at ground level and 48 feet (15m) deep. Crater B, the former Caterpillar, was 280 feet (86m) In diameter and 68 feet (21m) deep. All around the lip of both craters there were large lumps of blue clay, evidence that the Germans had previously been looking for, as evidence of the British deep mines. For 100 yards around both craters, any remaining trenches that had not been destroyed by the crater, had been crushed wall to wall, into nonexistence. They had been completely compressed, along with anything in them.

As soon as the men finished that day, at Hill 60 and Caterpillar, they were withdrawn, back to Ypres and then given a week of leave. They all loaded into the lorries that had been made available to them and were transported back to Poperinge. Once there they joined the remainder of their mates from sections one and four and were transported further then, to St Omer for their week's leave. St Omer was a town well behind the frontline, about twenty miles (33km) from Poperinge. These men needed a rest. The deserved a rest and that, is what they used it for. The two sections played a cricket match against each other, they slept, bathed, washed their uniforms, swam, and just wandered around as tourists, sightseeing. Sections two and three commenced work on rebuilding roads in the newly captured area.

Over the next three or four weeks, all the men of 1ATC had leave for R&R on a rotational basis. Whilst on duty they worked on the road rebuilding. At least that was not underground and by doing this, thousands would not die in a few seconds. These thoughts plagued many of the men from here on, some for the rest of their lives, however long or short that was to be.

For the next six weeks, all four sections of 1ATC, worked on road building and rebuilding over a large area, from Zonnebeke, four miles (7km) north east of Ypres, to Messines, six miles (10km) south of Ypres and about two miles (3km) wide. So much damage had occurred on these roads that at times, the road was in distinguishable, from the surrounding farmland. Much of the work they had to do, involve re-gravelling of the damaged surface. There was however, enough of the road system that was completely demolished and needed rebuilding from the base up that their progress at times seemed to be at a snail's pace.

Not only that, but the men also realised that at any moment, the frontline could change again, and all their work would be blown up once again. Mind you, the men did not mind all that much. At least they were not underground, but out in the sunshine. If they thought that being on road works behind the line was going to be a safer job, they soon learned otherwise. The casualties continued to mount in 1ATC. Each day that passed, so another one or two added to their casualty list, either wounded or killed, by war or by accident.

During this time, the company was based at a new camp on the Dranoutre-Locre road, about seven miles (11 km) south west of Ypres. It was considered a kind of rest camp, being situated away from the front line, although they were taken from here to do the work on the roads closer to the front. On 5th of July, the men were called to hastily form a sort of guard of honour along the roadside, next to the camp. They figured that this must be some dignitary to command such a guard. The men paraded along both sides of the road and waited. No one knew who their guest of honour was to be.

"Wha' the blazes are we doin' standin' oot here all bloody dae long, waitin' for god knoes who?" whinged Bill.

"Noe idea," replied Bob. "But whoever it is, it mus' be someone important. Dae ye think it mebee General Haig, or someone like that?"

"If it is, I should shoot the bastard," added Bill. "The man's go' noe idea how to run a bloody war. Give the job to Monash I say!" Bill was in no mood for any Sassenach general. He was in no mood for anything English. He believed Scotland, should be run by the Scots.

"Mebee it's the King," Bert offered.

"Yer right!" scoffed Bill. "Noe English bloody king is goin' tae set foot oot here for fear he gets shot. Too scared to come here I would think."

"Well one thing's for sure. Ye'll noe have to wait long noo. There's a car or two comin' noo," said Bob. The men all spun round and peered into the distance and sure enough, there were two cars headed their way.

"Atten—tion!" called the CSM, and all the men dragged themselves to the attention position.

The car drew level with the men and the officers saluted and the cheers started at the far end of the line and progressively made the way towards Bob and the boys.

"Holy smokes!" uttered Bert. "It is the bloody King."

"And the Prince of Wales," added Bob.

"Well, I'll be..." added Bill as the cheers drowned out the rest of his sentence.

Both the King and the Prince, waved to the men as they went past and the formality of the occasion was lost, as the men started waving back. Not exactly military protocol, but this was hardly a normal military unit either. After the cars had passed the guard, the men were dismissed and allowed to go about their daily activities. As they walked back to their tent, Bert spoke up.

"Ye knoe, he's noe as big as I thought he was. He's quite short actually."

"Aye," added Bob. "He's noe a big man. That's noe the first time I've seen him, ye knoe."

"Aye we knoe ye great lump," Bill gave Bob a whack on the back of the head as they walked, then added, "Ye've tol' us so many times noo that ye saw the King in Edinburgh, that we may actually be beginnin' tae believe ye noo."

"So noe English King is goin' tae set foot oot here are they Bill?" Bob was razzing Bill by now. "Too scared would he be Bill?"

The three of them laughed at this and ran back to camp. The mood around camp that afternoon was decidedly up. Most of the men there had never seen the king, so for them, this was a highlight of the war. Certainly, the war itself was no highlight.

Part 3

Chapter 17
Hooge

It seemed to the men that now that the offensive mining was at a close, that the army did not know what to do with them, so they got maintenance type jobs to do. The road works was one of the tasks they pointed at. None of the men were road makers, so why would they be building roads? It was explained to them that the Tunnelling companies were all part of the engineers and it was the function of the engineers or the engineering battalions, to build the roads, or anything else the army wanted them to build. They would soon find out that this would mean a huge variety of items. They would continue repairing and building roads through June, July and August.

At the same time, a small number would be taken to build dugouts in some of the captured German trenches at L'Enfer Wood and late August, they started work on the dugouts at Hollandseschur mine crater. Hollandseschur crater, was the second mine to the south west of Hill 60, along the Messines ridge. It was one of the nineteen mines that were exploded on the 7th of June. It was about three miles (5km) from their earlier engagement. Once again, they were to be building accommodation dugouts in this crater and its surrounds. It was not to be a large system but did involve a fair bit of timber work, so once again Bob and Bert found themselves constructing dugouts as they had done previously, at Hill 63 and Hill 60.

After about two to three weeks, their part of the work there was completed and handed over to the 2nd Canadian Tunnelling Co for continuation and completion. 1ATC receive orders to move back to an area east of Ypres, known as Hooge.

Hooge crater also carried a reputation. Not a reputation that the men were too pleased about either. It was only a couple of miles to the east of Ypres, along the Menenstraat, the Menen road and close to the front line. To get there from

Ypres, the men had to pass through the Menen gate and at about the one mile (1.6km) mark, through Hellfire Corner. Everyone knew the Hellfire corner. Shrapnel corner to the west of Ypres, was bad enough, but Hellfire corner, made Shrapnel corner, look like a tea party. It was close to the frontline and easily visible for miles around, with higher ground to the east, which the Germans held. It was a major road and rail intersection on the outskirts of Ypres, and the German artillery had it well and truly ranged.

In fact, that whole Menen Road, between Ypres and Hooge, was so well ranged that it was almost impossible to move along that road in daytime. Being an unsurfaced road, any movement along there raised dust, which gave the enemy the heads up on any troop movement. It used to be a sealed road but had been shelled so often that virtually none of the seal remained. To combat this the British army had erected hessian screens between the trees, or what remained of the trees, all the way along this road, where they could, in an attempt to block German vision of any movement. It was a ploy that was moderately successful.

Not unlike Hill 60, Hooge was situated at the top of Bellewarde ridge, a slight rise, but compared to the rest of the area, provided a vantage point overlooking the entire area to the west, right into Ypres itself, and like Hill 60, it was considered a desirable and strategic position to hold.

Hooge crater had been created by the British tunnellers of the 175th Tunnelling Company, on 19 July 1915, to dislodge the Germans from that part of their frontline. The charge of 3500 lb (1600kg) of ammonal, had left a crater 120 ft (37m) wide and 20 ft (6.1m) deep. This, and other attacks around that time, initially failed to dislodge the Germans from the Hooge Chateau or its stables. Occupation of Hooge crater (where the stables used to be) and the Hooge Chateau, alternated between the British and Germans until 1 August 1917 when a British push, moved them almost a mile (1.6km) to the east. A further push on the 22nd of August did push them back to that one mile mark.

Once the area had been consolidated, it was decided to turn the area at the old crater into a Brigade headquarters, and who better to dig it, than the men who done such an exemplary job, at Hill 63. No 4 Section of 1ATC was to take over from the British 177th Tunnelling Co and finish off the dugouts.

"Here we go again," thought Bob, and probably most of the rest of the No 4 Section. "Sometimes it may be better tae dae noe so good a job. A' least you wouldn't get asked again." Whilst they were not too pleased about being in the firing line again, they were proud that their efforts had indeed been recognised.

They were getting quite a reputation, not only amongst the Australians, but all the allies, even the British.

There was to be a big push coming up (eventually to be known as the third battle of Ypres or the battle of Passendale (Passchendaele) and the British needed an advance headquarters from which to work, closer to the frontline than their current position in Ypres. The crater at Hooge, had been a significant-sized crater, and under German occupation the inside of the crater had been levelled off, so it would look more like a crater that you might see on the Moon.

The plan, the men were told, was to burrow into the walls of the crater and descended 27 ft (8.5m) down access stairways, where there would be accommodation for two whole brigades and their admin. Part of the digging had been completed, by the British 177th tunnellers. 1ATCs job, was to finish digging the galleries and the fit out and ensure that it was ready for occupation. The dugouts were built to accommodate eighteen officers, twenty NCOs and five hundred and twenty fighting troops. There were half a dozen entrances off the east side of the crater that descended via stairways, to a preliminary gallery and after a couple of right angle bends, the main access gallery extended some 200 ft (61m) southeast, then turned left and extended a further 100 ft (30m) northeast.

Most of the length of these two galleries were double or parallel tunnels, each with many lateral galleries about 40 ft (12m) long branching off every 40 ft or so. These battle galleries contained triple level Timber bunkbeds. It was certainly crowded, but it was mostly for short term accommodation. Not only did this system have to have bunking for around five hundred and sixty men, but it also required eating areas, toileting areas, admin areas and staging areas, as well as adequate ventilation, so the whole infrastructure was quite extensive.

Once again, water was a problem, and although the crater and the dugouts, were situated on the Bellewarde ridge, the water table was still not too far down, so constant pumping of water was an issue. Again, it took manpower, to man these pumps. Two men were required for each pump and several pumps were required, to keep the area from going under water. A combination of hand operated pumps and electrically operated pumps was being used during the construction phase, but once completed, the pumping would be all electric.

Needless to say, as there was an abundance of water, there was also an abundance of mud. Just as sticky as the mud of Hill 60, but this time only the orange mud. After all this time in the mud, the men noticed that their boots were no longer lasting. The stitching was beginning to rot and many of the men found as they walked, or attempted to walk through the mud, their boots would get stuck deep with the gluey suction, and efforts to pull their feet out, resulted in the souls departing company with the rest of their boots. This resulted in the somewhat comical sight of men fruitlessly hopping around in the mud trying not to put their now socked foot, into the glue. The QM was kept busy replacing boots.

Meanwhile, underground Bob, Bert and the other carpenters, were kept busy building the timber work for the accommodation and all the other installations. They were glad to be back, just working with the timber, in an accommodation area, not on an offensive installation. Both men, had seen enough of the aftereffects of the offensive system. Enough to last a lifetime.

The men did not stay at Hooge during their off-shift time, so they travelled back and forward from their temporary camp outside of Ypres. Each time they went on shift, it meant travelling through Hellfire corner and Birr crossroads, an equally significant crossroad for artillery to range on. Sometimes they travelled by lorry, sometimes they travelled on foot but either way nobody dawdled along the Menen road. By now of course, the men were used to the shelling and just ducked and dodged as needed. There were surprisingly few casualties on these back and forward movements. Whilst on the job at Hooge crater, things were no better. As the work was on a tight schedule, they did not like to be held up but that was unavoidable at times.

For example, in the afternoon of 11 September, little work was possible due to the incessant gas attacks. These gas attacks brought virtually everything to a halt, until the air had cleared sufficiently. Most days on the job, the men were subject to shelling from the German artillery, but being low down in the crater, it required a close hit, to be of any hindrance. The men were protected by the crater wall, from any hits outside of that wall.

Bob and Bert had become close friends, during the time they worked together. With similar backgrounds and similar outlooks, they tended to back each other up, especially when it came to the things they had seen and done.

"I think this must be hell, Bert." Bob commented one day at Hooge. "It seems tae satisfy every definition of it. I cannae imagine there would be anything worse that the devil could throw at us, than wha' we have witnessed, these last few weeks."

"Aye Bob," he replied. "I think the devil himself must be behind all of this. This couldnae possibly be the work of God. It would take a very strange interpretation of the bible, tae come up with this lot, as the work o' the almighty. There must be one heck of a battle goin' on, at this moment, between the devil and the Lord himself, and unfortunately, it looks like the devil be winnin'."

"Aye Bert. I ken exactly wha' ye mean. But even though it be looking like the devil is winnin', I have faith that the good lord will win in the end. I have tae believe that, otherwise what point would there be in us bein' here? I just have tae believe it. I have tae."

"Too true Bob," replied Bert. "The Bosch be the mob that started this little affair, and they've got tae be made tae pay for it. We cannae allow, this kind of glaikit oppression tae shape the world for our bairns."

Bob was silent for a while and when he replied to Bert's musing, he agreed. "'Tis about the only thing that keeps me goin'. I dinnae want tae live in a world that is run by this kindae thinkin'. I just want tae get home tae ma Jean and get back tae the way things were. In peace. Sometimes it seems like a lot tae ask for though."

"Doesnae stop me asking him for that though Bob. I sure hope he's listenin'. Sometimes I wonder though," Bert said, "I dinnae ken Bob, all this kindae tests yer faith, I think. I cannae come tae grips with all this hate and devastation. It just doesnae make any sense tae me either." The discussion went back and forth for some time, not really coming to any conclusion. It was the sort of discussion that would always lead nowhere.

On Monday 17th of September, the section had a visit from Australia's official photographer, Frank Hurley. He took several photographs of the men at work in the crater and then went underground and photographed some of the work going on down there directed by Sgt Hood. These photographs are some of only a few of the 1ATC in action during the conflict. It was really quite an event. Hurley's equipment was quite large and bulky and required quite a deal of setting up time. He was still using glass plate negatives at this stage. The whole squad was asked to get up into the crater while continuing to work. Hurley was to comment later:

It is a wretched job as they are working 25 feet below the surface level and most of the time knee deep in mud, which they jocularly term 'hero juice' on account of it percolating through tiers and tiers of buried corpses. Most of the men are miners and they are applying their knowledge to supreme advantage whilst the Boche shells whiz and burst around them.

The following day saw an event that had a huge impact on Bob. The squad's shift had ended for the day and they were being returned to their camp. As usual, three lorries brought the next crew out to a changeover point, about halfway between Hellfire corner and Birr crossroads. At this point the incoming squad would jump off the lorries and start making their way towards Hooge. The outgoing squad would then load themselves into the lorries and head back towards Ypres. The changeover needed to be swift, so the trucks would not become targets for the artillery. On this night, the outgoing squad were a couple of minutes late, and the lorries had to wait. Some of the incoming squad were still on the lorries, when one of them took a direct hit from the German artillery. A single shot, right on target.

As mentioned before, this section of road was well ranged by the German artillery, and this shot was a perfect example of that. The lead lorry, disintegrated in the blast and four men, were killed instantly. A further four died of wounds the next day, and one a week later. The other two lorries were damaged by the blast, but no further injuries were reported from them.

Bob, Bert and twenty seven other members of the outgoing squad, stood transfixed, as the lorry flew into the air, in two pieces, just a few feet in front of them, silhouetted against the bright orange, of the explosion. Once the dust had settled, they had half a chance of seeing where they were going and dashed in to help the wounded. The sight that greeted them, was horrible. Those that were dead, had received horrific injuries. Those that had survived, were not much better. They did what they could for their mates, stemming the bleeding, packing their wounds but it was obvious to Bob that their efforts were futile. When Bob arrived at the scene some of the surviving unwounded men were already attending to some of their wounded mates.

Bob zeroed in on one of the as yet unattended men. "Hold on, Adam," he said, as he grabbed a number 15 wound pack from his backpack. "We'll get this on ye injury son. We'll get this bleeding stopped noo and get ye to the CCS quick smart. You're goin' tae be fine, I'll see tae that." Bob was getting the dressing tied on firmly, when one of the of the other lads came along and sat Adam up and used his own body as a backrest. Adam did not look good. He had a gaping hole in his abdomen, made by either a fragment of the shell or a part of the lorry. To make matters worse, the mud that the explosion had stirred up had mixed with the blood and guts as well. They kept the pressure on the injury and were able to slow the flow of blood. As luck would have it, a casualty clearing station, was only a couple of hundred yards back along the Menen road towards Ypres. Stretcher bearers and medics were on scene within a couple of minutes and took over from the men, to try and save the lives of their comrades.

They could not hang around, knowing the Germans already had the correct range for this position, so they bundled into the remaining two lorries and headed back through Ypres to their campsite, outside Poperinge. Bob sat in the back of the lorry, his hands now sticky and crusty from the blood. In their haste to leave the incident, none of them had a chance to clean up. Not much was said in the lorries, on the way home. They were stunned, and Bob was reminded of the faces of the Germans, who paraded through the Larch Wood HQ, after the blowing of Hill 60, three months previously. He now understood those faces.

Once they were back at camp, they all headed to clean themselves up, and then all went to the mess tent for a hot cup of tea. There they sat around the table and discussed what they had just seen. "If we were only 1 minute earlier, we would've been the ones being hit."

"If only they'd kept driving another 100 yards, maybe they would have missed."

"That could have been us."

"Why did they stay sitting in the truck?"

"The Corp is a good bloke, for an ex-navy man. I hope he makes it."

"I don't think there's much hope for any of them."

"I've never seen anything like it, and I hope to never have to see it again."

These and many more comments were made over the next half hour, all in a similar vein. Bob just sat there, staring into his tea, and looking at his hands. "That was Adam's blood," he thought. "I've just seen his insides. They are not meant tae be on the ootside. I couldnae do much for him. He must have been in so much pain and he just lay there, quiet, looking straight into my eyes. He knew what was happening." All these thoughts and more, raced through his head. He finished his tea, rose slowly, turned and walked back to his tent, without uttering a word. He wanted to tell the others; he did everything he could; he just could not speak.

Back at his tent, he sat and slowly unwound his puttees, placing them neatly beside his bunk, removed his boots, placed them next to his puttees, removed his jacket and breeches, hanging them on the peg behind his bunk and climbed into bed, in a vain attempt to have sleep block out the events of this evening. One by one, the other men filtered back to the tent and turned in, without a word being spoken.

The toll for that night, had a big effect on all of those who were there, and was as follows:

Campbell, Charles. 5502 Spr, 31 yo, KIA 18/9/17
Cooper, Walter. 91 Spr, 24 yo, KIA 18/9/17
Hodder, Arthur. 4103 Spr, 23 yo, KIA 18/9/17
Murrin, Albert. 5531 Spr, 32 yo, KIA 18/9/17/17
Hall, Edgar. 5335 Sgt 22 yo, DOW 19/9/17
Hendrickson, Charles. 3307 Spr, 26 yo, DOW 19/9/17
McGown, Adam. 3330 Spr, 24 yo, DOW 19/9/17
North, Thorne. 3656 Spr, 26 yo, DOW 19/9/17
Sawyer, Tom. 6644 Cpl, 39 yo, DOW 25/9/17

The work did not go way, so the following day they were back on shift again. They worked at a feverish pace, as the deadline was close. They worked day and night shifts over the two weeks to get all the installations completed. Capt. Woodward's records showed that in their two weeks, 1ATC completed 130 ft of 6 ¼' x 3' (40m of 2 m x 1m) stairway, 127' of 6 ¼' x 3' (39m of 2m x 1m) galleries and 140 feet of 6' x 6' (43m of 2m x 2m) dugouts. All in 288.5 hours. In that time, they removed a total of 465.4 cubic yards or 12,566 cu ft (355.8 cu m) of dirt, and they fitted all the timber work in there as well. They did manage it, and at 5pm on 19 September, the dugouts were handed over to the British army. They were in fact occupied that day by the members of the Australian first division, in preparation for an all-out advance to the east of following day.

The Cambridge Road dugouts, like the Hooge dugouts, were several hundred yards to their north and were occupied that day by the second Australian division, in preparation for the following day's attack. Once again, a squad under the lead of Sgt Alex Hood and sixteen of the tunnellers, remained behind for the next two days to oversee the occupation and to deal with any issues. The men all along the frontline in the region, received quite a hot reception, from the German artillery all night. At about 1100 hrs all allied traffic on the roads ceased, in preparation for the following morning's attack.

At 5am the following day, the artillery started up with a terrific barrage on the German frontline. This barrage lasted for forty minutes, so at 0540 hrs precisely members of the 22nd and 23rd brigade streamed out of the Hooge and Cambridge Road dugouts and attacked the German frontline. On their right, were members of the British 41st Division and on the left was the Royal Scots. Bob and the other tunnellers, manned the stairways and guided the troops up the stairways to assemble in the crater prior to their attack. Each man that went by, received "a Good luck" or a "Give them hell, won't you" or some other words of encouragement. The departing troops were remarkably upbeat, given that they may be going to their death. Many had been waiting for weeks for this chance to drive the enemy back.

By 1030 hrs, the ANZAC troops had accomplished all their objectives, with a noticeably light casualty list of their own. Over the next few hours, over 700 captured German prisoners, passed through the Hooge dugouts on their way to Ypres. Not only did the dugouts act as a clearing post for wounded troops but also is a holding facility for the prisoners until they could be removed to the rear, to a POW camp. The sergeant, Bob and the boys acted as marshals, directing the prisoners to appropriate parts of the dugout, as they understood the lay-out of the dugouts implicitly. Something was different about these prisoners though. They did not look like the ones they had seen previously at Hill 60. These ones were more animated. Some were smiling, most were chatting, in German of course, with the occasional "hello" or "thank you" in English.

Bob turned to the Sergeant and said, "Do ye notice anything different aboot these prisoners tae the last lot, Sergeant?"

"As a matter of fact, Bob, I do. This lot, actually look, alive. The last lot looked like they were the walking dead. It's kind o' strange, but they appear happy, to have been taken prisoner. Well, they're oot o' it noo."

Of course, what it did mean, was that they were going to survive this war. One can only assume that they were in fact, happy to be taken prisoner. After three years of war, they had probably had enough, and even though their homes may have only been a few hundred miles away, they too, would not have seen their families for the last three years.

Over the course of the next three weeks, British, French, Canadian and ANZAC troops, advanced in excess of three miles (around 5km), to take the villages and towns of Geluveld, Zonnebeke, Broodseinde, Passchendaele, Langemarck and Poelcappelle, as well as the strategic Polygon wood. October 3rd saw the battle of Broodseinde, and it was the only time in the entire war that a wholly ANZAC force, conducted a section of the battle. Here, the 1st, 2nd and

3rd Australian divisions and the New Zealand division, fought side by side, in what has been described as one of the most successful campaigns for the ANZAC troops, of the war. They showed what could be achieved, when they were allowed to work together, rather than just to fill in holes in the British army. Several military crosses, and two VCs were awarded to members of the AIF, in that three weeks.

Several important installations and landmarks were captured during this time. Landmarks that became known as ANZAC House, Halfway House and Polygon Wood, along with the important town of Zonnebeke and the village of Broodseinde. The village of Passchendaele, would not fall into Allied hands, until the second battle of Passchendaele, in early November, when the Canadians, with the assistance of a few Australians, took over from the exhausted Australians, in that sector and drove the Germans out. This final action brought to an end, on November 6th, the third battle of Ypres.

Whilst the third battle of Ypres, was a resounding success, it came at a high cost to the Australians. For the month of October 1917, the AIF lost a total of 6405 KIA or DOW as well as the further 19,194 wounded in action. Many of those wounded, would never really recover, and remained scarred for the rest of their lives either physically or mentally. These men were casualties, just as much as those who died, but were never recorded as such. Given that Australia's total commitment to the great war was around 400,000, this represents a casually rate of 6.25%, and 11% of the total deaths for the war.

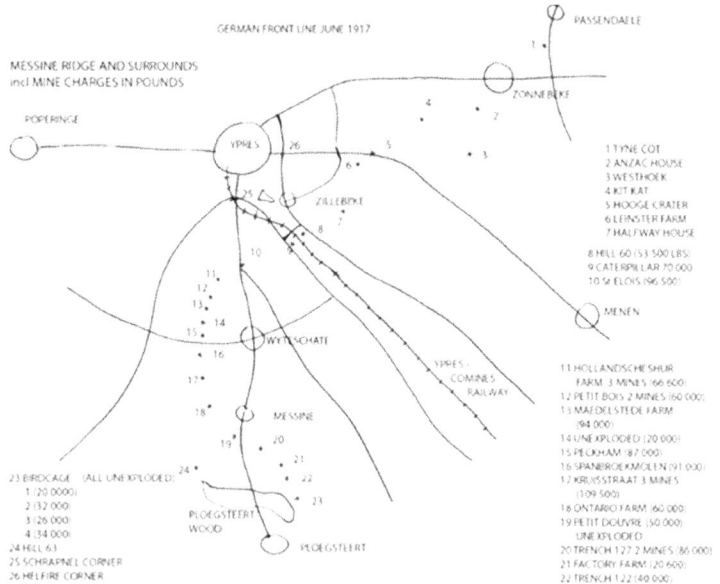

Fig 4

The southern part of the Ypres salient. Numbers 8-23 are the mines along the Messine Ridge. Ypres to Ploegsteert 8.5 miles (13.5 km)

It was now heading into winter so the entire area, from Ypres to Passchendaele, was nothing more than a sea of mud. Stories abound, of men, who slipped off the duckboard, into a water filled shell hole and because of the weight of their equipment, were never seen again.

By mid to late October, with the frontline moving forward, the men of 1ATC were spread over several different digs. Some remained at Hooge, some went up to the Cambridge Road dugouts, some to ANZAC House and Halfway House, and yet others to Leinster Farm. ANZAC and Halfway House were both German built pillboxes. ANZAC house had the distinction of being the only two story pillbox in the region, the upper story of which had been used as a German artillery spotting post.

One of the losses Bob was not expecting, occurred on 31st October. Halfway House was one of the dugouts under construction by 1ATC. It was located just south of the Birr Crossroads, about halfway between Hellfire Corner and Hooge crater dugouts. Being over five miles (8.5km) behind the front, the men were thinking they were fairly safe, from enemy artillery. On this day, on one of the rotations at Halfway House, the men found otherwise. Long range, High explosive shells, started raining in. Sgt Alex Hood dived into the cookhouse for cover, just as it took a direct hit. He was killed instantly, along with:

Sappers 3563 Joseph Bailey, 28 yo, Englishman, late of Adelaide

145 Archie Ivall 32 yo, Englishman, late of Laidley, Queensland

5579 Sgt Roy Mason, 22 yo, of Newcastle NSW

When the barrage was over, and the men rushed in to help, they found Sgt Hood, completely unmarked, by the blast. What this meant was that he had been killed by the percussion from the explosion, not the explosion itself. Bob knew all the men but was particularly saddened by the loss of Sgt Hood. Not only was he a fellow Scotsman and they shared a common surname, but Bob genuinely liked Alex. They had both wondered if they were related somehow. They got on well, with similar likes and dislikes. He was also particularly good at his job. Bob also knew that Alex left behind a wife and eight children, to fend for themselves. This loss, and those of six weeks before, were starting to have an effect on Bob. He was not sure how much more of this he could take.

During his time at Hooge, after the commencement of the battles, Bob saw many casualties from both sides, pass through the dugouts. As time went on, the men passing through, got thinner, dirtier and more vacant. From the eager, fresh faced boys that passed through on September 20th, to a month later, the shell shocked, filthy, emaciated troops of the AIF. The stories they recounted to him, shocked and horrified him. From mates drowning in the mud, to disappearing in a red haze, from a direct artillery hit. From bodies lying with no legs or no arms but just silently waiting to die, to men riddled with machine gun bullets, guts hanging out and screaming for help, when help was impossible.

Many of the men who were less wounded, suffering from what became known as, survivor guilt, to others who had no physical wounds, but suffered from some kind of traumatic brain altering illness that became known as "shell shock". At the time, many senior officers termed this condition as LMF. Lack of Moral Fibre. Usually, by officers who had not experienced the horrors of the front, in battle. Bob knew that in some of these men, moral fibre, was certainly not lacking and yet, these men exhibited all the signs, of some kind of real mind injury. Some of these men, just sat and stared into space, with the strangest of looks in their eyes. This look eventually became known as the "1000-yard stare."

Others were unable to walk, talk or eat. Yet others had a sort of obsessive behaviour, twitch or mannerism, which they seemed to have no control over.

Some thought that these men were just putting on these strange characteristics, just to get sent off the frontline. After talking with some of these men at length, Bob came to believe that there was nothing put on, about this behaviour. It was a genuine reaction to things they had seen and done, or in some cases, extremely near misses.

Chapter 18
Going Home

In the second week of November, Bob was informed that as of next week, he could take ten days leave. The men had been heavily involved over the last year and it was felt it was time they had some breathing space. The pressure was off now, so it seemed prudent, to allow the men some R and R. Bob immediately made plans to head back home to Scotland and catch up with his family. He had not seen them for five years, so it seemed like a good opportunity. He immediately wrote to his sister Mary, to let her know that he would be coming home but at the same time he was not sure if she would get it in time or not. Either way, he was sure it was going to be a great surprise for them.

On Tuesday, the 13th of November, he did not load up with the others on the trip out to ANZAC but instead headed for the bath house. He was going to enjoy this. A nice hot bath, clean uniform and a good shave and Bob was ready to take on the world. After lunch, he and a few of the others who were also going on leave, boarded one of the lorries headed for Calais. This trip was to be a couple of hours long, but no one really minded, because it was heading away from the front, towards Blighty. It was a rough ride, but spirits were high. The men sang and sang; mostly the usual songs that the boys sang together: Pack up your troubles in your old kit bag, It's a long way to Tipperary, Take me back to dear old Blighty and of course, Never Mind, along with a few others, but these were the popular ones.

They arrived in Calais late in the afternoon and set about finding a room for the night. That was not that difficult, as there were many rooms available down near the docks, for just this purpose. As luck would have it, Bob ran into one of his old mates from the Ardrossan Volunteers, who was also heading home for a break. He had joined up with a British army and was serving in an artillery unit outside of Lille, just south of the Belgian border. The two of them went into one of the photographic studios just back from the Calais docks, to have their portrait taken and then went and had dinner together. It would be an early start the next morning, so they both went back to their billets and turned in for the night.

He rose at 0600 hrs the following day and quickly walked two blocks, down to the dock, where he checked in for the boat ride to Dover. He had registered the previous day, so it was a simple matter of checking in, getting his ticket, and then waiting for the boarding call. In the meantime, he settled down in the café for tea and toast. While he was waiting, his friend Angus, from the Ardrossan Volunteer days, came in for his breakfast. They sat and chatted whilst waiting for the call to board their ship. With both being conversant with artillery, the conversation centred around that. Bob mentioned that there seem to be a high failure rate, in the Hun artillery shells.

"Aye, we've noticed that. Apparently, oors aren't much better," Angus replied. "No one seems tae know, just why it is, we're having such a high dud rate. We've inspected the shells and their fusing, and all seems tae be fine. Some o' the boys suspect sabotage at the factory level. I tend tae think tha's a little farfetched. If that were the case, then why are the Boche shells doing the same thing? Surely, we dinnae have as many saboteurs in their factories."

"Has got tae be something with the design o' the fuses surely," Bob suggested. "I mean, I know that ground is muddy and soft, but a properly fused shell, should still explode in those conditions. It has tae be the fuse."

"Aye, I agree with ye. Tae me, the fuse is either jamming up, on firing or it's simply not sensitive enough, tae trigger when it hits the groond. It seems an awful bloody waste, tae send all those shells over and only have two in three go off. That's a lot of wasted effort; and it's also a lot o' Huns, who are noe knocked."

At that moment, the steward started calling for all the passengers to board, for the trip to Dover. The two men rose and taking their kit bags, joined the queue. Half an hour later, with everyone safely on board, the ship gradually pulled away from the quay and turned its nose, towards the open water. Once out past the breakwater, the ship entered the straits of Dover, and set a line, for the port of Dover twenty five miles away (40km). It was certainly a choppy crossing, as it often is at this time of year but two hours later the ship pulled into the docks in Dover, England. They were back on British soil again, although admittedly not Scotland but certainly closer to home than France or Belgium.

On disembarking, all the troops on leave, headed straight for the Dover train station to pick up the train for London. The train ride from Dover to London, whilst predominantly soldiers on leave, also included members of the general public, which for the boys was a novel experience, as they had not had contact with the general public, for some time. For the soldiers on the train, the common jokes of the day, were things like, "Who are these people, these strange-looking people who are not dressed in khaki?"

"Do you mean these people don't have to do as they are ordered every day of their lives? Wow, that must be quite an experience. I wonder what it's like?"

There was lots of chatter and merriment all the way to London. The trip was quite slow, as the rail system had to use the LCDR line as the SER line had been closed for many months now due to a land slip. The LCDR lined consisted of many steep gradients which made for slow climbs but due to the extra traffic required to transport troops, even longer, thus heavier, trains were plying the route, which made them even slower. By the time they made it to London's Victoria station, it was already mid-afternoon.

Bob knew he had time to spare, before making the Glasgow train, so he decided to walk from Victoria Station to Charring Cross station and then take the underground to Euston Station for his Glasgow train. He made his way slowly up Victoria road. This was only his fourth time in London, the first two being on his ill-fated attempt to emigrate to South Africa and the third, on his way through to Southampton, when he migrated to Australia. He took his time, to take in all the sites, even stopping at a tea house for a hot cuppa.

His route took him past Westminster and the Houses of Parliament, as well as Clock Tower, usually called Big Ben, although strictly speaking, Big Ben, is the name of the largest of the bells, atop Clock Tower. He made his way along the embankment then, until he reached Charring Cross station. As much as he was a Scotsman through and through, he still thought that walk along the Thames, was beautiful. He purchased his ticket for Glasgow on the overnighter and then sought out a café, where he could have his evening meal. He felt quite strange, as this was really the first time, he had been on his own for the last two years. He had had leave before but had always taken it in France with a couple of his mates. Now, he found himself in a somewhat unique situation and while he was excited to be heading home, to see his sisters and brothers, he felt alone. The waitress came over to take his order and said to him, "Hello soldier! You from Australia?"

Bob looked up and replied, "Aye, I am lassie."

"Ooh," she said with a smile, "you certainly don't sound like it, luv."

Bob laughed and explained, "I was born and raised in Scotland, on the West Coast, but I moved to Australia, five years ago. Now I find masel' back here fighting a blessed war. I'm on mae way, tae see mae family in Glasgow."

She smiled and asked, "What's it like out there in Australia? I hear it's very hot."

"Not all the time. It's actually very pleasant, most o' the time, but it does have its hot days. You do get used tae them. The best bit is, it's nowhere near as cold and wet. Lots o' sunshine. Does you good." Bob replied.

"I'll bet it does," she chirped. "Anyway, how's your war going?"

"Ma war?" he scoffed. "Ma war is going bloody. I've already had enough of it. I've got 10 days off and I don't want tae think aboot it. I just want 10 days of peace."

"Oh, I'm sorry luv," she said apologetically. "What can I get you then luv?"

Bob placed his order and sat back to read the newspaper from that morning. As he read, he could not help feeling a little guilty about how he had answered her last question. When she brought his meal to him, he said to her, "Look miss. I'm terribly sorry about being so short tae ye a minute ago. I shouldnae said it like that. I'm sorry, you were just being nice, and I had tae go and say it like that."

"Oh, don't worry about that luv" she replied. "I understand. I have a brother over there, doing his bit at the moment and he feels the same way that you do. It must be really horrible."

"Aye lassie, it is. It really is."

Whilst he sat eating his meal, his thoughts wandered about 12,000 miles away, to a little street, in a little city, on the other side of the earth. He wondered what Jean would be doing at this moment. It would be coming up to about 11:00 AM in Perth right now. She would probably be working, in Robert's bakery, preparing for the lunchtime rush. Oh, how he missed them all. *It is crazy,* he thought. *I've only met these people for less than four weeks, but I feel like I've known them all my life. I so wish I was still with them.* These thoughts went round and round in his mind. *This stupid war. What's it all about anyway? All it's done is to bring misery to millions of people and has solved nothing. How can we keep doing this to each other?*

The things he had seen and done, played over again and again, until he was in such a state that he banged his fist on the table. It created quite a noise, with the jangling cutlery and crockery. It drew a couple of glances from some of the other customers, but Bob was oblivious to their looks. The waitress came over, to Bob and sat down beside him. She did not say anything; she just reached out and put her hand on his and smiled and nodded. After a few seconds, Bob relaxed again. He thanked her for her understanding.

He was saved by the call for the Glasgow train. He gathered up these things, slung his kit bag over his shoulder, and made his way to the platform. There he boarded his train and found an empty cubicle where he took up residence in the corner. He hoped no one else would join him, in that cubicle but realised the chances of this happening, were slim. At least for a while he would be on his own. As the train pulled away from the station, he pulled his slouch hat down, over his eyes and went to sleep. He woke sometime later, to find two more people in his compartment. He apologised to them, for sleeping through their arrival, explaining he had had a long two days of travel and was exceedingly tired. They said they understood and as this was the night train, it was their intention to do likewise. The trip would take them around twelve hours, so it would be about 8:00 AM when they arrived in Glasgow. They turn the lights out, drew the blinds and tried to catch as much sleep as they could.

Around 7.30 AM, the conductor walked through the car, to make sure everyone was awake and ready for their impending arrival into Glasgow central station. The train pulled into the station about 8:10 that morning. After checking at the office, he found that as their train had been delayed along the way he had missed the connection to the train to Saltcoats. He would have to wait for the next train tomorrow morning. "Blast," he thought. "Oh well might as well head up to the YMCA for a leisurely breakfast and a cuppa and a sleep." The YMCA had been so good to all the men at the camp in Blackboy Hill, back in Perth, and they had advised the men that if they got time in the UK, they should avail themselves of the YMCA accommodation whenever they could. It would always be at mates rates.

He took this opportunity to write to Jean as well. He took out the postcard of himself and his mate from the Ardrossan Volunteers and wrote on the back.

My Darling Girl,

This leading sounds very well don't you think so? Of course, I haven't had your permission, so excuse me please. All the same I like to call you so now Jean what do you think? Here am I again on furlough and disappointed as your much expected letter hasn't come along yet. Well if it doesn't I'm sending you a small present. I'm Going down home tomorrow for a couple of days and perhaps another in Glasgow with my sisters. Do please write me and as often as you possibly can. Months since I had a letter from you.

Love from Bob

P.S. What will your mother say when you show her this? Bob

Later that afternoon, he took the card and the jewellery box down to the post office and mailed it home to Jean. The following morning, he found himself on the train, passing through all too familiar countryside, and feeling that finally he was home. He passed many familiar sights. The Castle Semple and Barr Lochs, one after the other and then in the distance Kilbirnie Loch, before veering right through Kilwinning. Once the train changed tracks at Kilwinning, he knew he was only a couple of miles from home. When the train passed along the seafront, Bob got up ready to leave the train. Once he alighted the train at Saltcoats station it was only a short ten minute walk to his old home in Kirkgate, just off Chapelwell St.

When his sister, Mary, answered the front door to his knock, she was so overcome, she burst into tears and was unable to say anything. She just threw her arms around him and sobbed her heart out. She clung for what seemed an age, before finally leaning back to take a good long look at him, through teary eyes of course, "Oh Robert. It's so good tae see ye again. And jus' look at ye, all dressed up in yer Australian uniform. Oh, hoo I've missed ye bein' aroond."

"Hello Mary," he said when he finally got a word in. "How have ye been?"

"Och I'm fine and even better now. Come in. Come in. Don't stand on the doorstep all day," she laughed as she said it. "Why didnae ye let me know ye were comin'," she asked.

"Well, I did write tae ye. I only got a few days' notice, so I wasnae sure, whether ye'd get it in time or noc, so I'm guessin' noe," he answered.

"No! I havenae got a letter from ye in three weeks. I was startin' tae worry like."

"Och, ye've no need tae worry aboot me. I'll be fine. Most o' the time, I'm noe near the frontline," he said, slightly twisting the truth. It was true enough that he was not on the frontline, but he neglected to offer the fact that the artillery could still reach them where they were.

"That's good then," she said, then adding, "Would ye like a cup o' tea Robert?"

"Aye," he answered. "I'd love one. I havenae had one since Glasgow."

"Ye mustae come doon on the 8.05, did ye?" Being only 25 miles (40 km), from Glasgow, they pretty much knew every train schedule off by heart.

"Aye, I did. I got into Glasgow, yesterday morning but just missed the connection, so I stayed at the Y overnight, befoor catching the train doon here. It were braw, seeing that countryside again. It's so beautiful. Very different from Australia. Mind ye, that's also very beautiful but very different."

"I've read all your letters, o'er and o'er and but I'd still like tae hear it from ye aboot how different it really is," she queried.

"Well, it's grand, no mistake aboot that. It's a lot warmer, tha's for sure. The rain only tends to come in winter and in summer, the countryside is brown, all the green having dried oot. There's trees everywhere, even through the farmin' country, but they are very different tae oor trees. It's called the bush, and, in the bush, there are so many different types of trees it's incredible. The eucalyptus is the major type of tree, they call them gum trees, but there are hundreds of different ones it seems. They are a lot spindlier than our oak or beech trees and they hold their leaves all year roond. They don't lose them in winter. They are all hardwoods and some of them, are beautiful tae work with. Some of them are very, very hard too. Where I am there is no snow. It does snow up in the mountains but that's about the only place. I havenae been up there yet. It's a wonderful place though Mary. Lots o' opportunities."

"Sounds wonderful, Robert," Mary commented. "Now tell me aboot this Jean girl. Ye sound all dafty aboot her."

"Och Mary, she's bonnie. A real nice girl. She's only 20 noo, but she's a braw wee lassie. Short red hair, blue eyes, and a Scot tae boot. The family is an Edinburgh family. Strangely, they went oot tae Australia only three months after me, but they settled in Perth, on the West Coast. Robert, her father is a Baker, a braw Baker and her mother is Jemima, but they call her Mimey. Jean is the eldest, then there's Jack, who is two years younger, then Jessie, two years younger again and Roberta would now be thirteen. Jessie is definitely the outgoing one, but Jean is quite reserved and quiet. A real thinker. She's just lovely." Bob bubbled over with enthusiasm, which was not lost on Mary.

"So, what are ye gonnae do aboot it? Are ye gonnae go back there?" Mary was hoping to hear an answer to the affirmative and she did not have to wait long.

"Aye, I am. I think I'm gonnae ask her tae marry me," he replied.

"Ye THINK you're gonnae ask her to marry ye," she teased. "Ye heid over heels man. Sounds tae me, like ye'd better get canny, and ask her."

"Aye, it's a big step and I've only ken her three weeks. I made her a wee jewellery box, oot o' the oak from the Ypres cathedral. I sent it to her from Glasgow this morning, along with a photograph I got taken at Calais, two days ago. Thinking aboot her, is aboot all that keeps me going. So, I guess the answer is, aye." Bob was telling her all this, as he pulled a photograph of Jean from his pocket. He handed it to Mary after he finished.

"Och aye Robert, she does look a bonnie lassie and red hair ye say? She'd be a fine Scot."

They talked all morning, pausing only for the occasional cup of tea. They covered everything, from Bob's life in Australia, to the animals he had seen there, to the stipend he was sending her from his army pay. Mary was canny enough, to dodge any discussion on the war situation. She knew from his letters that things over in Belgium were upsetting him. So, it was not until late morning that she finally said to him, "I see from your letters, Robert, that things over in Europe are a bit tough for ye. I want tae know, how we are handling it?" There was a reason, Mary was Bob's favourite sister. Quite apart from being older than him, she also understood him. She had always been there for him, since their parents died, 9 and 13 years ago. She stood by him, whilst he finished his apprenticeship under Mr Wallace, and also supported him, when he decided to move to Australia. She knew Robert and she knew he would have a hard time dealing with the sights of war.

Bob paused for a while, to think. Mary said nothing more, she just sat and waited for when he was ready. "I really cannae tell ye, what have seen and been a part of. Some ae it, has been just horrible. I cannae believe, sane, thinking men, can dae these things tae each other, all in the name of freedom. Aye, what the Boche is doing, is wrong and they've got to be stopped; but Mary, the way it's happening, it's just insanity. That job at Hill 60, I was a part o' that, and they tell us we killed 10,000 men. Some o' them died a horrible death and I've been a part of that. Artillery: what that can dae tae a man, is indescribable. Some men that get hit, ye never find anything of 'em. There's noe even anything left to bury. There's nae doubt Mary, that when this is all over, I'll be a different man."

Mary just reached over the table and put her hand on his and gave him a knowing smile. He moved around the corner of the table and sat next to him now. With her hand still on his, she leaned against his shoulder, as if to say, "I understand, and I'm here to share your grief." She did not actually need to say anything. Two of them knew each other so well. They sat there for about 10 minutes without a word passing between them. The silence was broken by the sound of the front door opening.

"O lord!" cried Mary, "That'll be the girls home, and I havenae got the lunch on. There's gonnae be at riot if I dinnae git a wriggle on." Mary jumped up to start the midday meal, when Effie walked in.

"Hello Effie," said Bob.

There was a scream. "Robert? Och, it really is you?" as she flung her arms around him, giving him the biggest hug, she could muster. There were more tears, followed by more questions. "How are ye? When did ye get in? Why didnae ye let us ken?" etc. No sooner had he finished answering these questions, than the front door opened yet again and in walked Elizabeth. The scene that played out, was almost identical, only to be played out yet again, when Minnie walked in.

This time, however, Bob was ready and got in first. "Hello Minnie. I'm fine. I got in aboot 9.30 this morning. I did write but the letter hasnae got here yet. I'm here for a couple of days. I have ten days leave all up." They all laughed together, Minnie realising that Bob had probably had to answer these questions a couple of times before.

Mary need not have worried, about not having lunch ready. Everyone just wanted to hear what Bob had to say about everything. He did not go into detail, about the war, like he did with Mary. He just glossed over it, choosing to spend more time talking about his life in Australia and, of course, about Jean. He would not get to see his brothers on this leave, as they had all moved away from Saltcoats, either with their work or with their wives. The afternoon and evening passed quickly, as they all sat around the fire talking, until it was late.

Chapter 19
Furlough

The following day was Monday and the three girls had to go to work. All the travelling Bob had done over the last couple of days, finally caught up with him, so he slept late. After he woke, he took a late breakfast, then set off on foot for a walk around his old hometown. The house in Kirkgate, was only two hundred yards from the harbour so he headed in that direction first and just rolled around the waterfront. He worked his way around the harbour to the point where he sat and just watched out to sea. After a while he headed back along the street past the town hall and around the corner to the workshop of his old employer Mr James Wallace.

As he stepped through the door, the smells transported him back ten years to his time as an apprentice in this exact building. In his mind's eye he could see the times Mr Wallace had guided him, chided him and encouraged him, to be the fine carpenter that he was. As he stood in the doorway with his memories of those times, which seems so far away now, he was jolted back into the here and now, by a booming voice, that he recognised instantly as that of James Wallace. "Robert mae laddie! Is that ye? Is that really ye?"

"Aye Mr Wallace, it is. How are ye, sir?" Bob spluttered out.

"Well, I'll be laddie. Come in. It's so grand to see you again. Boys," he said turning to the boys working in the shop, "this is Robert Hood. He was apprentice to me right here, until aboot; well how long ago was it laddie? About seven or eight years ago?"

"Nine," replied Robert. "Nine years ago, ae finished my apprenticeship, and noo ae have my own workshop, in Sydney, in Australia."

"Well done laddie, well done. What's it like oot there?" Robert was well used to hearing this question by now, and he gave his usual answer about the weather, the trees, the animals and the people.

Mr Wallace told his boys to down tools for an early morning tea. They sat around the table, talking about his time with Mr Wallace and work he had done since he left his employ. He talked about the type of timbers used in Australia. How hard they were, the durability and their ease or difficulty of working and comparing it to the timbers he had been used to working here in Scotland. Of course, the topic of conversation eventually made its way around to the war and his involvement in it. The boys in Mr Wallace's workshop, were all still too young to enlist but indicated their willingness and eagerness, to do so as soon as they could.

"Dinnae be too hasty to enlist laddies," he said. "Ae can assure ye it's naw at all like wha' they try and tell ye it's like. Imagine, if you will, the three o' ye walkin' along together and a whizz-bang comes over and kills one o' ye, on the spot, blows the leg off one of ye and leaves the other one untouched. Which one will ye be? If ye are the one left, wha' are ye gonnae dae? That's wha' it's like. It's horrible. Damned horrible."

Mr Wallace chimed in at that point, "You listen to the man laddies. It's obvious he knows wha' he's talkin' aboot. Aye Robert, it's so braw to see ye again. How long the ye home for?" Mr Wallace could sense the pain Robert was experiencing and changed the subject.

"I'm only home for a couple o' days. I'm here to see ma sisters and I'll head back up to Glasgow to see two o' ma other sisters there and then I have to head back. I'd rather just go home." They chatted for a few more minutes, then Robert excused himself, saying he had best let them get back to work and he on his walk around, before his sister got worried where he was. He wandered around the town, reacquainting himself with old sites, for another half hour and then headed back to Kirkgate, to Mary.

That evening when the other girls got home, Mary had put on a dinner, fit for the prodigal brother. They sat around a table chatting and laughing long after their meal was finished. Robert regaled them with stories of Australia, this time including the stories of his time in Perth and Blackboy Hill. He had to explain to them what was, Blackboy Hill. Of course, his stories often included, either Jean or the Chappells. They were unbelieving that in a big city, you could have a house and enough land, to grow fruit trees and climbing trees. Their backyard was tiny, not much use for anything really. They made plans for the following day to take a picnic up to Ardrossan castle, overlooking South Beach. This was naturally, subject to the weather, which at this time of year was, at best, unpredictable. The west coast of Scotland, in winter, is renowned for being somewhat bleak and as Saturday morning broke their fears were realised. There would be no picnic today, not that that particularly upset them. This way they could just sit and talk all day if necessary, which they did.

Bob was awfully glad to be home, in his native Scotland, but even after two days there, he had seen enough to make him believe that his choice to move to Australia, was the correct one. Yes, he missed his sisters and brothers, but it was apparent to him that the reasons he left for Australia in the first place, were still present, the weather, the lack of sunshine and the poor employment outlook. What is more, they were unlikely to change. The employment situation had improved but only as a result of the war and chances were, it would revert to pre-war status as soon as it was over.

Quite apart from catching up with his family, he was satisfied that his trip back home had answered those questions that had been plaguing his mind for some time—about his decision to move to Australia. Once these feelings were confirmed, he was keen to move on, this time to catch up with his sisters in Glasgow. After that, it would be back to this damned war, get that over and done with and get back to Australia, and Jean.

Tuesday morning came around and Robert, accompanied by his four sisters. walked the couple of hundred yards to the Saltcoats railway station. At 11:30 AM they heard the whistle of the steamer, coming in from Ardrossan. A couple of minutes later it pulled into the station and Robert was saying goodbye to his sisters again. The hugs were long and intense, and no one wanted to let go. He saved the last one for Mary. The whistle sounded for their departure and Robert broke free of his embrace with Mary, saying he would be back. "I promise ye, I'll return and see ye all again. I will nae go back tae Australia without seeing ye again. Tek care and may the Lord be with ye and watch over ye. Goodbye!"

"Ye see that ye dae that Robert. Goodbye! Goodbye!" The girls talked over each other as the train pulled away, all with tears streaming down their faces. "Keep ye heid doon. Stay safe laddie."

Bob sat back in his chair, once the girls were out of sight. He sighed, staring out the window, as the houses and other buildings, slowly morphed into pastures and cows. Roads gave way to fences and rock walls that divided differing shades of green, into a patchwork stretching up the hills and down the glens. With his thoughts still dwelling on the time spent with his sisters, the train slowly slipped by the three lochs along the line. After the brief stop at Kilbarchan, the countryside commenced a slow reversion to roads, houses, businesses and the urban sprawl that had become Glasgow. Fifteen minutes later, the train once again pulled into Glasgow central station. By now his thoughts turned to his two younger sisters.

Bob was getting excited about seeing his sisters again. Jemima and Divina had moved into a housing unit south of the city centre. Jemima was two years Bob's junior and Divina, who was known as Ciss, was eight years his junior. They had both moved up to Glasgow from Saltcoats, for work. They had been living here for the last two years.

Bob exited the Glasgow central station and turn right to cross the river Clyde. He continued his way south, along Eglington St, for about one and a half miles (2km), past the blocks of business houses, then rows and rows of tenement housing. After a zigzag walk through the housing estate, he found himself standing in front of their door, wondering if they got his letter or not. He knocked on the door and shortly, it opened and there was the face of his sister Jemima. He beamed from ear to ear, on seeing her but at first, she did not react. *Who is this strange soldier standing on my doorstep*? she thought.

The moment she saw his smile though, she recognised him and screamed out. "Robert! Och mae! Robert," and threw her arms around his neck and gave in the biggest hug she could possibly muster. She quickly turned and yelled inside. "Ciss, oh Cissy. Come an' look who's here." Ciss had already heard the commotion and was already underway to see what the noise was all about. As soon she saw who it was, she too screamed out, "Robert! Is that really ye?"

"Aye, ma bonnie wee lassie. 'Tis me. Are ye gonnae let me in?" Bob teased. All this was said through the tears, the hugs, the kisses and multiple exclamations.

"Och aye, of course. Please, dae come in. Here, let me tek yer bag. Come in, come in. Ye shouldae let us know you were comin." Jemima got out through the tears.

"I take it you didnae get my letter then. I only got less than a week's notice, so I wrote, but I wasnae sure ye'd get it in time," said Bob.

"Och, it doesnae matter Robert. Wha' a wonderful surprise. Och, I'm so happy tae see ye again. How are ye?" Ciss was blurting out sentences, one after the other, hardly able to breathe in between. She was, they were, just so excited.

Ciss continued, "Wha' are ye doin' here? Are ye home for good? Are ye finished with the war? Wha's Australia like? Are ye well?"

Bob finally interrupted, "Whoa there lassie. One thing at a time. I cannae answer all o' your questions at once. So, I came tae see you. No, I'm only home for a week. I've only got ten days leave and I have tae go back. Australia's a lovely place. Ye'd love it. And yes, I am well, thank you." Bob laughed and Ciss went red. At that point, Jemima stepped in, "Would ye like a cup o' tea Robert?"

"I could murder a cup right noo. Thank ye." He answered. To the girls he was Robert. His name had not been shortened at home, so they had never known him as Bob.

They sat and talked for hours. The girls had so many questions for Bob. They wanted to know all the details of Sydney and of everything he had experienced since leaving there, including his time in Perth. At that point, Bob brought out a photo of Jean and showed his sisters. "Och, she looks lovely," they cooed. "And a Scot too, although she is from the east side." They laughed at that. East-west rivalry was alive and well, although, mostly in good humour.

"Aye. She's a bonnie wee lassie that one. See if you can guess, wha' her mother's name is?" he jibed. After a few failed guesses, he put them out of their misery. "It's Jemima, but they call her Mimey for short. And ye wouldnae believe wha' her father's name is. It's Robert!"

All three of them laughed and laughed. Bob could not remember when had laughed so much. It felt so good to laugh again. Here, amongst his family, away from the war and its horrors, already, he had started to feel human again. He felt that maybe, there was actually hope for him, to recover from all that he had seen and done. All that was needed, was a little space, a little time, and friendly faces.

They sat and talked, drank tea and ate, all afternoon long. There was hardly a time when the smiles left the girls' faces. They had their brother back, even if he did seem a little bit different, not quite as chirpy as he used to be, maybe. Bob did not give them all the details of what he had seen in Belgium. They did ask about Hill 60, however. They knew he had been there and wanted to know what it was all about. Bob described it the barest of details, likening it to coal mining, rather than what they were actually digging for. That was left, to be taken for granted.

Jemima spoke up and said, "The newspapers, said that in London the Prime Minister heard the explosion from Hill 60. Could that really be the case Robert?"

"Naw, that's rubbish." He answered. "He couldnae heard it. It was a deep undergroond explosion, 100 feet doon in fact, an' being underground, means it were very muffled. Sure, it were loud at the site but wouldnae been able tae be heard far away. He may well ha' been able tae feel it, as explosions like that would probably cause an earthquake. Tha' wouldae been possible. I mean, I were there an' I can tell ye, it shook the ground like nothin' I ever fel' before. It left a crater 270 feet at Hill 60 and 280 feet at Ca'erpillar across, an' nearly 70 feet deep. That's a lot o' dirt to move and muffle the sound."

Ciss added, "Aye I can see wha' ye mean Robert. Ye know wha' reporters are like, ne'er let the truth get in the way o' a good story." Again they laughed and then the questions continued.

Bob was experiencing a severe case of Déjà vu. All questions Jemima and Ciss came up with, were, of course, the same ones, the girls back in Saltcoats had asked. But Bob did not mind. He knew they just wanted to know, and they had not heard it from anyone yet. He did, check himself though. He had already given a bit much detail, from Hill 60. He did not want the questions on that topic to continue, so kept steering the conversation away, whenever it got too close. After dinner was over, they sat around the fire and talked mainly about life and Glasgow, as compared to life in Saltcoats. The girls had moved there, as there was little the work for them in Ardrossan or Saltcoats, so they moved up to Glasgow in search of work. They both found work within a short period of time, Jemima in an apparel workshop and Ciss in a munitions factory, up along the River Clyde.

Fortunately for Ciss, she was not one of the canary girls, the name given to the women who handled the explosives. They were called canary girls because the handling of the TNT (trinitrotoluene) turned their hands and hair yellow. Ciss certainly knew some of the canary girls that had become quite ill, but she worked in a safer, more administrative area. Unfortunately, they would both have to go to work tomorrow morning, so Bob decided to stay an extra day and to head back to London on Thursday morning. That would give him another evening with his sisters.

The girls had both gone to work by the time Bob rose the following morning, but waiting for him on the cooker, was a pot of lovely steaming porridge. After he dressed and downed the porridge, with salt of course, as every good Scotsman will know, a cup of tea and toast, he took himself off for a wander around Glasgow. Even though he had lived the bulk of his life only twenty five miles (40km) from Glasgow, he had not often travelled there. He knew his way around but by no means had seen all there was to see, not that in 1917 there was a great deal for a tourist to see in an industrial town, which is basically what Glasgow was. Shipbuilding and Steel Manufacturing were its main industries. Its capacity for steel manufacturing is why it was chosen as a centre for munitions production, as well as its normal capacity for building ships, only now it was warships.

He walked up to the river and followed it, until the Portland Street suspension bridge, where he crossed the Clyde, and entered the south of the commercial centre. He had a little shopping he wanted to do. Some luxuries, he wanted to take back to the front with him, and a few little things to send back to Jean. He had already mailed the jewellery box back to her when he arrived in Glasgow the other day, but he wanted to send some truly Scottish bits and pieces back. Ornaments, cruet sets and trinkets, were on his list. It took a while to find all the things he wanted. This was wartime Scotland, so commodities were in short supply, but he did find them eventually.

After stopping in at the Post Office, to pack and send them, he continued east through the city and worked his way back to the river through Glasgow Green. He had not seen Nelson's monument close up before, so he wandered over to the column to take a closer look. He had always thought that it was an impressive looking column from a distance, but when standing at its base, leaning on the railings and looking up its 144 ft (44m), bronzed looking sandstone spire, he realised just how impressive it really was. The day was cold and partly cloudy, so when the sun came out briefly, he looked at its shadow, pointing across the green.

Being November, with the sun low to the south west, it cast a huge shadow, stretching almost all way across the green. It must be twice its actual height he thought. To the right of its shadow, his attention was taken by the People's Palace. He remembered then that it contained a winter garden under its huge glass structure, so he wandered over for a look through.

This was also about time for an afternoon cup of tea. *What a pleasant way to spend an afternoon*, he thought, as he sat, sipping his tea and eating those beautiful scones. *I could sit here all day in this warmth, looking at the wonderful indoor gardens*. It was not long before the locals started asking him questions about the war. They had read all the newspapers, but they also knew that they only tell them what they were supposed to hear. Robert engaged them in conversation alright, sticking well to his now practiced bland version, of what was going on in Europe.

The big purple T with a golden 1 on it that was on his upper arm, was a bit of a giveaway, that he was a tunneller; an Australian tunneller at that. Everyone had heard of the battle of the Messines Ridge and the mines that had blown beforehand. They wanted to know if he was involved in that, to which, of course, he replied that he was. Again, he stuck to the facts of the digging and the resulting crater but did not touch on the scale of the human carnage that he witnessed. He was not prepared this time, for the visions that appeared in his head, whilst describing to the people that part of the campaign. It disturbed him, to the point, that he had to excuse himself from the conversation, saying he had an appointment to keep. He rolled the collar of his greatcoat, up around his neck and set off outside, into the cold.

By now, the sky had completely clouded over, ironically, to match his mood. He headed straight for the river now, passing by the statue of James Watt, without even a glance. A minute later, he was on the St Andrews, suspension bridge, again crossing the Clyde, heading back for his sisters' residence. He walked through the industrial area on the south bank and was shortly winding his way through the tenements towards the bridge over the rail line. It was not long before a found himself back at his sisters Govanhill block. Once inside he tossed his greatcoat and slouch hat to one side, sat down and took a deep breath. He needed to calm down, before his sisters got home and start asking questions. After a few minutes he rose, set a fire in the grate, and got that started. The kitchen cooker needed attention too, but that just needed opening up and more coal, to get it fired up. It was not long before the house was warm again and no sooner had he got it to that point, than his sisters came home. He was glad to see them again. It took his focus from his thoughts.

Jemima and Ciss, started to prepare the evening meal, while Bob explained to them his day. It had been good to reacquaint himself with Glasgow. At the same time, they felt that not everything had gone according to plan. Ciss especially understood her brother, not unlike Mary, and sensed that something was not right. When Minnie ducked out, Ciss asked him "Are ye alright Robert? I feel as if something isnnae quite right."

"I'm oright Ciss. I had a bit of an episode this after' that I wasnae quite expecting. People were askin' me aboot the Messines mess, an' I had to get oot. This war has mucked me aboot a bit I'm afraid. I'll be oright though, when it's all over." Bob at least hoped that would be the case. "Are ye sure Robert," asked

Minnie as she came back in? She had heard the previous exchange. "Ye dinnae seem the same as I remember."

"Och, aye Minnie. Sorry! I am a bit doon aboot it all, there's nae doot. That's the nature o' war though. It's horrible, be noe mistake. But once it's all over, havenae fear, I'll be fine. I'm sure of it. In the meantime, there's a job tae be done. An' I'm goin' tae see that it's done."

This exchange seemed to satisfy the girls. "War certainly is a horrible thing, but these Boche need tae be told tae get back home," Ciss said. She went on, "Well this tea is not going to cook itself, so we'd better get on with it. Robert, would ye peel the tatties for me please?"

"Certainly," he replied. "How many would ye like me tae peel?"

"Just the one each," she answered, handing him peeling knife. He set about peeling the tatties, whilst the girls prepared the rest of the meal. He even put them in the pot of boiling water on the cooker and mashed them when they were ready.

Once again, when the meal was over, they retired to the table in front of the fire and talked and played cards and just enjoyed each other's company. Whilst Bob, promised to return before he went back to Australia, all three of them knew that there was always a chance he may never come back. After all, he was going back to a war zone and there were no guarantees of survival there. When their evening drew to a close, Minnie said her goodbyes to Bob. Her work in the munitions factory, included an early start and no flexibility of start time. She would be gone by 5.30. Ciss however, had negotiated a late start in the morning, due to Robert being home on leave.

Bob and Ciss both rose around 6.30 and sat together through their breakfast. Little was said this morning, both deep in their thoughts. After breakfast, they both cleaned up the kitchen, and Bob got his belongings together, slung his kit bag over the shoulder and the two of them headed up to Glasgow Central station. There was still thirty minutes until Bob's train, so the two of them sat in the café, with yet another, cup of tea.

When the time came to board, Bob stopped on the platform by the door of his carriage and took Ciss by the shoulders and said to her, "Cissy, I am comin' back tae see ye, at least one more time, before I go home. Who knows, how long this war will goe on, so we may well have more than one chance to come back but I will come back."

Ciss burst into tears and flung her arms around him. Through the tears she managed to say, "I pray that is the case, Robert. May the Lord goe with ye and keep ye safe. I'll wait tae see ye again. I'll still be here."

He boarded the train, as the whistle blew and the train hissed and chuffed as it started to pull away. "Good luck to ye Ciss. Look after Minnie won't ye? Bye now." Ciss was unable to speak, she just nodded vigorously, and waved to him. She kept waving until she could see him no more.

Bob sat back in the carriage, just staring out the window, as the train crossed the Clyde and worked its way through the southern suburbs of Glasgow. It chuffed along slowly, until the housing began to spread out a little. As the train gathered speed and the city slipped into the distance, Bob started thinking about his two visits to Saltcoats and Glasgow. He reflected on his last comments to both lots of sisters, about returning to see them. He sure hoped he would be able to see them again.

After a while he settled back in his seat, opened his newspaper and tried to catch up on the latest news. This was going to be a long train trip back to London. Much longer than the trip up to Glasgow. As this was a daylight trip, he would at least get to see the countryside on the way down. Apart from the newspaper and a book he brought with him, he spent his time talking with other passengers, answering the same questions as usual about the war and about Australia. He did not mind though, it helped to pass the time, and he did not have to go into great detail on the war.

Chapter 20
Anzac Buffet

It was late that evening, when the train finally pulled into Euston station. Bob left the station and walked the three blocks, to a boarding house address he had been given that was used to taking passengers from the late train. He settled in quickly and before too long, was sound asleep. After breakfast, the following morning he headed to the underground station near Euston, to pick up the circle line train for Victoria station. Some of the other soldiers returning from leave had previously told him of a serviceman's club near Victoria station. It had moved a couple of times but the address he had been given was 94 Victoria Street, only 200 yards from the station.

Good reports had been made about the ANZAC buffet. He had decided to check it out for himself and maybe to spend the day there, while he waited for the train back to Dover. He found it without any trouble it all, exactly where they said it would be. It was hard to miss, at the Australian blue ensign flag was flying outside. He turned in, and on the doors leading to the buffet were the words "Welcome to the Australian and New Zealand troops." He pushed open the doors, walked in and he was greeted with open arms and warm smiles.

*

The Anzac Buffet was an establishment set up and run by women wanting to support ANZAC troops on leave in London. It provided a quiet location for troops either on leave or convalescing from hospitals in the area. They could use the buffet as a quiet place to sit, talk with fellow Australian troops, read the newspapers, or just have a quiet sandwich and cuppa at no charge, between 9:00 AM and 6:00 PM any day of the week. The buffet was staffed entirely by volunteer Australian women, many of whom had their own men at the front.

They were available to sit and talk as well, and many of the men made use of that service. Here, they knew they could talk to someone who would listen, without making any judgments and allow them to unburden their minds. At around this time the ANZAC Buffet was dealing with up to 1000 servicemen a day.

*

On walking in, Bob saw women in green coveralls, darting around, delivering tea or coffee, with sandwiches or cakes to men from all different units, of the AIF. The aroma filling the air was a mixture of sweetness and coffee. He could have sworn he could also smell the gum trees as well, and whilst that would seem ridiculous to many, he was convince he could. One of the women came up to him and he noticed that on the coverall she was wearing, was embroidered the yellow wattle, the native flower of Australia. She said to him, "Hello Dear. Have you been here before?"

"Noe," replied Bob. "I havenae bin here befoor but some o' my friends ha' recommended I drop in here."

"Well, they got that right dearie," she said. "You might not sound like an Aussie but you're wearing the uniform of the Australian army, so that's good enough for me. A tunneller are you," she asked?

"Aye. First Australian Tunnelling Company lassie," he answered.

"Oh!" she sighed. "Hill 60 eh?"

"Uh huh! Hill 60. Seems like years ago noo."

"Well, I think you need to come in my friend. What's your name? Mine's Emily."

"Hello Emily. Pleased tae meet ye." As he held out his hand he added, "Mine's Robert, but they all call me Bob noo."

"Well Bob, let me show you around and explain everything to you. You're welcome to come in any time you're here in London. If you have to go into the Commonwealth offices, just up the road and you find you have a wait on your hands, you can always spend your waiting time in here. There are newspapers from home, plenty of books to read, quiet rooms, snooker table through there; we've tea, or coffee if you'd prefer, cakes and sandwiches all day long and if you're here between eleven and two, there's even a light lunch put on. There's no charge for any of this, we fund raise back home, and we're supported by sponsorship. Of course, if you wish to make a contribution, there is a donation box over by the door but that is entirely voluntary."

"Fantastic," exclaimed Bob. "Wha' a wonderful place ye've got here."

"Yes, it is." Emily replied. "Oh, and if you just want to sit and talk at any stage, just give us a call and provided it's not too busy, one of us will only be too happy, to sit and listen. Many of us here, have our own men over there. Some of the girls here, have actually lost their men over there, so we all have a pretty good idea, of what you've had to put up with. We have heard lots of stories and whilst not experiencing it ourselves, we have heard enough to understand. OK?"

"Thank ye so much Emily. I'll have a bit of a wander around. I'll see ye again soon." Bob felt he was in a place of safety and with friends.

"Good-oh then Bob. I'll be back over there, with the other girls, so if you need anything just give me a call. Now, just relax. Bye!"

"Thank ye. Bye!", and Bob turned to have a look around. In the main room he saw rows and rows of tables and chairs, with men sitting at some of them, in ones, twos and threes. There was one table with five men and one of the girls and they were all sitting chatting merrily and sipping on tea. Through the archway on the other side of the room was a snooker table where two men were playing pool. Another room off that, had rows of chairs and a small, raised stage. There was also a piano in the corner. It looked like this was where they held small concerts.

On the other side of the passageway, off the snooker table room, was a series of rooms, with newspapers and books, scattered around, on the central table. There were a range of comfortable chairs, scattered around the room and several men sitting there smoking and reading. One of the rooms with the newspapers in it, was labelled a non-smoking room, apparently for those men they preferred not to smoke. That room had nobody in it, so Bob, browsed through newspapers, looking for the Sydney Morning Herald. He found several copies from different dates, all at least two months old but he was glad to see news from home, so he sat down with one of newspapers and read the news of that day. The railways and tramway strike was over.

He thought, *That's good. Pity I didn't know they were on strike in the first place.* He chuckled to himself. *Ah, Mr Hughes is providing 20,000,000 pounds of jam to the English, for us workers. That's good. We won't run out of jam.* He then read the article on the overseas mail to the troops. Now he understood why he had not been getting many letters from Jean. It was all backed up, with many tons waiting to be sent by ship. "Two million American troops to be in Europe by next June? Bloomin' Yanks. We need them now, not next June. They're not even trained yet. It's not like they haven't had plenty of notice. Three cheers for President Wilson. My fat..." his thoughts went round and round. "They have known for three years they were gonnae be into this dashed war. Why the heck had they not prepared for it?"

One of the many discussion topics, in the trenches and dugouts, had been around when the yanks were coming into this war. It was an inevitability and many of them thought they should have been preparing for years. Bob got a little annoyed at this article, so tossed the paper back on the table and went out to get a cuppa and a cake. It was still early, but cake was a luxury, and a luxury he had seen little of, in Belgium. "Hello Emily," he said as he approached the counter. "I'd love a cup o' tea, if I may?"

"Hello Bob," she returned, "You most certainly can. White?"

"Thank ye. An' may I have a wee cake? We dinnae get much cake over there."

"You sure can," replied Emily. "We like to try and provide some of the things that you don't get over there. I saw you found the newspapers. Find anything interesting in there?"

"Aye, apparently, there is gonnae be two million yanks here, bae June next year. They're not even bloomin' trained yet. Can ye imagine this place, with two million yanks screaming around. Och my lord." It was obvious, Bob was frustrated by this.

"Yes, I did hear that," said Emily. "Us girls have been talking about it, wondering what difference it's going to make to us. We're set up specifically for Australian troops. I suppose someone will have to set up something for them too, but it won't be us. Do you not like Americans, Bob?"

"Och, it's nae tha' I don't like 'em," he answered. "It's just they're so loud and pushy. I dinnae like that, in any of race of people. Jus' look at the Germans. Ye've go' tae be considerate o' others, and it seems, they jus' think o' themsel's."

"I know exactly what you mean, Bob," said Emily. "Unfortunately, I think we might just need them though."

"Aye lassie. I think ye're right, unfortunately." Bob sighed.

Emily sensed a deal of exasperation in Bob's voice. She wondered then, just what had brought him to the ANZAC Buffet. Remembering he was at Hill 60, she went on, "Are you alright Bob? Would you like to sit and talk about things a little? It's very slow this morning, I have the time now, but I mightn't later."

"Aye lassie," he replied. "I'm doin' ok, but I would like tae sit and chat if ye can."

"You go and get a table and I'll bring your tea and cake over. In fact, I might even have one with you," Emily said with a big wide smile on her face.

"Thank ye. I'll dae that," he replied.

He wandered over to the corner and sat at the table there. He was trying to gather his thoughts, when Emily arrived with a tray with two cups and two cakes on it. She set it down on the table and lifted the cups and plates onto the table, one in front of Bob and the other adjacent to him, around the corner. She sat and leaned her forearms on the table so she could lean towards him. "Was it really rough at the Hill 60?" she asked?

"Aye!" replied Bob. "Aye it was. What have you heard about it?"

She started to explain, "I heard it was one huge bang. They say it was even heard here in London, so it must have been huge. I've spoken with some of the men who went over just after both there and further down the line and some of them recon they will never be the same again. No one said what they saw but I guess it was pretty horrific."

"Aye lassie, it was." Bob sighed. "It's rubbish 'boot hearin' it here though. They couldnae possibly heard it. It wasnae that loud. I think they probably fel' it though. Was a massive shake. It crushed everything for 100 yards around. I'll nae say wha' I saw either. No human should ever have to witness tha'." Emily just shook her head displaying incredulity. He went on, "I jus' dinnae understand, how we, as educated humans, can dae that tae each other."

He paused for a moment to think. Emily let the silence play its part. "I were there, at the HQ, when they brought the prisoners back through. Hundreds o' 'em. Ye shouldae seen their faces. They were already dead. They jus' dinnae noe it yet. There weren't nothin' in those faces." He paused again, and again Emily sat silent. She knew when to just let them speak in their own time. "Tha' were bad enough," he said, "but then we moved on tae another area, an' it were night time on a change o' shift. 3 lorries we were, waitin' for oor swap, whun a big Hun whizz-bang scored a direct hit on our lead lorry. Jus' a few yards in front o' us. Blew it to smithereens it did."

"Four o' mae mates died on the spot. I dashed in tae see wha' I could dae, but they were so badly injured. Good lord it were horrible. I did wha' I could, for one of them. I packed his wounds and talked to him; but those eyes; he jus' stared at me. He said nothin'. He knew he was dying and there weren't nothin' I could dae for him. He and three others died the next day. All the way back tae camp I just sat and stared at the blood on mae hands. Back at camp, I couldnae scrub hard enough, to get it all off. I dinnae think, I'll ever forget that sight. It'll haunt mae to mae grave."

"Now I understand, Bob," Emily spoke up. "Ever since I first saw you, I felt you had something, weighing you down. Now I understand. All I can say to you Bob, is that you did do your best. I have no doubt about that, and that he was lucky to have you there, to hold his hand. Just remember that one of the last things she saw, was the face of one of his mates and to an Aussie, you can't ask much more than that. Do you understand what I'm saying, Bob?"

Bob paused to take in what Emily had just said to him. Slowly, he starts to nod his head.

"Aye lassie. I dae," he answered. "I havenae been in Australia very long, only four years, before I shipped oot here, but one thing I have learned in that time, is how important yer mates are. Noe sure I completely understand it mind ye, but I dae know that it's important."

"It is, Bob. It is." They sat in silence for a while, each thinking, "What comes next? Where does this conversation go from here?" Emily finally broke the silence, "So, how long ago and did this happen Bob?"

"Jus' two months hence," he replied. "And then mae friend and Sergeant, Alex, took a direct hit from their damned arty tae, jus' two weeks ago." Bob instantly realised he had said a word one simply does not say in front of a lady. "Och, I'm sorry, Emily. I shouldnae said tha' word."

"Thank you, Bob, but don't worry," she said. "I've heard a lot worse than that in here. Some of the things I've heard would curl your hair."

Bob laughed at that, then added, "Surely, they dinnae bring their trench language in here, lassie."

This time, Emily laughed. "Yes, Bob. They do. The lady in charge is not too fond of bad language but it's just the way it is, at the moment. I think we will find, a lot of things have changed, when this lot is over."

"Aye Emily, I think yer right there. For better or for worse, I dae think yer right." Again, he paused before adding, "I have tae ask ye this Emily. When I first walked in, I could swear I could smell the gum trees. Have I imagined it or noe?"

Emily chuckled and answered him. "No Bob. You are not imagining it. We get a bag of gum leaves sent over from home regularly, and we burn them here to give that smell of home. We find it is such a comfort for everyone involved, including us. We are all such a long way from home, and we have even had some of the men burst out weeping, just at that smell, as it reminds them of their own family back home."

"Well I have tae say Emily, it is a wonderful thing, and there is noe doubt, it is certainly unique. As I said befoor, I'm only 4 years an Australian, an' I picked it up straight away and it did feel like home." Bob was genuinely impressed.

They talked for over half an hour, not just about war stuff but families, Sydney, Bob's time in Perth and all sorts of other things. They needed to talk about some happy stuff, to try and lift Bob out of his funk. As time went on, Bob's mood did indeed lift. By the time they had finished they were both laughing and joking. More and more men drifted in as the morning went on. It got to the point where Emily had to excuse herself from their conversation and go and help the other girls. Before she left him, she asked Bob to check in with her before he left. Bob agreed, then took himself back up the reading rooms, where he checked in a few more the newspapers. He even checked out copies of 'The West Australian' and the 'Western Mail' to see if there was anything in there he might have known about. There was nothing there of any interest that was not already in the Herald.

His train for Dover was to leave at 3.35 pm, so he still had time. He took up Emily's offer of lunch and joined a couple of the other former Scottish fellows who were sitting on their own. The AIF, included around one third, expat Brits, which included a lot of Scotsmen, so it was never difficult to find another Scot. They continued to chat for an hour or so after lunch had finished and then Bob made his apologies saying he had a train to catch. He sought out Emily, to say goodbye. She smiled a warm genuine smile and came out from behind the counter. "Thank you so much for coming in today. It was a good thing you have done, coming in here. I hope you found the day useful Bob, and I hope you find peace."

"Och aye," he replied. "It were a nice change. I think ye are all doin' a wonderful job. An' I have tae say, I really appreciate the time you spent listening tae mae goin' on. It's made quite a difference I can tell ye. Thank you. Ye're a bonnie lassie."

"I hope everything works out for you Bob and if you're ever in London again, please feel to drop in and let me know how you're going. I'll pray for you. Now, you stay safe Bob. Please?"

"Dinnae ye worry Emily. I'll keep mae heid doon. I've made a good practice o' keepin' mae heid doon. Thank ye again and I will be back, dinnae ye worry boot that." Bob shook her hand and she clasped his with both of hers, as she bade him goodbye.

It was a short one minute walk to Victoria station. He purchased his ticket for Dover and went through to the platform only to find it teaming with khaki. He wandered through the mob and eventually found half a dozen other members of 1ATC. Their leave was coming to an end as well, so he joined them for the rest of the trip back, to the battlefields of France and Belgium. All of a sudden, the peace of the previous week, evaporated and once again he was back in the war. One member, of a group of men, who all dressed the same, all looked the same and all had a similar goal. To survive. Sure, they wanted to drive the Hun back to where he belonged but that was secondary to survival.

When they arrived at Calais, the following day, the group headed to a prearranged point in behind the docks and found a lorry that had been marked as being destined for Poperinge. Once they climbed on board, the lorry was full, to the point of overflowing. They headed off for Poperinge, at 0930 hrs. The 40 mile (60km) trip, took them over two hours. two hours of pounding, bone crunching discomfort. Whilst it was faster than walking, the men often commented, it was probably better for their health, if they had walked.

For most of the ride, there was little sign that this was a war zone. Villages still operated, farmers still worked their land and people went about their business as normal. With about ten miles (16km) remaining, the scenery slowly changed. There were less people, much less activity in the villages and evidence of bombardment. The mood of the men on the lorry changed, with that change of scenery. They were back in the war zone, there was no doubt about that.

The Miners from the four sections of 1ATC, or the diggers, as they were now known as, were spread over the four jobs at ANZAC House dugouts, Halfway House dugouts, Leinster Farm and the Cambridge Road dugouts. At each of these locations, extensive networks of accommodation and headquarters, were dug out over the remainder of the year. Bob spent the initial couple of weeks at Hooge, and then as work progressed on ANZAC and Halfway House, he moved between them as the work required. The Cambridge Road dugouts, he discovered, were even bigger and the Hooge dugouts. Initially they had been dug by the British 177th tunnellers, but now 1ATC tunnellers had extensively extended the system.

Christmas and new year came and went, but with the successes of the last three months, the men started to think that maybe, just maybe, this year, it may all be over by Christmas 1918. The majority of the men were optimistic that this might be the case this year. The men often joked with each other that those men, in 1914, who had rushed to enlist for the adventure, thought the war would probably be over by that Christmas (1914). They hurried to enlist, so they would not miss out. Well, they did not miss out, and by now, most of them were probably dead.

One of the big things that happened for the men this Christmas, however, was the arrival of parcels from home. Not necessarily parcels from family but from community groups, from many of the towns all around Australia. Many church groups, CWA, Red Cross and individual town progress groups spent a lot of a time putting these packs together, in the hope that it would reach one of the men from the AIF and just for a brief moment or two, give them some of the comforts of home. Most of the women back home, were frustrated at not being able to do much for the men overseas, as they were just too far away. Many community groups formed in most of the Australian towns, for the sole purpose of putting these aid packs together.

For some of the men, it was the only thing they received from "home." Many of the men, predominantly the ex-miners, had no family back in Australia, well, none that they kept in touch with anyway. So for them, these packs were not only a surprise, but hugely welcomed. They did not all arrive at the same time but were waiting for them when they came off shift, back at camp. "What did you get in yours?" was the most common question asked.

To this, Bob replied, "I got some chocolate, butter and jam, some biscuits for the butter and jam, and cheese. I havenae had cheese for … well, I canna actually remember when I last had cheese. Oh, and look, sardines, raisins and prunes."

"Prunes?" laughed Bill. "Anyone need prunes?" The tent erupted in laughter. "The cheese is more likely to be o' use here. No one needs anything to make 'em go. The hard part is how to stop!" again more laughter.

"Aye," replied Bob, "I think I might keep them for later, an' have 'em maybe only one at a time. They will be a nice change of flavour though. Hey, looky here, I've got Corned Beef too!" Again, the tent erupted in laughter. Corned Beef or Bully Beef, as it was called in the Army, was not something the men had in short supply. In fact, they had it so often, many of the men had sworn off it, for the rest of their lives. "But to offset that, I've got some tinned salmon, powdered milk and some salt and pepper."

There were some things in common in the packs that they all got, but they sat around that afternoon in a jolly mood, swapping and sharing many of the treats they received. Some got Christmas cakes or plum puddings. These travelled rather well, so were particularly desirable. Bob did get stuck with his bully beef though.

"Are ye sure I cannae tempt ye, with the corned beef? Anyone? Please? Oh well, I suppose a have tae eat it masel'."

Chapter 21
Passchendaele

Back on the job, there were advantages to working underground, none the least of course, being the whizz-bangs and minnies could not get them there. More so though, at this time of year, when temperatures above ground were in the minus degrees centigrade (less than 32° F). Underground tended to keep a nice even temperature, and the cold only became an issue, if you had to go above ground to collect materials. One of the real luxuries the men enjoyed underground, was to a brew up a nice hot cup of tea, without the fear of their fire telegraphing their position to the enemy. At this time, the conversation went something like this. "Well boys, what do you think? Do you think will be out of this place by Christmas?"

Answers ranged from "Not a snowflake's chance in hell" to "At the rate we're driving them backwards now, we've got them on the run. I think this lot will be over by the middle of the year. They can't have much fight left in them now surely?" Bob was not convinced by either side of the argument. He just thought, one day longer was too many more days. It was not so much a matter, of how much fight the Hun had left in him, as much as how much fight he had left in himself? He was beginning to wonder.

Mid-January saw yet another change in orders, with number 4 Section ordered forward to Zonnebeke. Here, they were to build a new accommodation dugout, right next to the Zonnebeke church. This was not to be an overly large dugout system but an important one all the same. The diggers by now, knew exactly what they had to dig and got straight onto it and had it dug in under 3 weeks. Bob and the other carpenters had it all fitted out a couple of days later, so that the entire project only took them twenty one days. A decision was made only a month later to expand the Zonnebeke dugouts and most of the four sections of 1ATC worked on this project over the next two months. The dugout was beneath the foundations of the church and consisted of a main gallery 95 ft (29m) long, with side corridors and five rooms as well as two access stairs all about 16 ft (5m) underground. [These dugouts still exist to this day and were opened to the public in 2017 for the 100th anniversary of the battle of Passchendaele but have since been permanently closed. They are some of the best preserved dugouts, of all those on the Western Front.]

Until October, Zonnebeke had been constantly in German hands, for the last three years. It too, had suffered the same fate as Ypres, in that it had received intensive bombing, but this time by the British artillery. There was however, a little more left of Zonnebeke than there was of Ypres, but not a huge amount more. By the end of the war, virtually nothing of Zonnebeke would remain standing. Between the British and the Australian troops, Zonnebeke and the surrounds were turned into a mass of trenches and dugouts. It became one of the highest concentrations of underground facilities on the western front. This gives an indication of the strategic importance, of this area, to the overall outcome of the conflict.

Throughout February and March, the priority lay with the Cambridge Road dugouts, Halfway House dugouts and ANZAC house dugouts. This was where the majority of 1ATC efforts were to be concentrated. There were other installations that the men worked on as well, such as Muhle, just south of Zonnebeke, North ANZAC, Kit Kat Dugouts, Cemetery North and South and several dressing stations, but the top three, absorbed most of their efforts. It was a difficult time though, through the first two and a half months of 1918. It was one of the coldest winters, the men had ever experienced, with snow on average, every second day and some of those falls being enough to cover the ground, with 6 inches of snow in the one fall.

Thankfully for the diggers, most of the digging was underground, so was not frozen solid like it was on the surface. When they did get some beautiful days, all that meant was, the snow would melt and the ground would turn to slush, making walking around the surface or along the trenches, exceedingly difficult indeed. Not that anyone really felt like walking around up top anyway. The Germans, having previously occupied this area, knew it well and constantly bombarded all three installations with their artillery. Not that it was overly effective, but you never knew where it was going to hit or, for that matter, when it did hit, whether it was even going to explode or not. It was evident that many incoming shells, landed and buried themselves but did not actually explode.

A common saying among the men was "So much for superior German expertise!" Little did they know at that time that their own artillery shells experienced a similar failure rate. Occasionally one of the shells did land close enough to the dugouts to cause damage but it was usually minor and was quickly repaired. Considering the number of shells that were sent over, it was not a particularly effective strategy. Mind you, it did make you keep your head down and that slowed the pace of work, so from that angle it did have its use.

On March 17th, the sergeant came in whilst the boys were on shift, at ANZAC House and called them all together. "It seems Fritz has become very fond of using gas again. Word has just come through that work over Kit Kat have been interrupted, by heavy shelling and use of mustard gas, a couple of days ago. Almost the entire squad of No 2 Section that were working there, have been affected by it and thus have been evacuated. They have seconded several of the boys from No 1 Section to fill in on the job there. I'm sure it won't be long before we start attracting the same attention, so I want you boys to make sure all your gas precautions are in place and we need those gas doors installed as soon as the tunnel is ready for them. Any questions?"

"Aye Sergeant," replied Bob. "How are the men from number to?"

"There's none that are critical, that's the good news but a lot of them have been exposed to the mustard gas, so some are blistering quite badly, but as you know, that will heal in time. It will keep the field hospitals busy though. At least it wasn't the chlorine. So, keep your eyes and ears open and your masks handy. How long do you fellows think until the gas doors will be ready?" enquired the Sergeant.

"I'd say they will be ready to go in in a day or two. No longer," was the reply.

"Alright then keep on with it then and we can keep us all safe."

The carpenters had to prepare the framework and sealing of the door enclosures before the doors themselves could be installed. That was what Bob was working on with his mates at that time. They were still working on them on their next shift the following day, when the Hun artillery started up on them again. This time however, they included several gas shells, so the sergeant's warning of the previous day, was fortuitous and the men were ready for the gas and donned their masks immediately, as they were all at hand. Whilst they did all avoid exposure to the gas it did hold them up for two hours, ironically preventing the installation of the gas doors in time. Once the gas all clear was given, installation of the doors was completed so for any further gas attacks, they would be ready. This included the installation of backup gas doors, in the event of damage to, or failure of, the first set.

The installation at ANZAC house was getting larger by the day. A second, connected dugout, had also been commenced called Wattle, so the men were kept busy between the two installations fulltime. On the 23rd, No 4 Section was involved in draining crater holes on the surface, preparatory to commencing the third dugout system also attached to ANZAC and this time called Gum House. They had to be cautious when dealing with these shell holes, as not only could they contain water but could also contain the heavier than air gases that the Germans had been using. Not only were these hazards for them but of immediate danger, was the almost constant shelling they had to endure. It is incredible to think, that twenty to thirty men, could be running around on the surface, dodging whizz-bangs and leftover gas, and yet the major inconvenience to them at the end of that shift was how filthy they had become trudging through the mud. There had been no injuries through their efforts this shift.

On days like this they all mucked in to get the job done, regardless of their trade. The quicker the job can be done, the quicker everyone can get back to safety. By the time they finish their shift, they were all in high spirits, having dodged everything the Hun could throw at them. As the men assembled underground, ready to be moved out of the shift change they were laughing and joking with each other. "Tek a look at yoursel', Bert! Ye're all mawkit. From heid tae toe, ye're all the same colour. Mud colour," Bob said pointing at Bert.

"Ye can talk, Bob. Tek a look at yoursel'. Ye've turned into a black fella. Now ye can go home to Australia and feel right at home." Bert laughed at Bob now too.

"I cannae wait tae get back tae camp tae get this lot off. Recon I'll lose ten pounds (4.5 kg), by the time I get to bed tonight." He desperately wanted a bath too, but knew that was going to happen for a few days yet.

The following day, on shift, word came out that they were to be prepared to move at a moment's notice. So, the day was spent tidying up as best they could, in preparation for a hand over of the workings to somebody else. The men had not been told who they would be handing over to just yet, or indeed when they would be handing over. That night they found out handover would be tomorrow, and they had in fact finished their time at those installations.

News had started filtering through of a huge German offensive commenced a couple of days before. This would ultimately be known as the German "Spring

Offensive." The German army had been bolstered by the addition of some fifty divisions of soldiers, after they had been redirected from the Russian front. The fighting there had finished, due to the Russian revolution deposing the Czar, and the Russians suing for peace. Whilst the eastern front was not yet completely over and done with, upwards of half a million German infantry had been released for conflict on the western front. There were already stories of large German successes down on the Somme River. Bill was discussing with the others that evening and offered, "Well I guess this move is aboot us going doon tae the Somme tae help oot there. What dae ye recon, fellas?"

Bert agreed with Bill. "Aye Bill. Unfortunately, I think ye might be right this time. We wouldn't have tae mek such a drastic pack up, for just a standard change of venue I think."

"Yep I recon them bloody Poms 'ave realised, they need the experts down there, to show 'em how it's done. Not sure I fancy too much time down there though. Sounds like it's been a bit rough down there over the last couple o' years." Bluey was never backwards in taking an opportunity to sledge the English.

"Aye ye right there, Bluey," added Bob. "I know we've had a lot tae deal with ourselves, wha' with Hill 60 and Hooge, but they were isolated hotspots. From what I've heard the whole of the Somme region is a hotspot."

"Yeah, with a bit o' luck, we'll be diggin' the accommodation holes for them troops behind the lines," Bluey commented.

"I think tha's a bit o' wishful thinkin' there, Bluey." Bob was drawing on his pipe now. "When have we ever been 'behind the lines' digging holes and staying oot of danger's way?"

Bluey thought for a minute, "Hill 63!"

"Tha's yer definition of 'behind the lines', is it, Bluey?" Bill was showing his distaste for Bluey's obvious ignorance.

"Yeah, well I 'spose it is wishful thinkin. But, ya never know ya luck?" Bluey was ever the optimist.

Bob spoke slowly now, "Dae ye really think, the army is going tae drag us halfway across the country, just tae dig holes for resting troops and peely-wally officers? Sorry Blue, we are aboot tae be chucked in the deep end again, mek noe mistek aboot that. I jus' hope it's not back into diggin' mines again. I dinnae think I could dae that again."

There was general agreement amongst the men for this last remark. The rest of the evening was a somewhat sombre affair as the gravity of their plight sank in. Bob wrote letters to Jean and Mary that evening. He told Jean that everything was going well, he wished he was at home with her and that tomorrow they were off to "somewhere in France." He told her, he could not wait to be able to get back to her and he was trying everything within his power to make sure he would do just that. In contrast, he told Mary, he was fearful that the move would mean more pain and sorrow. The mates he had lost continue to climb and he was sure there would be more.

The 25th was spent dismantling camp, packing everything up, kit inspections and parades whilst the following handovers were taking place. Halfway House, Cambridge road, Birr crossroads, Leinster Farm and Mud lane, were all handed over to the third Canadian Tunnelling Co, along with all plans, materials estimates and orders. The British 171st Tunnelling Company would take charge of, Kit Kat, 186, 226, ANZAC, Wattle, Gum House, Waratah, Westhoek, Cemetery north, Cemetery south, Molehoek, Muhle and Zonnebeke church.

When the men were informed of this information, Bluey laughed out loud and said, "See fellas, it takes two of them pommie companies to take over where one of us Aussie companies was doin' the job." The men gave out a hearty laugh at his comment.

"Oi!" someone else chimed in. "Don't lump them Canadians in with the poms. They're nothing like the poms. They are good blokes and can work as hard as us."

"I wouldn't be too hard on them poms either," said one of the other men. "They we here before all of us and got the systems worked out for us to use and abuse." There was a good deal of laughing and jibing, given that at least a third of the Australian troops were expat British. One thing they all agreed on was that the Canadians were not to be lumped in with the British. It was felt, the British were still stuck in the ways of the old military systems and both the Canadians and the Australians had moved on from that, to encompass all the aspects of military conflict. This was the first war, to use machine guns, artillery, tanks and aircraft. That they should not be used in isolation but together, seemed so obvious to the average thinking man. Thus, it was felt that the English were neither average, nor thinking, when it came to military strategy. Eventually that had to change though, if they were to win this war.

Chapter 22
Moving South

The following day, Tuesday, was the day of the big march south. The men all breakfasted at 0700 hrs and then and spent time preparing for 1000 hrs march off. No 1 Section was to lead off first and subsequent sections, at fifteen minute intervals. At 1100 hrs 138 men of No 4 Section stepped off for their long march south. They marched via Bailleul, through to their lunch stop just short of Hazebrouck. After lunch they continued their march through to the evening stop at Pradelle. The men were all billeted out in farms close by. The following day they were picked up at 0900 hrs AM by a lorry train and travelled south through Strazelle, Merville, Robecq, Gonnehem, Chocques, Gosnay, Houdain, Hermin Caucourt, Villers Chatel and finally their stop for the night at Cambligneul.

The talk along the way confirmed the boys' worst fears. Headed south, they were destined for the Somme. They arrived at their day 2 destination, around 6:00 PM and were all fed by 8 PM. Once again, they were billeted out of local farms, but these people had never seen an Australian before. They were incredibly surprised to find that these people from this far away foreign land, spoke English. Some of them had never even heard of Australia. By the time this war was over, they would never forget, Australia.

The next day was not quite as long a day. With breakfast over by 0900 hrs, the company commander called a rifle and gas inspection for 1000 hrs. The rest of the morning was spent around camp with an early lunch and an appointment to meet the lorry train at 1230 hrs. Today they travelled south through the Aubigny en Artois, Avesnes le Compte and Barly to their final destination of Saulty. By the time they arrived at Saulty, the day had turned miserable and bleak. It was cold, it had started raining and the wind was blowing right through the men. Billets was sorted for the men and officers and all was completed by around 1900 hrs.

The following day the men were allocated their work details. Each of the four sections, was detailed to dig one mile (1.6km) of trench, along with its communication and support trenches and lay double runs of wire along the aprons. It had been decided at this point, behind the frontline to establish a non-fallback position. A position, beyond which there would be no backward movement. One ATC had been rushed down here for that purpose. The men relished working in a new area and new dirt. There was not so much of the same old, same old feel. There was a sense of urgency to their work here, so they got on with it and were making some particularly good progress when orders came through for yet another move. At least at this point in time there was no stifling mud.

This was to be their lot over the next few weeks, move after move. It seemed to the men that No 4 Section was moving more than any of the others, and to a degree they were justified. They never seemed to get one job finished before they were off to the next digs. At one time 1ATC was spread over a twenty five mile (40km) front, digging, wiring and timbering, dugouts, machine gun pits, artillery bases and trench after trench. They found themselves working at Saulty, Warlincourt-le-pas, Hautville, Vimy, Harbacq and Bouvigny-Boyeffles. The last of these was not so much a dugout emplacement as dugout caves.

A series of caves had been discovered underneath the back road from Bouvigny to Boyeffles and Capt. Woodward was dispatched to survey and assess the caves for use as a troop accommodation dugout. The cave system was a rough truncated triangle shape, oriented along the road with about a 250ft (76m) base and 250ft vertical axis. It was not unlike honeycomb in its layout, with an average 8ft (2.4m) head height and 47ft (14.3m) overlay. This would make an exceptionally safe underground accommodation unit. With some extra work by 1ATC, this could be made into an accommodation unit suitable for several hundred troops if needed. No 4 Section set about cleaning, timbering where necessary and expanding.

On their second day down there, they managed to clear enough, to walk through the whole system. Bob and Bert were trying to work out what timber would be needed and where when Bert said to Bob, "Dinnae 'bout ye, Bob, but I'm not feelin' too good."

"What's ye problem, Bert?" Bob stopped and came back to Bert. "Ye dinnae look to good man. What's up wi' ye?"

"I dinnae. Just feel like I cannae breathe. Like there's sommat asittin ona mae chest," he said gasping by now.

"Aye I can feel it too noo. Best we get canny an' get oot a here, an' fast." Bob said as he grabbed Bert and headed back towards the entrance.

As they got back there, their breathing improved, and Bob reported to the Sergeant. "Sergeant, there's an area o' bad air back there. It's nae good for man nor beast back there I can tell ye. It nearly took poor ol' Bert to the groond. He couldnae breath properly, an' I have tae say, it started tae get me too."

The Sergeant replied, "Some of the others thought there might be some bad air, so I'll let the captain know and get something done. Once we get both shafts in, we'll be able to give it a good blow out."

They already had one access point on the southern edge, and Capt. Woodward had planned for another access shaft, at the northern end of the complex but the men had not yet started on that. "I think we might have to make that second shaft a priority. I'll speak to the captain about that too," added the sergeant.

"If ye're gonnae speak to the captain, can ye ask aboot some more timber? We're gonnae run oot fairly quickly, at the current rate o' use." Bob added.

"Righto Bob. I'll let the lieutenant know and get that passed on to the captain," the Sergeant promised.

"There's quite a bit of roof tae chisel away at, on the way doon there too. There's gonnae be a few cracked heids if we dinnae dae that," Bob laughed as he spoke.

"Yep, the boys are onto it now. They're workin' in the east section right now and will be working their way around there soon. I'll let 'em know about the bad air though. Might have to restrict ourselves to this entrance area for the time being though." The sergeant moved off towards the sound of picks on rock to the right, to let them know about the air.

True to his word, the next day Capt. Woodward arrived at the caves and investigated the air situation. The Sergeant was telling him of the incident with Bob and Bert from the previous day. The captain sought out Bob. "Good morning Bob."

"Mornin', sir," Bob replied.

"What can you tell me about this air situation? Where was it?" the captain asked.

"I'll tek ye doon there masel' if ye like. Mind ye, I wouldnae stay there too long. It affected Bert more than me." Bob led the captain to the area from yesterday and explained what happened. They had only been there less than a minute, when Capt. Woodward said, "Actually Bob, I think we better get ourselves out of this area. I'm beginning to see what you're talking about." The captain had begun to feel the effects of oxygen deprivation. As they moved away things began to improve. "I have to say Bob, I didn't experience any of that when I was surveying the caves, but I guess that was because I moved through this area fairly quickly, just taking measurements. Standing there for that short period of time, I started to feel a bit breathless myself, so we'll get some ventilation down here and get that second shaft dug as a priority. In the meantime, I'll get you to steer clear of this area and as work in the areas where the air is OK. The sergeant also mentioned about the shortage of timber."

"Aye, sir. We cannae get done wha' we've got to get done, with what we've got," replied Bob.

"I understand that, Bob. The shortages have been noted. The other sections are having similar problems and we're doing what we can do get more timber." He paused, "We seem to have had this conversation once before, if I remember rightly Bob?" they both laughed.

"Aye, sir, we have. Only this time there's no wrecked Cloth Hall to salvage from," Bob replied.

Captain Woodward smiled and added, "No Bob, there's not. I can only ask you to do what you can and be patient. We'll get you timber soon as possible."

"Thank ye, sir. I know ye will."

Captain Woodward moved off and checked in, on the other workers underground, then took the sergeant to a point on the surface, where he wanted the second shaft dug. As soon as the captain had gone, the sergeant went back underground, he selected a group of miners and took them up top to commence the shaft. The shaft was completed the following day and the air began to flow through the system. They did need to add a couple of blowers to make sure that all the galleries were safe for working and living in. That is where the AEMM&BC came into their own. They arrived as soon as the entrance was dug, with generator and fans and got that air situation sorted, as well as getting lighting installed for them, which made the working much easier. That week in May, saw the whole of 1ATC dig the equivalent of 1456' (442m) of 6' x 3' (2m x 1m) trenches and milled 11,600 sq. ft (27.4cu m) timber. Not bad work for a group of men who were experiencing difficulties sourcing enough materials.

Chapter 23
The Somme Commences

The men knew they were nearer the front now, when orders were issued, to the entire sector that stated, an enemy attack is expected anytime now and all troops, need to be on full alert and ready to defend their positions. They had spent so along behind the lines that their only reminder they were in a war zone, was the incoming artillery fire and the occasional aircraft overhead. Now, they had to have their rifles at the ready and not just rely on the attached infantry. The attack, however, did not eventuate but it must have sparked some interest at command level, because late in May yet another order came out stating the following:

The whole company will go through a course of infantry training and general discipline. The period of training will be a fortnight at a camp situated at company HQ, and after that each squad will have had least one half day a week when they re-join their section; this will be carried out as far as possible on the same day as bath parade, when the mining operations will cease for the day.
(Special instruction number 4 of 23/5/18)

There was a mixed variety of reactions to this when it was read out to the men. Some laughed heartily, some groaned and someone even yelled out. "So, they finally think we're actually soldiers, do they?" This drew a great deal of laughter from the men, and even a smile from the officer reading it.

He went on, "Each section of the company will be divided into four training squads and you will receive two weeks infantry training, including weapons training, tactics, formation drill, gas precautions and bayonet skirmishing, from the company sergeant major (CSM)"

At the sound of this last drill inclusion, the laughter stopped. Everyone was taking it seriously now. They all had bayonets, they all knew how to use them, but no one had ever imagined that he would have to use it. The last lot of infantry training that most of them had had, was at Blackboy Hill in Perth, 2 years 3 months ago. A week later, the first squad from each section marched out for their fortnight training camp. Each fortnight after that, one squad was to march out, as the other marched in, until all the men of 1ATC had been through the training.

Some were not all that disappointed at having to do this training, as it meant a total change to their normal routine. The thing that concerned them most, however, was they could see a situation now, where their mining activities had come to an end, and they may be needed to act as infantry troops in future. That was not what the signed up for. Still, they would cross that bridge when they came to it; if they came to it. The course was not that arduous. The day was broken up into six instruction sessions with ample break time. A typical day looked something like this:

6.30 to 7	physical training and fitness
9 to 10	squad drill with arms
10 to 11	musketry instruction
11 to 12	bayonet fighting
2 to 3	musketry instruction
3 to 4	lecture musketry

The first 10 days of the course looked like this, with a few extras thrown in. Platoon drill, eyesight training, aiming and judging distances were some of the other inclusions. The last four days of the course, were spent on the shooting range, bombing and field exercises. It was felt that, as there were several men in the units that had previous military training, they would be left until last, in case the situation changed, and the courses had to be stopped or postponed. This meant that Bob, Bill and Bert would have to wait for the last school.

"Wha' are ye thinkin', Bill?" Bob asked when they found out they would be last.

"Well laddie," he started, "I'ma thinkin' that I hope this bloody war will bae o'er by then. The wae I see it, it's yet another one o' those dafty Sassenach ideas, where they're getting tae the point, where they dinnae ken wha' tae do with us. They mus' be getting' short of fightin' troops, so they have tae get 'em from somewhere an' that somewhere, is us. I'm happy doin' wha' I'm doin' here but I'll bae damned if I'll want tae go oot there shootin' Fritz."

"I ken what ye mean Bill. I'm nae too keen on the idea musel." Bob did not relish the thought of coming face to face with the enemy and having to shoot or bayonet him. He'd seen enough dead by now, to last a lifetime.

In the meantime, the work continued at the caves. There were floors to level out, ceilings to chip bits off, walls to timber up occasionally, stairs to build and bunking to set in place. Morale was on the up. Small gains had been made, along the frontline and being midsummer, the weather was far more conducive to getting work done. No longer knee deep in mud, simply moving around the site was so much easier. On July 4th, news came through that bolstered the Morale even further. About thirty five miles (58km) to their south, lay a small village of le Hamel. It occupied the high ground to the west of Corbie, on the Somme River.

A small-scale attack on this area was undertaken by Australian and American troops, under the command of the newly appointed chief of the Australian third division, Major General John Monash. It was the first time that a wholly coordinated, integrated attack, had appeared during the great war. It was a new tactic devised by Monash, to include not only infantry but tanks artillery and aerial reconnaissance. All previous attacks during the conflict had opened with massive artillery bombardment, which simply signalled to the enemy, an attack was about to take place. Monash dispensed with the artillery bombardment, at the opening, in favour of a sudden charge by brigades of tanks followed by the infantry. Once that had started, the artillery joined in, with a creeping barrage.

A creeping barrage is where artillery fire is concentrated on the frontline of the enemy, which forces them underground or backwards for safety. Guns then increase their range marginally, to force the enemy even further back, when they increase their range again. This had the desired effect of turning the enemy on their heels, in a continued retreat. Monash believed that the infantry should not bear the brunt of the attack, but the artillery and tanks should do that, leaving the infantry to follow up and occupy the objective. This way the loss of human life should be minimised. He felt this was important.

Famously, General Monash predicted a ninety minute battle. He was out by three minutes, with all the objectives of this stunt taking precisely ninety three minutes. It showed the rest of the Allied armies, what could be achieved by a coordinated campaign. Never, had such a successful action, appeared in this conflict, to this date. This battle would result, in 1400 Allied killed or wounded and 2000 Germans killed and 1600 taken prisoner.

When news started drifting through, in the afternoon of the fourth, the men started celebrating. Bill came rushing into the cave complex, "Have ye heard boys? The third divvy have just had a massive win up near Corbie. Monash and the boys have pushed them back 2000 yards already, an' taken the village o' le Hamel." At this news all the men in the cave system gave a hearty cheer and crowded around Bill for any further news. "Great news," said Bob. "Can ye tell us anything else?"

"Naw a lot really," replied Bill, "But what I can tell ye, is they've got rid o' that nasty salient bae the river. I guess they'll keep pushing further east noo."

"Och, that's grand news Bill," said Bert "I wonder what that'll mean for us? Things will probably get a move along noo."

Bluey piped up at this point, "See what 'appens when you put an Australian in charge. Them bloody Fritzes turn on their heels and run. We been sayin' for months that those pommies have been doing this all wrong. Now there's your proof." Once again, the boys joined in in a round of cheers and backslapping.

Just then another voice joined the conversation, "All right lads, you've had your celebration, now let's get back to the job. This only means we've got a lot more work to do." It was, of course, the voice of the sergeant, ever so understanding and tolerant.

Back to work they went, but this time, mostly with smiles on their faces, albeit intermittent, from the toil. Such a resounding victory could be the beginning of the end. They most certainly hoped it was. The German Spring Offensive, known as 'Operation Michael' had indeed come to an end. Whilst it appeared on paper that the offensive had been spectacularly successful, the reality had been a little different. Yes, they had captured much ground, and in places gained up to twelve miles (20km), but it was mostly ground of little strategic importance. In doing this the German army had overextended itself and was now experiencing supply problems. Allied command had expected this to happen, hence the new push to drive them back had waited for this moment.

The work throughout July went on much the same, with some record volumes of dirt excavated per man. They were down to about half strength through the month due to infantry courses and leave. The former changed its format, in the second half of the month, with the training taking place at the workplace. The trainers now travelled to the participants instead of the other way around.

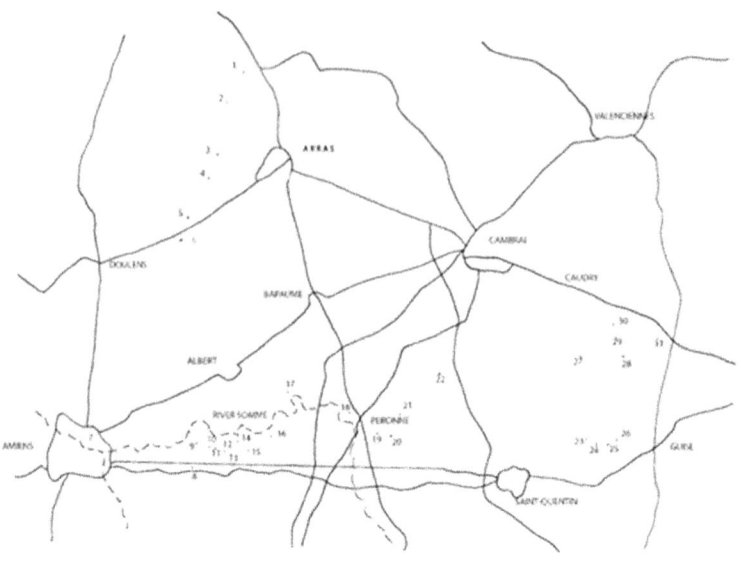

Fig 5

The Somme Campaign March 1918-Armistice

1 Bovigny-Boyeffles caves

2 Camblibneul 27.3.18

3 Chateau Harbacq

4 Hauteville camp

5 Saulty camp

6 7.4.18

7 1ATC camp HQ Rivery

8 Villers Bretonneux

9 Brigade Dugout Le Hamel

10-15 captured Dugouts

16 HQ end August 18

17 With the Canadians 4.9.18

18 Checking rail lines for mines 7.9.18

19 Co HQ 12.9.18

20 Rest Camp Cartigny 19.10.18

21 Roadworks 21.9.18

22 Advanced Depot

23 Temporary HQ with 11th Engineers

24 Gun valley dugouts

25, 26 Captured dugouts

27 4 Section HQ 10.10.18 and

27 Camp site when bombed at night

28 La Vallee-Mulatre

29 Bridge repair 19.10.18

30 Bridge repair

31 Rejet-de-Beaulieu. Sambre Canal

It was around this time that Bob started to feel a little more optimistic about the outcome of the war. Things were looking up. In a letter he wrote to Jean, he told her of his optimism and the likelihood of him returning home soon. He was a lot more upbeat in this letter then he had been in recent times. He even surprised himself, with his more positive outlook. By the time he finished his letter, he was feeling even better so he finished it off with, "Oh by the way Jean, when I get home would you do me the honour of marrying me? I feel that you're the only one for me. I love you, and want to marry you." He wrote that letter but did not post it immediately. He hung onto it for a few days, to make sure of himself. In the end, he decided, nothing ventured nothing gained. He posted it.

At the beginning of August, another move was ordered for No 4 Section, to take over from 2ATC further north. The following day thirty six of the section were ordered up to Le Hamel to dig a brigade HQ a mile (1.6km) west of the town. As this one was a rushed job, and had to be finished by 8 August, the men travelled to the job by lorry with all their equipment. They were to live and work on the job. The men chatted as best they could along the way. The Sergeant commented, "Looks like this must be an important job, don't you recon lads?"

"Aye sergeant," Bob answered. "With what went on las' month there, I recon they will be getting' organised for the next push. It's bin a month noo, an' it soonds like they have gained a tad more ground than on that first day."

"Very true Bob," replied the sergeant. "Looks like they have now taken an area about four miles (6 Km) long by a mile and a half (2.5 km) wide. And yes, I believe we will be an important part of the planning for this next push, so let's make our mark with this job. We'll be being watched very closely I bet."

"Yeah," one of the others commented, "it's only a Brigade HQ so shouldn't take all that long. I'll bet all the materials will be available for this one." All the men smirked at this, waiting for the sergeant's reaction. When he broke out in laughter, they all followed. They had been experiencing a drastic shortage of materials at their recent digs. The saving grace down here was that the ground being chalk and flint, was much more capable of supporting itself, thus requiring less timber. The downside was that they had to work harder to camouflage the spoils. It stood out from the air and high ground really easily.

When they arrived at the site, they immediately got to work. The diggers started on the entry stairway and Bob and Bert got onto sorting the timber, ready for installation as soon as the digging was deep enough. Once the timber was sorted, they all mucked in to get the job running smoothly. With only five days to complete the job it was all hands on deck. "Well boys, here we are again. Shoved onto an important job, to be completed in no time at all. Nothin' like pickin' on the best class in the school eh?" It was Bluey again. Never short on putting the boot in where he could.

"Aye," said Bob. "Sometimes it would be nice tae noe be the best on the front though. Would make for a quieter life, I think. Still, it's got tae be an honour, tae be chosen, all the same."

"Mebee so," Bert added, "but it's good tae be part o' this. Think aboot how we felt when we heard aboot Hamel. Hopefully, we will be able tae say we were a part o' something big here this week too. Let's hope so. Might bring the end a little closer."

"Sure hope so, Bert." Bob really did hope so.

They got the HQ dug to the point of occupation by the 7th. They continued to expand the dugout even while the big wigs moved in. There was top brass everywhere, and yet the work went on. The attack, they learned, was to commence tomorrow morning, at 0400 hrs. The Australian 2nd and 3rd division would be attacking from this point with the 18th British division on the left of them and the Canadians 1st, 2nd and 3rd divisions, on their right. The French were even further to the right (south). On the north side of the Somme River, were parts of the American 33rd, with the British. Major General Monash, was now Lieutenant General Monash, and his plan from Hamel last month was the basis of the assault tomorrow.

"Well Bert, you got wha' ye wanted then." Bob whispered to Bert. "We are a part of this stunt, an' it looks tae be a big one. 10 divisions in the first wave."

"Aye Bob, we are. If we can tek 'em by surprise again, we should give 'em a damned good hidin'. Can't wait tae see the results."

Not long after this, men saw some of their mates from all four sections, and Lieutenants Irving (1 Sect), Nye (3 Sect), Mayoh (4 Sect) and Armstrong (2 Sect), join them. "What are you blokes doing here?" asked one of the boys.

"Hello lads. We're here, to follow up the advance tomorrow, to report on likely dugout situations. Whatever we find in the way of Boche dugouts, we've got to assess them quickly and report back to these guys," their mate said, tilting his head towards the top Brass.

"Well, that's a turn up for the books, there's no mistake." Bert said "Imagine that. 1ATC is really in the thick o' it on this one is it noe?" he went on.

"So, four lieutenants. Are ye four different groups or all together?" asked Bob.

"Nar, we're four groups, going in four directions, to cover the ground quicker. We've gotta have a report back here, by 1000 hrs, so the brass can work out what to do next."

"Half your luck boys," Bob said. "Ye make sure ye keep your heids doon. Follow me back here, an' ye can toss your gear down with ours," he added, as he walked a short distance to their sleeping area in the back of the dugout. "It's kicking off early tomorrow morning, so you'll be needing your beauty sleep."

One of the new group added, "We'll have to wait for our instructions from the lieutenants, before we turn in. Once we've got that it'll be good night sweet prince."

"Why thank ye, young James. I never thought ye thought of me that way before," Bob said with a demure, mocking smile.

"Not on your bloody Nellie mate." James replied. "You are simply, not my type at all. I prefer blondes." At this they all had a hearty laugh. Spirits were high and anticipation of tomorrow's offensive added to their mood. Shortly the lieutenants came back and discussed tomorrow's tasks, with their respective groups. They spent some time pouring over the maps of their escapade. They were to follow the initial assault, at about 20 minutes after step off and remain that distance behind the lead troops. As the infantry cleared the way, they were to analyse any trenching, dugouts, or emplacements that they manage to find. They were to then gauge the suitability of these facilities, for use by the Allied armies and report back to HQ on their findings.

There was not much sleep that night, as all the final preparations were formalised and messages back and forward to the attacking troops. At 0400 hrs, the tanks rumbled past, the sound being muffled by the drone of dozens of bombers flying around over the German lines. These particular bombers, Handley Page bombers, were chosen for this task, as their engines sounded similar to those of the tanks in use, at this time. The element of surprise was essential to the success of the plan and the tanks would certainly telegraph their approach, so the bombers were tasked to make as much noise as possible and mask the sound of the tanks, to delay the discovery of the attack.

Twenty minutes later, the infantry followed the tanks and then the creeping barrage commenced. The battle of Amiens had begun. Even underground where the men stayed, the noise was thunderous. They manage to keep out of the way whilst still continuing to expand the HQ. At 0440 hrs, their mates who were surveying for the dugouts, stepped off as well.

"Good luck laddies," Bob bade them. "Mind ye keep your heids doon noo. Good luck and good hunting." The whole of the HQ working party, wish them well and saw them off.

"They'll be alright Bob. Dinnae ye worry aboot that." It was Bert, right by Bob's shoulder. He placed his hand on Bob's shoulder, as they watched them leave. "They will be alright laddie. They are a good bunch, with good officers, an' they will look after 'em. They will be well behind any action."

"Aye Bert, I ken that. Doesnae stop me worrying aboot them though," Bob said, as he turned back to their bunks. They would spend most of their time back there today, out of the way, chipping away at extending the bunker as required, but most of the time keeping an eye on the progress of the battle. They would also be of help as the prisoners started coming back through, helping to marshal them and guide them in the right directions.

Somewhere around 0700 hrs, the prisoners started filtering back, through the command post. It was not long until it was a continuous stream of troops and officers. Many of them looked like they had been caught unawares, as some of the officers were not even fully dressed. It turns out, the attack was so sudden and unexpected that this group of officers were taken prisoner as they ate their breakfast. Bob noticed, once again, that many of these prisoners seemed almost glad to have been taken. They had indeed, had enough of this war.

At 9:00 AM, the 4th and 5th Australian divisions, leap frogged the 2nd and 3rd, who consolidated their positions. Similar moves will be made all up the line except for the British who were having a little more difficulty penetrating the German frontline, due to harsher terrain and less tank assistance. Just after 10:00 AM, the first of their reconnaissance mates, returned to the HQ, with news of the dugouts they had found. The runner was from No 2 Section, bringing a message from Lieutenant Armstrong that they had found an extensive dugout just 1100 yards (1km) along the road south east of Le Hamel. The next runner to return was James from their own No 4 Section.

They had found a dugout system about 2,000 yards, down the same road. These were not particularly good dugouts and the CO of 9th brigade, informed them that they were not going to hang around, they were pressing further forward, and these dugouts would not be suitable for them anyway. James gave his information to the intelligence officer, and then came back to join his mates of the back of the dugout. "Not very happy, boys," he said, puffing loudly. "I've run all that bloody way, to bring this information back, and no one's interested in using and dugouts. Good news is, it's going smashingly out there. There already further ahead than they'd planned to be by this time. So bloody Fritz is on the run."

"Poor auld James," said Bob laughing. "Ye'll get fit noo, will ye noe?"

"Thanks a bloody lot, Bob, ya Scottish git!" was the somewhat terse reply.

"'Tis good news about the stunt though. How far did ye get?" enquired Bob.

James' breathing was starting to settle down now. "Not all that far really. We only had to cover about a mile south of here, then east a mile, but the ground's pretty rough, so wasn't easy. I took a couple of tumbles on the way home, dammit. The other fellows, they're still checkin' the area, in a bit more detail, in case we missed anything. The other two sections have a lot further to go. They'll be a while yet."

"OK, well ye just settle yesel' doon. We've got a brew on, so we'll have a cuppa, while we wait."

They did have a while to wait for the next reports. It was another hour, before the next runner came in. He was from the Lieutenant Nye's No 3 Section. He too, was breathless, after the long run to bring his report back. They had been all way over to Morcourt, on the south bank of the Somme River, about 4 miles (7.2 km), to the east. They had more success, finding at least four emplacements, in the bank of the river, as well as a number of bivouac opportunities along the bank, all the way north, to Cerisy. Just as he was finishing his report, the fourth runner, from Lieutenant Irving's No 1 Section, arrived just as breathless as the other three.

They had been a similar distance to Nye's section, but covered an area 1000 yards south of 3 Section. This section, had the most success in finding dugouts, having found eight, to this point. These were in two groups of four. The first was 1100 yards (1 km) south west of Morcourt and the second, was a mile (1.6 km), west south west of Morcourt. This was only a preliminary report, as further work was required to survey the entire area.

"Have you guys got a cuppa going by any chance?" This was the first thing they said, when they got back to the tunnellers dugout. "I'm as dry as a wooden god."

"Sure have boys. Settle yeself' doon here and take the weight off yer bones," said Bob holding out a cup to the first of them. "Hoo far did ye fellows goe?"

"I've been four miles east to Morcourt," said the first of them.

"I've done the same but further to the south. Found a lot of dugouts though. Some of them pretty damn good," said the second runner.

The first runner went on, "One of the good things we found, was heaps of timber, just lying around all over the place. Looks like they weren't giving a damn, about conserving timber. We'll have to scout around and collected it but there is an awful lot for us to use."

"That will be grand," said Bob. "We've bin so short o' timber lately. We can sure use some extra." Again, the two runners confirmed that the battle was going well. The advancing troops were encountering less resistance, than they expected. The attack had taken the Germans, completely by surprise.

By 11:00 AM there was a huge bulge in the centre of the frontline, where the Australians and Canadians had penetrated three miles (4.8 km) from their start point. By the end of the day, a rift had been torn in the German frontline, fifteen miles wide (28 km) and almost seven miles deep (11km). By the following afternoon, this line had been pushed even further back, to form an arc, stretching from Albert in the north, to Montdidier in the south, and east almost to Chaulnes. All the way through this second day, prisoners continued to stream through the command centre. Australian corps estimated that at this point, they had taken between 10 and 12,000 prisoners of war.

Also significant was the amount of hardware taken in the action. The amount of timber was significant, adding to their meagre reserves. The amount of artillery taken, must have had a significant impact on the central power's capacity to wage war. Add to that, machine guns, weaponry, ammunition, food stores and associated equipment, and this action had to go down, as one of the most successful campaigns of the conflict.

It is fair to say that the 3thirty sixmen, who were working on this brigade HQ, felt privileged, to have played a part, in this significant battle. They still had more work to do, to get the HQ to the desired specifications. Late on that second day, Capt. Woodward, and a few of the other officers, came through the HQ, to check on their men working there and to have a look around the captured ground, from the point of view of troop dugouts etc.

The men were working in the back of the dugouts, extending as per the plan, when the heard a familiar voice, "Good afternoon men." The men spun round to see Capt. Woodward standing there with the other officers. They naturally snapped to attention.

"Good afternoon, sirs," answered the sergeant.

"As you were, men, relax." The men did just that and gathered around in a group.

"G'day John, Alex, James, Bob. All of you. I have to say to you all, you have done a fantastic job here, especially given the time scale. I've been talking to the brigadier and the other officers out there at the command post, and they can't speak highly enough of you, or the work you've done. Hey Bob? I hear there's plenty of timber out there in the captured ground," he looked Bob fair in the eye as he said it, with a huge grin on his face. Captain Woodward had an unusual face, but when he smiled, his whole face lit up. Everyone laughed at this latest comment, as they all knew Bob always complained, about the lack of timber.

"Thank ye, sir. Aye, James here tol' me aboot it all, an' I have tae say, I have even thought about goin' oot there an' grabbin' some, but then I thought better o' it in the end," Bob said with a sheepish grin on his face.

"Was just as well, you didn't go out there Bob, because we're finished here you know. The advance has been so successful that this headquarters, is now too far behind the lines, so they're going to have to move up a few miles. Sorry about that boys, but you'll need to pack up your gear now. The lorry will call for you in the morning, to take you down Villers Bretonneux, where you're going to become railway engineers." He made this last comment with a hearty laugh. "So, what do you recon about that?"

"What?" barked one of the other men, "You mean we did this all for nothing?"

"Far from it, son. Far from it," the captain swiftly replied. "This dugout, has been an extremely important part of this campaign, and whilst its use has been short-lived, that does not for one second, diminish its importance, nor the contribution that you men have made. All rights fellas, we have to go and check out this new won ground, so you'll get your gear together, and have a quiet evening. The lorry will be here tomorrow morning at 0800 hrs to pick you up. See you all down at Bretonneux."

"Yes, sir," came the reply from the men, as they watched the officers turn and leave.

"Well, what dae ye think aboot that?" said Bob. "We're on the railways noo. I always wanted tae be a train. Whoo!" he added mimicking the actions of the train whistle.

"I be thinking you'd better head that train tae the funny farm, think ye nae?" said Bert laughing. The others all joined in then, with all sorts of trained noises.

"It will be nice to work out in the sunshine for a change though, don't you reckon boys?" One of the other men added. The general consensus of the group was, it would be nice to work up top for change. It was after all summer, and they could do with a few rays of sunshine. They gathered all their gear together in a stack and settled down to a nice brew of tea. The troopers' answer to all ills—a nice hot cup of tea. It cures everything.

Chapter 24
Reassignment

At 0800 hrs the following morning, the company's Daimler lorry arrived at the dugout HQ. The men threw on all their gear and climbed aboard. It certainly was a tight fit, but it was really only a short drive down Villers-Bretonneux, so they were prepared to put up with thirty minutes of discomfort. Finally, they manage to catch up with all their mates from the remainder of the section. They had not seen them for over a week, so time was spent catching up as they pitched camp in preparation for the new task.

The 4th Canadian Railway Company (4th CRC) was already hard at work, on the broad gauge railway, passing through Villers-Bretonneux. In the afternoon, the men joined the Canadians on the job. This was the first, broad gauge railway that 1ATC had worked on. Up until now all their work had been on the light gauge supplies railways that were usually only temporary constructions. There was a variety of work to be done on this railway. Much of it had been extensively damaged and required rebuilding from the sub-base up. Some of it only needed the tracks re-laid, and that is where the bulk of the men started their work. Others were taken by the Canadians and shown how to rebuild the base, bed the sleepers and fix the tracks.

Once they all had their techniques organised, the men of 1ATC were able to work on their own. This, of course, allowed for much greater section of line to be reconstructed, in a shorter period of time. There is no doubt it was hard and heavy work. It was certainly a lot warmer out in the sun, than it had been underground, but most men relished this change. During their time and Villers-Bretonneux, the men found themselves working on more than just the railway. Roads required repairing, water supplies to be reconnected, wells to be cleaned and relined and general clearing of roads to make them more accessible.

These activities, continued throughout August, with little change, to the daily routine. One thing that did happen around this time, was the discontinuing of the infantry training schools. Things were advancing so quickly now that the men could not be spared for this purpose. The men who had not yet been on the courses, were mightily relieved by this. The big thing as far as the men were concerned however, was that all four sections of 1 ATC were working together on this project, the first time it happened in an awfully long time. It was not however, all the men of 1 ATC, as the company was going through a cycle of leave for the men.

Bob's turn came up, on August 27, where he managed to score a fourteen day leave pass. Because of this, he managed to fulfil his promise to his sisters, to revisit them before he went home to Australia. Being so far inland now, two days each way, was taken up in travelling just to get up to Boulogne and back. This time his boat across the channel would leave from Boulogne and arrive at Folkestone on the Kent Coast, south east England. Once again, he managed to catch up with his sisters, both in Glasgow and Saltcoats. This time however, he managed to give his sisters in Saltcoats enough warning that he was coming that they arranged for him to also meet up with his brother, Alick and sister in law, Janet.

While he was away, the company underwent a few changes. It had two location moves. The first was to a position 1000 yds (0.9 km) north east of Chuignoles and the second to a position one mile (1.6 km) west of Cartigny. They completed the work on the Villers-Bretonneux railway line. No 4 Section moved its headquarters to a site at Billon Wood, five miles (8 km) south east of Albert and then on the day of his return from leave, to a position on the banks of the Somme River, with company HQ, west of Cartigny. Also, due to the changing nature of the company and its work, thirty eight men had been marched out for reassignment to the infantry. Many of the others had gone through job changes too.

Bob arrived back at camp, in the second week of September, to find that his section, was now working with the 1st CRC, on the Perrone to Roisel railway line. At Peronne, the river Somme, divides in two. The main branch of the river, leads south, eventually sweeping in a big arc back north, through St Quentin, and then runs east into the mountains and its headwaters. The smaller branch at Peronne runs east northeast through Roisel and into the higher farmland, as its source. It is only a short branch and is really not much of a river at this point, being only a small tributary of the river Somme. The railway from Peronne to Roisel, follows this tributary, crossing it twice, before reaching Roisel. In winter this would have been particularly boggy ground, almost swampy, but as this was September, the ground was firm underfoot and made the job easier.

When Bob reported back from leave, he spoke to Lt Mayoh, who asked him to hold off reporting back to his unit.

"Bob, I want you to hold off heading back to the section work, for a bit. Capt. Woodward would like a word with you before you head back. OK?"

"Aye, sir." Bob replied.

"If you want to head to your tent and settle your gear back in, that's fine. I'll send a runner for you when the captain gets here," the lieutenant said.

"Thank ye, sir. I'll dae that." Bob saluted and headed off to his tent.

He had not been long back at his tent, when runner came and said the captain wanted to see him.

"Thanks Alex. I'll be right there," he said grabbing his hat. He put on his hat, pulled the chin strap under his chin and made sure there was a downward tilt to the right, as had been the way with the slouch hat. He headed up to the section command tent and waited outside. He was called in almost immediately, so he marched in, halted and saluted the captain.

"Sapper Hood, reporting as requested, sir." He barked.

"At ease Bob and stand easy," said the captain, as he sat calmly at his desk. "As you may have noticed, Bob, there's been a bit of a reorganisation while you were on leave. We've broken out of the stale trench warfare that we been involved with for the last three years and it's become a more fluid, open style of warfare. As such, we've had to look at our structure."

"Aye, sir, I have noticed," Bob was getting worried now. He had already been told of the men who were reassigned to the infantry. He most certainly did not want to do that. The captain's words bounced around in his head, 'reorganisation'. "Oh No! Where am I going to be sent?" These thoughts were being repeated in his head, even while the captain paused between sentences.

"So, I have a question for you Bob. You've been pretty resourceful when it's come to finding timber, when we've run short, so I thought you might be useful in the supplies area, helping out Cpl Tiley. What do you think?" The captain was looking him straight in the eye by now, and Bob was sure his pure relief, would be visible to anyone looking on.

"That will be fine, sir. I'm sure I can be o' some use there," he replied.

"Good on you Bob. I'm sure you'll do a great job there. If you want to head down to the Quartermasters tent and report there, he's already expecting you," the captain said with a smile on his face. Bob must have had a somewhat quizzical look on his face at that point, as the captain then laughed and added, "Yes, I figured you'd say yes, so we've already organised it. Good luck Bob."

"Thank ye, sir." Bob took a pace backwards, saluted, about turned and marched on out. Once he was outside the tent, he let out a massive sigh of relief. He knew, this reassignment meant he would no longer be on the frontline. That pleased him greatly, as after coming back from this leave, he was not sure how much more of this he could take. He took himself off down to is tent, hung his hat, finished organising his kit and then flopped on his bunk. It was by now late afternoon, but he was going to take a few moments to get his thoughts together, before heading over to the supplies tent.

He lay on his bunk and his thoughts turned to the last two weeks with his family back in Scotland. Again, he wondered if he would see them again. He was feeling a little more confidant now though. Fritz was on the run and he was off the front line. This greatly improved his chances of surviving this war. It could not be much longer now surely? His thoughts turned to Western Australia, in particular to Jean. He thought back to the postcard he sent last year, in which he had been rather forward with his introduction; "My Darling Girl." Yes, that had been forward, but it had had the desired effect. Jean had written back in the positive, to his introduction. She indicated that her mother had found the line somewhat amusing. Oh, how he wished he was back there right now.

Eventually, he shook himself out of his funk, donned his hat again and headed off to the supplies tent to report to the 2nd corporal. He arrived at the tent, to find the 2nd corporal checking stock off against an inventory. "Excuse me Corporal." he said, "I'm tae report tae ye for duty in the stores area."

The Corporal looked up, "Oh yes Bob, come on in. I've been expecting you. You can start right now by giving me a hand with this."

"Sure thing corp. What dae ye want me tae dae?" Bob replied.

"I'm trying to match the stock with the inventory. With the move we've just made, it is all in a mess. Oh, and by the way, so long as no one else is around, just make it Frank."

*

304 2/Cpl Frank Trump Tiley was a storeman before the war, in Woolahra, Sydney, NSW. He was born in 1882, so was five years older than Bob. He was only a little fellow, at 5'7" (170 cm), with a shock of sandy coloured hair. Frank too, had piercing eyes but his were eyes of grey. He had joined up less than a month before Bob, but because of his stores experience, he was made lance corporal, on their arrival in France, in May 1916 and attached to the supplies section. For almost the next two years, he assisted 2nd Corporal William O'Dea, until O'Dea's death in action in April 1917. Tiley was promoted to 2nd corporal, on 17th of April 1917. He had continued as quartermaster for the company from that date. Now he had the added assistance of Bob, for which he was grateful.

*

The two of them spent the next couple of hours reorganising the supplies tent, checking off the stock against inventory and generally just getting things into shape. Whilst the two of them knew each other, they had not had a lot to do with each other over the last three years. Bob had certainly checked in with Frank, to get supplies of timber, nails, tools and anything else they had needed for the timber work in the mines, dugouts and trenches, but never really stopped for a chat at those times, due to the pressure of work. The two of them found that afternoon that they had a lot in common. By the time mess time came around that evening, they had licked that tent into shape and were ready for the following day, when all work orders went out.

"Well, I have to say Bob, I didn't think I was gonnae get this job done today," Frank commented. "We've worked well together, and I think we're ready for tomorrow now. We need to be down here, tomorrow morning, as soon as morning parade is finished. We'll get some advanced warning, of what will be required for the day, so that'll give us time to get organised. Most of 4 Section, it is still working on the railways with the 1st CRC but there's a lot of splinter work going on as well, a few here a few there. But we'll worry about that in the morning. I'll see you then."

"Ye will indeed, Frank. Thanks very much. Enjoy yer tea," Bob said with a big laugh. Enjoy, was hardly a word you used to describe the evening meal. It quelled the pangs of hunger but hardly satisfied the wants of the men.

That first week flew by quickly with both Frank and Bob setting up the systems and refining them as best they could. The sections were all working close together on the rail lines and on local roadways as well. There was also work done on wells and water supplies again. One of the jobs that was beginning to take more of their time now, was on mine detection and disposal. Not the kind of mines they had been used to working with, but the explosive kind. Now that the conflict had moved to a more open style warfare, retreating troops tried to slow down the advancing armies, by mining roads, rail lines, bridges, towns and ruins, by using artillery shells, raw explosives and custom made land mines. In later days these would be known as IEDs. Improvised explosive devices.

As the Germans were driven further back, each day, more prisoners would continue to file through the HQ, at West Cartigny. For that week alone, more than 2000 exhausted German soldiers, were ushered through. Before they were passed back down to POW camps, they were relieved of any kit that the men of 1 ATC could make use of. Frank and Bob made sure all this was catalogued and stored. Likewise, anything that could be salvaged from the battlefields was stored for reuse.

By the second week, it was clear that things were building for yet another offensive. More troops were moving into the area, including, this time, lots of troops from the USA. Late in the week, a conference was held at the company HQ that included high ranking officers from not only the Australian companies, but English, American and Canadians. The conference was all about how to deal with the transport network, before, during and after the coming offensive. The road and rail networks were in great need, of a lot of work to bring them up to a usable standard, for the rapidly advancing armies. The coming offensive was aimed at a wide front. Lines of demarcation of responsibility, for all the participating engineering and labour regiments, were required, to ensure a smooth and rapid repair system, of all those networks.

Frank and Bob, needed to be included in any planning, to ensure that there were enough supplies, for the men to use on these jobs. The offensive was set for the 29th of September, only four days hence. The two of them had to organise to get enough supplies to ensure there were no holdups in the company's allotted tasks. Fortunately for them, Peronne lay only three miles (5 km) to their north west. Supplies from Albert and Amiens had been moved forward to Peronne over the last three weeks. This made it a fairly simple task, to bring supplies forward to their base.

Frank explained to Bob, "Looks like the plan, Bob, is for the American 30th division to attack first in our sector and once they've achieved their objectives, our 5th, will jump over and drive Fritz off the Hindenburg line. What that mean for us, is our boys will not be required immediately the offensive commences, but couple of hours after. From then on, it's aimed to be pretty fast moving, so we'll need to be well on our toes."

"I dinnae ken aboot these Americans. I dinnae think they put up much o' a show last time. I'm noe sure they've learned enough yet. I hope I'm wrong but I dinnae think so." Bob was sceptical of these American troops. He felt them to be arrogant and ill prepared.

Frank agreed but added, "I'm told command wanted the Australian troops to lead the battle, due to the resounding successes we've had previously, but Monash told Rawlinson that they're tired and exhausted and needed a rest. Apparently Prime Minister Hughes himself, has insisted they be rested. So, Rawlinson promised Monash that he would give the Australian troops a rest after this action. He gave Monash, the American 27th and 30th, so Monash put them up front and our boys behind on the second line. What surprised everybody, was that Major General Reid, has put his American boys under the command of General Monash. They said at Hamel that they wouldn't allow their troops to be commanded by anyone from another country. Bloody arrogant lot they are, but at least Reid has recognised the advantages of Monash commanding this stunt."

Bob thought about this for a moment, then commented, "Aye, oor boys are due a rest. They've been hard at it noo since June. Certainly showed the Sassenachs how tae win a war. If the Americans have our boys assisting them, an' behind them, they should bae oright one would thenk."

"Yep! The boss said that the yanks were so short of experienced officers that we have loaned them, over 200 officers and NCOs, to assist them with this stunt. Let's just hope they listen to them. Don't know where they got 'em from though. I'm guessing from the 1st and 4th." Frank was referring to the 1st and 4th Division, who were being rested for this offensive.

It was true that the Americans were indeed short of officers, and the Australian army seconded two hundred and seventeen officers and NCOs to them, to help with the impending offensive. The US troops were delighted to be involved in this, as up until now they had only been used in reserve. Their CO was Major General George Reid, and he understood the enormity of the task at hand and asked that Lt Gen Monash command the operation. The St Quentin Canal was a part of a canal system that ran from the north of France to the Somme River. The section from Cambrai through St Quentin to the Somme, was known as the St Quentin Canal, and formed part of the famous Hindenburg line, a supposedly impenetrable defensive line laid down by the German army.

The canal was, in many places, extremely deep, with exceptionally steep sides, and too wide for tanks to cross. A 6000 yard (5.5 km) section of the canal that ran from Vendhuile to Bellicourt, ran below ground through a tunnel known as the Bellicourt Tunnel. It was in this section that Monash proposed to attack the Hindenburg line and break it. His plan involved similar tactics to his previously successful attacks, with the exception that a massive artillery barrage, would attempt to soften up the Hindenburg line first. If he could break the Hindenburg line here, it would severely impact German morale, which was already felt, to be an all-time low.

A plan was now for the American 27th and 30th Divisions to attack the Bellicourt tunnel crossing and drive the Germans back beyond the canal. They would then dig in, and the Australian 3rd and 5th divisions would leapfrog the Americans and push the Germans further back and fan out to the north and south, breaking the Hindenburg line wide open. Two British divisions, would attack north and south of the tunnel at the same time, attempting a crossing of the canal. The Australian 2nd Division would sit back behind the lines in reserve.

On the afternoon of the 25th, Corporal Tiley hurried into the supplies tent with papers in hand. "Okay Bob, we have a move on our hands. The main offensive is to start on the 29th, but there will be a minor offensive, conducted by the Americans, to get us into a prime kick off position, for the 29th. The boss has given me a list of supplies and we are to move up to St Emilie tomorrow. We will be only four miles behind the proposed front line, so we'll be in the firing line, but we will have cover there."

"Och, I see," said Bob with a deep sigh. "I was hoping this job would keep me off the frontline."

"Yeah, me too," replied Frank, "but I'm afraid it hasn't, and we have got a job to do, so, we'll just get on and do it. The sooner we get this stunt over with, the sooner we can all go home."

"Aye laddie," said Bob. After a pause, he added, "Well, what dae we need tae dae?"

Frank and Bob scanned over the list and started putting everything that was requested outside, ready to be loaded onto the lorries that would be needed transport the supplies. Everything was sorted by dark and stacked up ready for loading. The tent was struck and rolled. As soon as the evening mess was over, they headed for their respective tents for an early night. Most of the men who were involved in tomorrow's move, did the same. Bob and Bert were sitting on their respective bunks, discussing the next few days action.

"Well Bob," it was Bert, "wi' a bit o' luck, this may be the end o' the Boche. This lot might be over, before the year is oot."

"I hope so Bert, I hope so. Ye make sure ye keep yer heid doon laddie, o'er this next week. I want us all tae make it back home. What will ye boys be doin'?"

"Ah," Bert was speaking in a mocking tone now, "we have the delightful job, o' getting' the roads ready for the advance, an' then after they push off, we have tae follow behind them and repair the roads again, so we can keep the supplies up tae them. We have been told, there will be a big artillery barrage to start with, so there'll be plenty o' damage tae deal with, I think."

"Dash it Bert! You'll be closer tae the action than I am even. Och, please tek care, wont ye?" Bob was speaking seriously.

Bert smiled and looked down at the ground. "Aye Bob. I have naw desire tae be knocked at this late stage, ma friend. Naw desire at all. Hopefully, our boys will frighten the pants off o' Fritz and he'll turn an' run back tae his Fatherland, where he belongs. Anyway, it won't just be us working on the roads. A couple o' American Engineering companies, will be there too, so we won't have tae do it all oursel'."

They chatted on for another 30 minutes, discussing the likely outcomes, of the next week or so and then turned in for the night. They were woken not long after by the drone of aircraft. Enemy aircraft. They managed to drop 8 bombs on the HQ but did no damage.

"They must be bombing ba guesswork Bob," Bert commented.

Bob replied, "Aye Bert! I think they are gonnae need a bit moor practice, if they actually want tae dae any damage. Mind ye, I'm naw complainin'. Jus' ruined ma dreams though."

They both had a good laugh and went back in the tent and went to bed. Again.

Bob and mate from Ardrossan Volunteers

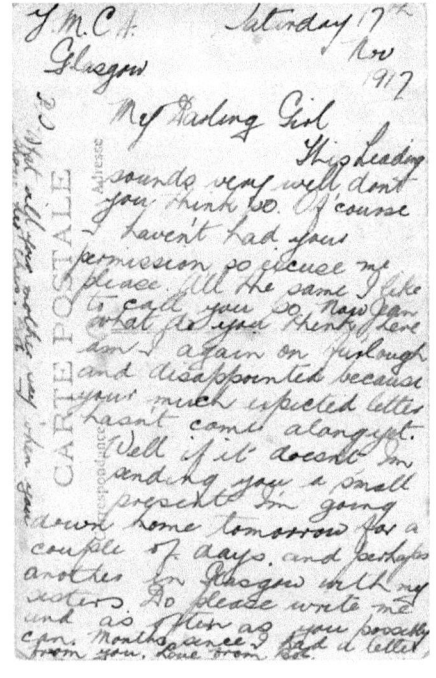

Reverse side of postcard. Bob is becoming forward

Hooge crater pumping water out

Bob, Bill and Bert 06-08-1917

Salvaging timber Ypres. Note remains of Cloth Hall at right and St Martin's Left

Hooge crater Entrances to dugouts

The Bencubbin Bakery before and after the fire.

AUSTRALIAN WAR MEMORIAL   P02333.002

ATC Officers Back (L-R) Lts Royle,
Boury, Carroll
(Front) Capt. Woodward, Maj. Henry,
Capt. Clinton 23-06-1916
Photo Courtesy AWM

Hoo

Road to

Ypr

Road

Hellfire corner looking toward Hooge. Note hessian screens and horses at the gallop. You did not waste time getting through here.

Bob and two Belgian boys

E05412

Type of Lorry used

Ypres 1918. St Martin's Cathedral, centre. Cloth Hall, right distance

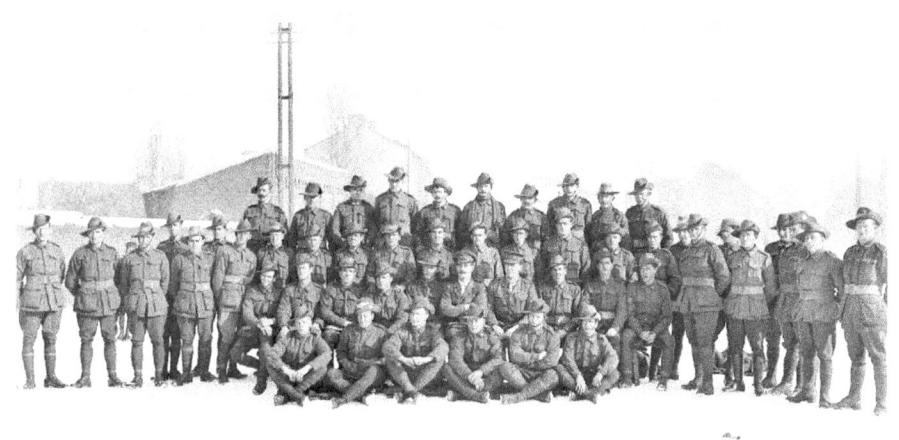

1 ATC March 1919. Bob seated on chair second from right

QM NCOs from 1 ATC. Identified front row, L-R
365 Charles Strelein,
either 312 John Levi Watts or 17 Edgar Tatham Shores, unknown,
Bob, 9 William John Hammond

Wedding Day 1919
L-R Bert Carr, Bob, Jean, Jessie

The Chappells.
Back (L-R) Roberta, Jean
(Centre) Mimey
(Front) Jack, Jessie

Jean and Bob (below) in front of Illawarra St Hurstville, House 1920

The Jewellery box Bob made for Jean

Reconstruction of sleeping arrangements

Florence St House today

Medical facility at Zonnebeke Dugout Museum

AUSTRALIAN IMPERIAL [crest] EXPEDITIONARY FORCE.

Certificate of Discharge of No. *118.3* (Rank) *W.O. hr d*

(Name) *HOOD Robert*

(Regiment or Corps) *1 st Tunnellers Cy*

born at or near the Town of *Ardrossan*

in the State or County of *Scotland*

Attested at *Casula N.S.W.* on the

6th January 19 *16* for the **Australian Imperial**

Expeditionary Forces Regiment or Corps at the age of *28 ½* years.

He is discharged in consequence of **Termination of his period of**

Enlistment,

		Medals	
Service towards completion of engagement	*THREE* years *229* days.	Medals and	
Service Abroad	*THREE* years *135* days.	Decorations	

Signature of Officer Commanding Regiment or Corps. *A.R.F. Ferguson Lt for Capt.*

S.O.I & R.S. 2nd M.D.

Returned Soldiers' Badge Place **Sydney, N.S.W.**

Issued *No. 223* Date *25th August 1919*

Discharge confirmed at **Sydney, N.S.W.**

Signature *A.R.F. Ferguson Lt for Capt.*

for Dist. Com. 2nd M.D.

Date *25th August*

(left margin, vertical) Civilian Suit and Cap Issued. SHOULD THIS CERTIFICATE BE LOST OR MISLAID NO DUPLICATE OF IT CAN BE OBTAINED

(right margin, vertical) Entitled to and Issued with Red Blue Chevrons.

Bob's Demob Papers

Memorial Arches at Blackboy Hill today. Axis points to sunrise on ANZAC day April 25

Chapter 25
Hindenburg Line

The G S wagon arrived first thing the following morning, and with the help of several of the other men, they loaded up the wagon. The new campsite would be along the road between St Emilie and Ronnsoy, ten miles (16 km) north east of their current camp. They would then have the American 27th and the Australian 3rd on their left and the American 30th and the Australian 5th on their right. They would be right in the middle of the action. The company settled in by late afternoon, ready to go into action the following day.

There was an artillery battery only 200 yards (180m) to their left and that evening the enemy artillery pounded it constantly for nearly two hours, averaging one shell every ten seconds. They did manage to drop a couple of shells fairly close to the HQ trenches, but little damage was done. One Sapper was wounded that evening. For the first two days all the sections worked on the roads, getting them up to a useable standard. Some of the jobs needed to be done at night so as not to semaphore the coming attack to the enemy, but the majority were concealed enough.

Frank and Bob worked overtime to keep the necessary supplies up to their mates. The G S Wagon continued to go back and forward to keep their reserve supplies up as well. All the time, 1ATC was under intermittent bombardment which ended with two more Sappers wounded and one KIA. Being on the frontline now, Frank and Bob did not rely on their tent for a supplies depot. This time, they were in trenches again.

The morning of the 29th, broke with the sound of an artillery bombardment, the likes of which, the men had never heard before. It was the sound of 1600 guns, pouring almost one million artillery shells down on the Hindenburg line, in a truly short period of time. By now, the British had sorted out their fusing problems with their artillery shells, so that now, they were far more effective at destroying the German defensive wire. Once the barrage lifted, the American troops commenced their advance. The 27th division on the left had a target of 5000 yds (4500 m) to cover before the Australian 3rd division would move through to continue the attack. The attack did not go well from start, and by the time the Australian 3rd arrived, instead of leapfrogging, they had to join the skirmish, in an attempt to make the first objective.

The 30th division on the right, were more successful and achieved their objective, so the fifth moved through to take the attack through the Hindenburg line. Unfortunately, with the attack on the right being successful, and the left, not yet a success, the 5th had to contend with fire from their front and their left. Naturally, that made the task more difficult. Further south, against all expectations, the British managed to cross the St Quentin canal, and captured the Riqueval Bridge intact, disarming demolition charges before the Germans had a chance to blow the bridge. The capture of the intact bridge was a huge and unexpected bonus.

It took a week, but eventually the combination of British, Australian, Canadian, US and French troops, broke a seventeen km (11 mile) wide gap in the Hindenburg line. This offensive signalled the end for the Central powers. It was now, only a matter of time until the war would be over. By the time, this battle was over, the British would lose nearly 9000 dead and wounded, the Australians 2500, the Americans over 13,000 and the Germans 36,000 taken as POWs. It was an unfortunate mix of inexperience and lack of effective leadership that led to the high American toll.

Whilst the attack was underway, other changes were taking place, away from the line. The position of CQMS, was created and the rank, would be that of a staff sergeant. It would take nearly a month for the official notifications to come through and take effect though.

As promised, once the main offensive was over, the Australian corps was withdrawn from the frontline. General Rawlinson ordered them back behind the frontline for, a period of rest and recuperation. The Australian corps had been on the frontline, in several offensives, from early June and were finally relieved on the 5th of October. They were utterly exhausted. Once behind the lines, they were able to re-outfit their uniforms where necessary and most importantly, get some good food into them. Living on frontline rations, for the last four months, had taken its toll. Most had lost some weight; many had lost too much weight. They desperately needed a period of rest.

This period of rest, however, did not apply to the Tunnelling companies. Their work continued unabated. An advancing army, especially a rapidly advancing army, needs an effective transport system, so throughout October 1 and 2 ATC, along with British Tunnelling companies and American Engineering companies, worked on repairing roads, bridges and railway lines throughout this region. Every day, the Germans were being pushed further and further back, which meant supply lines got longer, so the roads needed to be in good condition.

Bob and Frank continued to supply the men with all the equipment they required to do the jobs. Every so often, they would pack up their gear, load it onto the GS wagons and move their quartermaster store further forward. One of the jobs that Bob had not counted on, nor prepared for, arrived on his table on October 10th. Two days previously, a group from No 4 Section had been working on a road between Premont and Becquigny, with the 105th US engineers. A German artillery shell landed in the middle of the group of men, killing one instantly and wounding five others. 3339 Spr William Nolan was killed instantly, although once again, there were no marks on his body from the explosion. He had been killed by the percussion. The other five men, all showed multiple shrapnel wounds but survived. All five were classed as serious. Bob knew William well, having worked with him on several occasions.

On this particular day, Bob learned of one of the other functions, the Quartermasters had to perform. William's personal effects were handed to him at the store, to itemise and to pack, in preparation for sending them home to his mother. Bob just stood there looking at them. There was nothing special about them, nothing unusual about them. They sat there on the table, in front of him. Once again, his thoughts started going round and round in his head. "Is this all we amount to? Is this all we have to show for a life and a struggle?" On the table in front of him, lay some photos, 1 wallet brown, 1 book devotional, 1 pad writing, 1 YMCA wallet, 1 mirror, 1 pack of cards playing, 1 set of colours and one handkerchief white.

Frank came over and put a hand on Bob's shoulder and said, "Yep, we have to do that too. If there's not too much stuff, just place it in an envelope, with the deceased's name on the front, then write out a list of the contents in duplicate. We'll keep one list here, on file and the other goes in the envelope. We then pass it on to the lieutenant. If there's too much stuff, you'll need to use a box, but the same process applies." Bob stood there, still staring at these personal effects and slowly nodded his head. He said nothing.

"It's alright, Bob. You'll get used to it." Frank understood. He had felt the same way himself when the first fatalities came through, back in 1916.

Slowly, Bob lifted his head, then turned it to look at Frank. "I dinnae think I'll ever get used tae it, Frank. Never in a million years. It's noe right!" Frank left him to it. He would let him deal with it, in his own good time. Eventually, Bob got out the pad and wrote down the list of items in front of him and did as Frank had instructed.

Once he had finished packaging the personal effects, he put them aside to send up to command later that day. He had little time to dwell on the significance of this task, as there was so much to do, which was probably a good thing for him at that point in time. What he did not need, was time to think and to brood. That afternoon, a dispatch rider stopped by.

"Number 4 Section Quartermaster store?" he inquired.

"Aye it is," replied Bob.

"Delivery for you," said the rider, as he thrust the paperwork in front of Bob to sign.

"Thank ye for that," said Bob and the rider handed over two small bags. As soon as Bob had taken them the rider it took off, back in the direction from which he had come. Bob looked at the paperwork. 'Quartermaster No 4 Section, 1 ATC' was written on the top. Below it were the words 'From: 61st CCS'. Bob's heart sank. "Not more dead surely," he thought. Just as he was to open the bags, Frank was beside him. "Was that a delivery rider?" he asked. "He sure took off in a hurry. What did he …?" His voice trailed off, as Bob opened the bag. "Oh! Who this time?" was all he said.

Bob pulled the paperwork out of the first bag. "Damn and blast! Corporal Mooney."

"Shit," Was all Frank could say.

"Och naw! Noe Charlie Cuthbertson!"

"Bloody Fritz!" barked Frank. "The sooner we stop these bastards, the better. I'm getting tired of this. Well, you know what to do with them. Just process them like the others."

"Aye," replied Bob. "That's three we've goe tae send up tae command today. Three!"

Frank walked away shaking his head. Bob got on with the inventory, packaged up the effects, labelled them and place them with Nolan's. Three more of his mates gone, in the one day.

The next day, they again got orders to shift camp, further forward still. This time they were to set up camp by a bridge on the road between Becquigny and Busigny. The Germans were in fast retreat, but they were not going to make it easy for the advancing troops. Every bridge they could demolish, they would. Every road and rail line they could mine, they did. They blew up water supplies. Anything that could be of use to the advance was destroyed. Absolutely anything that could slow them down. The last two miles (3.2 km) of their journey from Bohain-en-Vermandois had been destroyed so their route took them by Premont, Serain, Elincourt, Maritz and Becquigny, a distance of eleven miles (17.6 km). Capt. Woodward and one hundred and twenty sappers made the journey to this rail bridge, which had been destroyed, leaving at 0545 hrs, arriving at their destination at 0730 hrs.

The men immediately set about constructing a diversion around the bridge site. The new crossing was suitable for all traffic use by 1030 hrs. This had been a waste of time as far as the retreating army was concerned. It did use up manpower to affect the advance, but it was manpower that would not affect the advance. Whilst on site, they were subjected to almost constant artillery fire. Not that it was particularly effective. For all their efforts two injuries were sustained by 4 Section, one of which was serious.

The plan was for the bulk of the men to arrive and the equipment would follow in lorries and G S wagons. Frank and Bob set off from the former camp an hour after the men did. They were slower than the advance party and still had to go the long way around. They made it as far as the town of Elincourt but were unable to travel any further. Enemy mines had cratered the road, and they were also subject to blocking artillery. The men at the bridge were in need of the equipment to get on with the bridge rebuild but just had to sit and wait. Their tents, bunking equipment and rations, were also on these lorries. It was a bitterly cold October night and the men just had to grit their way through it, as best they could. The bridge was over a rail cutting, so that provided them with some shelter from the wind, for part of the night. By the time the lorries arrived on site the next day the men gave them hell for taking so long. They were cold and hungry, but they were so glad to see them.

Capt. Woodward Spoke with Frank, "So what was the holdup, Frank?"

"Well, sir, between you and us on the Elincourt-Maretz road, just outside of Maretz, a Fritz mine had cratered the road. Mustae been a delayed action job," Frank explained.

"Bugger!" replied Capt. Woodward. "You all ok?"

"Yes, sir. It happened before we got there, but while we were waiting, the Hun started up with his whizz-bangs, so we hi-tailed it outta there back to Elincourt. Couldn't risk this lot getting hit," Frank indicated with a flick of his head to the lorries.

"Fair enough, Frank. You're right, we'd be up the, you-know-what, if we lost this lot. Ok how about the first order of the day is some food. Better break that out," the captain said. Whilst they were unloading, with the help of some of the men, the captain asked Bob, "Hi there, Bob. So, Frank said what happened. How did you get through in the end?"

"Well, sir, we had enough equipment here, so between us an' the other drivers, we just go' oot the shovels an' started filling holes. We only did enough tae ge' us through though. We left the rest for 2 ATC to fill in when they ge' up here," he said with a wink to the captain.

Woody laughed and added, "Good job then. They have to have something to do. We can't do it all. I know sometimes it looks like we are the ones doing it all, so well done."

The men spent the next two days consolidating and widening the diversion. They added turning base at either end of the crossing, for the larger vehicles and horse drawn vehicles. The captain by now, has surveyed the old bridge structure and instructed the men on what to remove in the way of brickwork and rubble. Some of the remaining structure need to be removed as well, so they used guncotton charges to remove that. They then set about shoring up the abutments in preparation for the new top. During the afternoon of the 12th, a Hun artillery shell landed near the job and a corporal and sapper were wounded. They were both moved to the nearest CCS and both survived. The shelling continued with a pasting of the village of Busigny but as it has not been used for accommodation, there were no casualties.

The following night, the men were treated to a gas attack but once a gain there were no injuries. That day the men witnessed a somewhat one sided affair in the air, to their north. Eight Hun aircraft were seen buzzing around, and 1 British plane happened onto their little party. It was a poor move by the Brit, and he was forced to land a short distance away, somewhat damaged. The misguided chivalry of the flying corps was evident, as each of the Hun craft performed a flyby and saluted the downed flier.

"I jus' dinnae ge' it, Frank," Bob said of the observation. "One minute they're trying to kill each other, the nayxt, they're salutin' each other. They even used tae have parties wi' their captured opposite flier. I jus' dinnae ge' it."

"So true Bob. It's quite amazing really. I guess they think that coz they are fliers, they are better than anyone else and are special. The bastards get to go home at night and have a nice comfy bed as well. Nice work that. I recon I could do it," Frank was laughing by now.

Bob snuffled and added, "Ye'll naw catch me up in one o' those infernal machines. It's naw right. If god 'ad wanted us to fly," at this point Frank joined in and they chorused, "he'd have given us all wings," and Bob added, "like the birds."

At this moment Lt Nye walked in, "And what are you two laughing at?" he said in a mocking rebuke. "Ah, Bob here was saying it's not right for men to fly, sir," Frank said as they snapped to attention. In the field it was not advisable to salute your officers. It identified them to any observing enemy and labelled them targets. Besides, in the commonwealth forces, if you are not wearing a hat, you do not salute. You just stand to attention.

"As you were gentlemen. I don't know Bob, I recon it would be a bit of fun flying around up there, don't you?" asked the lieutenant.

"Och naw, sir. I dinnae. I cannae think of anything I'd like tae do less," Bob replied.

"One day Bob, one day I recon we'll catch you up there," the lieutenant smiled. "I just popped in to let you know that there will be another offensive on Thursday. You've probably guessed something's up. This is the first push, where our infantry haven't played a role, since June, but Australia is still represented by us. We will still be doing the same work. So, keep it up lads."

"Yes, sir," they both chorused, then the lieutenant left.

"I guess this time they'll be looking to push 'em back to the canal. That's the next major landmark over the Selle river," Frank mused.

"Aye," said Bob, "they cannae have much fight lef' in 'em noo."

By this time, it had become obvious to all that another push was coming up. The amount of artillery, lorries, troops and officers, who were using their deviation around the demolished bridge, was a bit of a give-away. This was confirmed for all the men when on the afternoon of the fifteenth, the camp was paid a visit by the incoming CRE, Lt Col T.E. Hill, as well as the Lt Col A.M. Martyn, the outgoing CRE and Capt. McBride. A little later, the area got a little hot, yet again, on a cold, bleak and windy day, with a visit from a good deal of incoming Hun artillery. Once again, they did little damage and there were no injuries. On the 16th all the men of 1 ATC had to stand by, for an attack by the U.S. Army 2nd corps, the following day.

Lieutenant Nye dropped in again on that afternoon, with some more information for Frank and Bob. "I just dropped by to let you know, to check out the notice board. There is a rather good letter there, from General Rawlinson. It applies to all of us in this company, as much as the infantry when they were part of the 4th Army. Go and check it out. It's one to write home about."

"Thank you, sir. We'll do that," answered Frank.

They both immediately walked up to the command tent where the notice board was posted and, on the board, was a carbon copy, of a letter from General Rawlinson, to all the Australian troops.

Since the Australian corps joined the fourth army on the 8th of April 1918 they have passed through a series of hard and uniformly successful fighting, of which all ranks have every right to feel proud.

Now that it has been possible to give the Australian corps a well-earned rest I wish to express to them my gratitude for all they have done. I have watched with the greatest interest and admiration the various stages through which they have passed from the hard times of FLERS and POZIERES to their culminating victories at MONT ST QUENTIN and the great HINDENBURG system, at BELLICOURT canal and MONTBREHAIN.

During the summer of 1918, the safety of ARMIENS has been principally due to their determination tenacity and valour.

The story of what they have accomplished as a fighting army corps, of the diligence, gallantry and skill which they have exhibited, and of their scientific methods which they have so thoroughly learned and so successfully applied, had gained for all Australians a place of honour amongst nations and amongst the English speaking race in particular.

It has been my privilege to lead the Australian corps in the fourth army during the decisive battles since August 8 which bid fair to bring the war to a successful conclusion at a distant date.

No one realises more than I do the very prominent part they have played, for I have watched from day to day every detail of their fighting and learned to value beyond measure the prowess and determination of all ranks.

In once more congratulating the corps on a series of successes unsurpassed in this great war I feel that mere more words of mine cannot adequately express the renown that they have won for themselves and the position they have established for the Australian nation not only in France but throughout the world.

I wish every officer, NCO and men all possible good fortune in the future, and a speedy and safe return to their beloved Australia.

Signed H.S. Rawlinson General commanding fourth army.

14-10-18.

(NB Reproduced as it was typed up in Company orders)

The source of the Selle river, was by the village of Molain, just four miles (6 km) to their east. It travelled north through Saint-Souplet, Saint Benin and le Cateau, before turning northwest and joining the Somme, at Douchy-les-Mines. Le Cateau, was presently in German hands. As the area in front of the troops was near the beginning of the river, it was not particularly wide, but was still a barrier. Not only that, but there was a railway bank and line just over the river and then the ridge immediately east of that. the Germans were entrenched on the eastern side of the river at the top of that ridge. The battle was to kick off at 0615 hrs, but Gen. Rawlinson was concerned about the troops crossing the river, so he got them to do that during the night, using timber planks placed across the riverbanks, allowing the troops to quietly cross in single file and then assemble on the east side of the river, before zero hour.

The battle commenced right on 0615 hrs with the advance of Infantry and tanks, preceded by a creeping barrage. It was aided by the presence of thick fog, blanketing the area, masking their advance from the defending Germans. The front line, of the advance, stretched over ten miles (16 km) from le Cateau to Mennevret, five miles (8 km) to their south east. It was executed by the British 1st, 2nd, 3rd and 4th armies, consisting of British, Canadian, South African and New Zealand troops. Over the course of three days, they managed to push the Germans back, in excess of five miles (8 km) to the Sambre-Oise canal despite some determined resistance from the German Troops. The mopping up went on until the 26th of October.

Capt. Woodward and the engineers from the US corps headed off at the same time as the infantry on day one, to survey the roads in their sector with a view to establishing the need for road repairs, over the next week or so. There was a large area that would be needing attention and he needed to assess them in order to allocate resources of manpower and equipment, but it would be No 3 Section that would benefit from Woodward's appraisal. No 4 Section was to head back to the base at Cartigny for six day's rest.

Once again, the men of No 4 Section, packed up all their gear and loaded it onto five lorries, and headed back for familiar ground. They departed the Busigny camp at 0730 hrs. It was only twenty miles (36 km) as the crow flies, but due to damage, poor roads and air bombing it took all day to travel the distance back to Cartigny. It was late afternoon when they arrived, so the priority was the tents for the men and food for the mess. The setup was like clockwork these days, they had done it so many times. Everything went back where it was last time. It was just automatic. The next six days were spent with the occasional kit inspection and reprovisioning and a lot of resting. They were exhausted and needed the rest.

Due to losses and transfers to infantry, the 4 Sections of the company were disproportionate in their distribution of troops. During their rest week some transfers were affected. nineteen sappers from No 2 Section were transferred to No 4 Section and twelve from No 3 Section were transferred to No 1 Section. Given the friendly competitiveness between the four sections, the men were not best pleased by this move. The receiving sections were fine with it all, as it meant more sappers to do the work but the men doing the moving were not. They had to leave a lot of their mates behind. The following day, more changes occurred, as notification of the position of CQMS became official. Frank Tiley was promoted to the rank of CQMS backdated to 29th September and Bob was promoted to the rank of 2nd corporal. (The rank of 2nd corporal is no longer used and is a rank between that of lance corporal and corporal).

Capt. Woodward and Lt Nye both came around to the quartermaster's tent later that day.

"Well gentlemen," Capt. Woodward spoke first. "Congratulations on your promotions. Bloody well deserved, the both of you." Each of them extended their hands in turn and shook each of them, with genuine intent.

"Thank you, sirs," each of them replied.

The captain went on, "It's fair reward for a job well done, to the both of you. I have to say that the effort you two have put in, over the last few months, has been nothing short of fantastic. What, with lots of moves, pack, unpack, repack, changing roles, I don't think; I know we couldn't have done it without you."

"Thank you very much, sir," Frank replied.

"Aye, sirs. Thank ye so much," Bob said. "It has bin a long war, but I think I can see an end in sight. Would I be right in that thinkin', sir?"

"Yes Bob, I think you are right in thinking that. The generals think that maybe one more push, two at the most and we will have 'em by the balls." The captain made a grabbing motion with his hand as he said it. They all gave a hearty laugh.

Woody looked at Lt Nye and nodded. Lt Nye explained, "Yes one more push, and I'm sorry to say fellas, but we are going to be a part of it. We are getting a few reinforcements from No 1 Section as well. Lieutenant Thompson and twenty sappers will be joining us, for this next move. We move back up the line in two days, back up to the Becquigny-Busigny road."

"Ok, sir," Frank said. "One more push, we can handle. Especially, if it will see the end of those damned Huns."

"Good on you, boys. This one won't be road making but bridging. We're waiting on a list of requirements now. We'll let you have it as soon as we get it. There'll be some specialties on this one," the lieutenant finished with.

"We have some of the list at the moment, and it will come down to you shortly. Ok? Congratulations again, boys. We'll see you later," the captain bade them goodbye.

"Yes, sirs, thank you again," Frank said.

After a pause as the officers left, Frank said, "Well there you go, Bob. How about that then?"

"Och aye, Frank. 'ow aboot that? Ye a Sergeant an' me a corporal. Who'd o' thought? 'Twas nice o' the boss tae coom doon an' tell us 'imsel' weren't it?"

"Aye Bob, ye'd be right in thinkin' that," Frank answered in a mock Scottish accent. They laughed together. They did not have far to go, to obtain their stripes. They drew them themselves from their own store and before too long were both outfitted appropriately. They had a good laugh about that too, as they sewed them on.

The new list of requirements came down later that afternoon and the two of them set about working out what they already had and what they needed to get. The following day they started to pack up yet again, ready for what they hoped would be their last move. They had passed a list onto corps of the items they still needed, and they were to be dispatched to them at Busigny. The company HQ was at the same site the men had vacated only the week before. They would set up a staging camp nearby for the night, before moving again to their assignment.

The four lorries departed the Cartigny campsite, at 0900 hrs. This time, the trip was a lot faster. Further work had been done on the road, and they did not have to contend with any artillery this time. They arrived at camp at noon and set up the tents. The extra supplies had not yet arrived but there was no concern there. They were not expected, for a couple of days yet. The new CQMS and 2nd corporal, set about preparing the supplies that they did have and getting their loading schedule together. They now knew, what test they were about to embark on, so everything had to be meticulously prepared. The following day, 29th, saw two inspections. In the morning there was a company gas preparedness inspection, and in the afternoon, the full kit inspection. Any shortages would see the men at the CQMS store for replacement of defective or missing items, after explaining why they were short.

Chapter 26
Regretful Promotion

Bob still liked to bunk down in the same tent as Bert and his mates from before his move to the QMS. Yet again, it was a cold, wet and blustery day. Being late October now, the days were much shorter, less than ten hours long. The sun set at around 5:30 PM. On this evening of 29th October, as the men were in their tents after evening mess, trying to stay warm, they had a visitor, at 1830 hrs. Visibility was not great, being an hour after sunset and no one was really sure, whether their visitor was deliberate or lost, but a Hun plane flew overhead and dropped two bombs. For once, they landed where they could do maximum damage, right in the middle of No 4 Section's camp.

It was thought that maybe the Hun bomber was trying to bomb the road, as others had done previously. Bob, Bert and their mates, were reclining on their bunks, when they heard the whistle of the incoming bombs. They all hit the deck, lying prone covering their heads. The bombs went off not twenty yds (19 m) from their tent. There was a terrific explosion, and their tent was riddled with holes from shrapnel and the dirt blown out by the bomb. It was only seconds and it was all over.

"Is everyone alright?" yelled Bob, brushing all the dust and dirt off his tunic.

There was a chorus of, "Yeah mate," and variations, from all the boys in the tent, followed by, "What the fuck was that?" It was Bluey, as articulate as ever.

"Has tae have bin a Hun bomb," Bob said, stating the obvious.

The men then became aware of screaming and yelling coming from close quarters. They dashed outside to see a tent two up from theirs, shredded to nonexistence. There were bodies everywhere. The tent between that one and their own, was not in much better shape and that is where the screaming was coming from.

"That's Frank's tent!" yelled Bob, as he dived in to find Frank. He found him; he was alive but covered in blood. He looked around for a webbing pack, to find a first aid kit. He found one under some rubble and ripped open the pack. By now the other men from his tent, were doing the same with the other men from this second tent. There was nothing to be done, for the men from the first tent. Bob pulled the number 15 field dressing from the pack, opened it up and pushed it firmly under Frank's major wound. This was an abdominal wound and he pressed it in, to stem the flow of blood. He took the long tape, attached to the dressing, and wound it around Frank's body. He then took out the number 13 field dressing, pressed against frank's head, and wound the tape around his head. The whole time, he kept talking to Frank, telling him what he was doing, and that he was going to be alright. He sure as hell wished that were the case, but looking at him, he was not so sure. Bob had a quick look around, to see what else was happening. Bert and Bluey were both working on Will Reddan, as he had lost an arm and a leg. Strangely, he thought, Bill was just lying there, saying nothing, not yelling out but just allowing them to do what they had to do. Blood was still squirting from the arm, but they had the leg under control. Bill was working on George Mortimer. He gave Bob the thumbs up for George.

By now, all men from the section were there, as well as staff from the HQ, over the road. Corps medical staff, now took over, treating the men as best they could, before loading them into one of the lorries and heading for the nearest CCS. There was no shortage of volunteers to assist in loading the men into the lorries. The casualties were whisked away to the 48th CCS. Now the men could stand back and survey the damage. Two dead horses, their GS wagon was destroyed beyond recognition. It had taken the direct hit from one of the bombs. Next to that, the first tent was nowhere to be seen and three bodies lying amongst the rubble. The second tent, Frank's tent, had been partially destroyed and that is where the bulk of the injuries had occurred. Over the other side of the central lane several of the tents there were holed, and a couple of the injuries occurred there, from flying bits of shrapnel and GS wagon.

It was nothing short of a miracle that no one in Bob's tent had been hurt. The two tents between the blast and theirs had absorbed or deflected most of the debris. The four of them were now standing in a group, just looking at each other. Bert and Bluey looked a sight. They were covered in blood from head to toe. Bill's hands were covered in blood but the rest of him was not. Bob looked at himself now. His hands and arms were covered with Frank's blood and his grey back shirt and breeches were also covered. Once again, he found himself standing there, contemplating this sight. He just stared at his hands again.

Eventually, Bluey broke the silence, "Well fuck me! Wasn't expecting that." He paused and then went on as he looked at Bert, "I don't think Will is going to make it. Do you?"

"Noe no' a chance I feel. He's lost too much blood," replied Bert.

Bill broke in, "Sure looked that way from where I was. George will be alright. He's only go' a slight wound, on his upper arm. Should heal oright. How aboot Frank Bob?"

Bob was silent for a minute. The others said nothing, they just waited. Eventually he spoke but quite slowly; particularly measured.

"This is naw meant tae happen. Ye knoe there'll be a chance ye'll be killed or hurt. Ye knoe there is a chance yer mates could get killed or hurt; but naw this. Tae be standing here, covered in yer mates blood an' innards, is naw wha' thus is aboot. It cannae be. It jus' cannae be." He started, in a futile attempt, to try and wipe the blood off his hands. Eventually, realising the back of his breeches, would not have any blood on them, he wiped them vigorously over his backside.

Whilst he was standing there, Captain Woodward came up to them. This time no one really snapped to attention, although they did acknowledge his arrival. Bill made a half attempt to come to attention, but Woody just waved him down. "Don't worry about that lads. This is not the time or place for formalities. Are you boys all right?"

"Naw really, sir," offered Bert. "It was pretty horrible. The dead ones are really the lucky ones here. Will Reddan, will probably noe make it. He's lost an arm an' a leig, an' a lot o' blood. Ye'll have tae ask Bob about the CQMS, but I think the others will be ok."

"Well Bob. What about Frank?" Asked the captain.

It was like he had not been listening to the conversation. Bob did not answer at first. He was just looking at his breeches.

"Bob?" repeated the captain.

"Och, I'm sorry, sir. Um, aye, um Frank. Aye, he's naw too good. I dinnae know if he'll make it or noe. He was pretty bad. His guts were opened. I managed to get a dressing on it, and one on his heid. That one wasnae too bad." Bob tried to answer as best he could but could not really concentrate.

"Thank you for what you've done here tonight. None of you got hit?" the group around the captain had grown quite sizable by now, with all the others who were helping out joining in. "No, sir, we didn't," one of them answered. "Who are the dead, sir?"

"Looks like it's Bodinner, Grehn and Watson," replied the captain.

"I tek it there were others injured?" Asked Bert, "We had Tiley, Reddan, Mortimer, Davies and Comer in this tent."

"Yes, over the way were Sargent, Deakin and Wherry, hit by flying debris. They will all be ok. This whole thing is bit bloody though eh?" The captain remarked.

"Aye, sir, it is that," answered Bert.

"Bob, can I see you for a moment please?" said the captain as he walked away a short distance. Bob joined him, and the captain continued. "You know what this means don't you? You will now be temporary CQMS, until we know how Frank is going to be, but if he is as bad as you say, you will get permanency as soon as we are notified of his fate."

"Aye, sir. I guess so." Bob answered. He went on, "The men's uniforms, sir. Have I yer permission tae issue replacements for the ones soaked in blood tonight?"

"Of course, Bob. I'll get Lt Nye to bring me the list to authorise, if you'll make it up for him."

"Thank ye, sir. I'll dae that." Bob replied.

"Are you OK to carry on?" the captain asked.

"Aye, sir. We've noe really much choice, have we? There'll be plenty o' time for recovery, once we have these sods beaten," Bob answered in a determined manner. He was starting to feel angry now. Angry that these Germans had killed and injured, so many of his friends.

"Not really Bob," the captain agreed. "But it won't be long now. We've got the buggers well and truly on the run. I recon this stunt on the weekend, will see the end of them. I don't think they're going to be able to run fast enough. We just need to be really prepared. Are we?"

"Aye, sir. As far as we can be. We're still…." Bob paused, then restarted, "I'm, still waitin' on the delivery o' the large girders. I'm told they'll all being delivered to La Valee-Mulatre Thursday, sir."

Woody smiled to himself. He still loved the way the Scots so eloquently rolled their Rs. Gurrrrders. "And that's everything then, is it?"

"Aye, sir it is," answered Bob.

"Good-oh then. I still haven't been told what the job is yet, but from the list of supplies, it has to a bridge. I just don't yet, know where. I think you and the others had betterer go and get yourselves cleaned up. I'll get the lieutenant to organise a detail, to clear away all the mess, as soon as the bodies have been removed. You fellas have done enough for one day. Go and take it easy." Capt. Woodward was known by the men as a real bloke. A compassionate man; a man no different to themselves. He was a captain, due to his engineering knowledge and experience, but he was still, a good bloke.

"Thank ye, sir, I will," Bob replied, and the captain turned on his heels and left them to themselves.

Before he went and cleaned up, Bob went and checked the QM store, just to make sure there was no damage there. The tent had gained a few holes and a few of the stacks had been knocked over but apart from that, everything was fine. There were no facilities in camp, for a bath, just a washhouse. So, he cleaned himself up as best he could, removed his breeches and shirt and headed back for the supplies tent. The others had done the same and were waiting for him by now. He saw to his own uniform, so that he was not just wearing his long johns and then dealt out the replacements for the men. He kept a list of everything he handed out, to pass on to the lieutenant. By the time he made it back to his own tent, his mates had cleaned the place up again they had even managed to tack a patch, over one of the holes and were working on another. It was yet another cold and bleak night, and few in the tent got much sleep.

The next morning the section paraded in full uniform and marched the mile and a half (2.4 Km), to the Busigny cemetery. They marched with pride and determination. These damned Huns were not going to get them down. In a separate plot, alongside the Busigny cemetery, on the north western outskirts of town, they interred the three men who had died instantly the previous night:

6102 Spr Bodinner, Charles Edward. 21 yo

3302 Spr Grehn, Charles. 37 yo

8217 Spr Watson, William. 19 yo

After the service, they were all marched back to camp. While they were away, the extra men from No 1 Section had finished the clean-up of the previous night's bombing. The debris was cleared away, the crater filled, and the tents repaired. The men of No 4 Section were grateful for them for doing all that. It was bad enough having to attend a funeral for their friends, but the thought of coming back and having to clear up that lot was just too much.

In the afternoon, Captain Woodward came down to see the boys again. He let them know that after the funeral this morning, he took a ride over to the 48th CCS, to check in on the wounded from yesterday.

"I thought you'd like to know that the injured boys from yesterday, are all doing good. They asked me to tell you, thank you for all you did for them. They were all in pretty high spirits actually."

"What, even Reddan, sir?" asked Bluey.

"Yes lads, even Reddan. In fact, he was in pretty high spirits considering, he was someone who had lost an arm and a leg," replied the captain.

"Wha' aboot Frank, sir?" Bob Asked.

"Frank wasn't there Bob. I was worried at first, of course, but they told me, he has been moved on to the Base Hospital. He will live alright, but he won't be back. So, Bob, that's it. You're the new CQMS for the section. Congratulations," he said, and the captain held out his hand to shake Bob's.

"Thank ye, sir. But I didnae wan' it this way," Bob answered.

"I know Bob but that's war, isn't it?" The captain understood.

"Aye, sir. It is. An' the sooner it's noe, the better for all," Bob sighed.

"We'll keep you posted with any further information we get. OK, we'll see you later boys," and the captain continued on his way.

The following afternoon, they all received news from the 48th CCS that Will Reddan passed away that morning. Later that afternoon, the party of men from the No 4 Section repeated the process of the previous morning, the funeral procession down to the Busigny cemetery, where they laid to rest, 8193 Spr Reddan, William, 43 yo, alongside his mates, who were lain there yesterday.

Chapter 27
The End

Friday morning Capt. Woodward called the crew together to explain what they would be doing in the next few days. Rather than address them on parade, he called the men together in a group.

"Right-oh fellas, I've just got the details of why we are here. We have no date yet, but it will be very soon. The CRE 1st Division, has given us a rather important job to do. It's a tough one, make no mistake, but in a way, it is a real honour that we have been chosen to complete this job. To our east, is the Sambre-Ouise canal. We are going to build a tank bridge, across the canal, at the No 1 lock, outside Rejet-de-Beaulieu. Now that sounds easy enough, except that, the opposite side of the canal, is occupied territory apparently." There was an audible groan from the group.

He continued, "Yes, it is going to be dangerous, but if we can get this stunt done, in good time, it will allow us to push the Bosch, all the way back to Germany. I have the plans for the bridge now, and it is probably the most important construction job we've done so far. We had been given a list of items we will need and your CQMSs have been compiling those stores. Those items we don't have here, are being delivered to La Vallee-Mulatre as we speak. We will all move up there shortly before the stunt. I will let you know, as soon as I know. Carpenters, I need you to be on standby, to move at a moment's notice. You and I will go forward first, to prepare the timber for placement."

"Whilst you are doing that, the rest of the section, will pack up the camp and move up to La Valee-Mulatre. We will only be there, long enough to make camp and then we will move forward, under cover of darkness, to a predetermined point, 250 yards from the canal. Silence in this manoeuvre, we'll be of the utmost importance. The CQMS will be responsible for getting all our equipment on the site, in the correct order, at the correct time. The British 1st division will be responsible for keeping up withering fire on the enemy, so that we can get the bridge built. We believe, the Germans occupy the lock buildings, on the other side of the canal. They will have to be subdued before we can even start, as those buildings look down on to the lock, we will be working on."

"I don't have to tell you how important it is to clear those buildings first. Members of the first division will be responsible for crossing the canal, initially by the lock gates and driving the enemy out of those buildings. Those of you not immediately involved in the bridge building will join those brits of the first division, in eliminating the enemy. You will be crossing the lock, but you will be providing covering fire from our side of the lock. So, make sure your weapons are well serviced ahead of time and ready for action. Squad commanders will have all the details of the construction soon, and will assign each of you, your tasks. At this moment in time, we only know the basics of the bridge but not the specifics. I will hand over to them now to brief each section individually. So, you will see your lieutenants around behind you, head to them and listen closely. Thanks, off you go."

The men split into their squads and got all the information that they needed. As soon as they had finished these meetings they were directed back to the tents, to make sure they had everything they needed ready to go. For many of them that meant checking their rifles and making sure they were clean and ready to go, although nearly all of them were sure they were ready anyway, but just to be sure, they got cleaned and oiled again.

It was not until late on Saturday, when Captain Woodward returned from a meeting with the CRE that the specific details were known. Zero hour for this bridge building stunt, was to be 0545 hrs, Monday morning, 4th November. He was assured the girders for the bridge would be delivered to La Vallee-Mulatre, first thing tomorrow morning. At 0700 hrs the following morning, a boxcar turned up at the camp, with four HQ carpenters on board. Captain Woodward joined them, and they headed off for La Valee-Mulatre, to do the pre-work on the timber girders. For this job, they used HQ carpenters, as they had been trained specifically, to prepare the timber for this kind of job. Once he was satisfied that they had everything they needed there, he headed back to camp via the CRE at Vaux Andigny, about halfway back to camp.

An hour and a half after his return to camp, three lorries and five GS wagons arrived the camp. At midday, Lieutenants Sawyer and Thomson and ninety men, rations and supplies were loaded on to these eight vehicles and transported the five and a half miles (8.6km) to La Vallee-Mulatre. There, they picked up the girders and decking at 1600 hrs. With all their equipment on the lorries and GS wagons, the men then marched the four and a half miles (7.5 km), to Rejet de Beaulieu, arriving there by dark.

The men were starting to think that Fritz must know what was going on, as the last part of their march was completed, under fairly heavy bombardment by the Hun artillery. They could only take the wagons so far, without alerting the enemy to their presence, so they parked the wagons at a crossroad just north of Rejet de Beaulieu. The men quietly unloaded all materials, including the girders and carried it all to their assembly point, 200 m north. Here they met up with their compatriots from 23rd company RE of the BEF and the British infantry. They were all milling around, nervously waiting for the order to move forward. It would be a little while yet, however. The captain came over to check that everything was ready. "Aye, sir. Everything is ready as ordered. Ba naw, everyone should know their jobs an' wha' is expected o' them," Bob replied.

"Good. By the way Bob, do you know that English poet, Wilfred Owen?" the captain asked.

Bob thought this was a rather strange question to be asking right in the middle of a major action.

"Er, aye a dae, sir," Bob answered. "That's a strange question tae be askin' noo though."

"True, but he's here, you know. He's one of the English Lieutenants over there. He's with the 2nd Manchesters, and it's their job to get across the canal, to allow us to get the bridge built."

"Well, I'll be," said Bob. "Imagine that, us here wi' probably the greatest war poet ever. I didnae think he was on active service any moor."

"Apparently, he went back to active about six months ago, so I hear," said the captain.

"Dafty beggar!" Bob exclaimed. "He shouldae stayed oot o' it all if he had the chance tae. He'd better make it through this stunt noo."

The captain continued his rounds of the men to check everything was alright.

At 2230 hrs, they once again loaded up their gear and moved forward about 350 m and settled down to await zero hour. At this point, they were now only 250 m from the lock, being shielded by the patch of trees at the lock and a small ridge between the lock and their position. Here, they dug in for a wild night. Once again, it was cold and wet night out in the open with constant heavy shelling all night. The worst barrage the men had to endure, was between 0200 and 0430. This was by far the worst barrage they had ever experienced, worse than Hill 60, worse than Hooge.

Astonishingly, they survived this barrage with no injuries. In the hour before zero hour, the enemy got a return pasting by the British artillery and heavy machine gun fire. At 0545, all hell broke loose, with rifle fire, machine guns, grenades and artillery. The men wondered how anybody could survive this onslaught, but survive, they did. At zero hour plus fifteen, Sergeant Hutchinson went forward to observe the bridge site and report back. It still was not safe to move forward. It took three attempts by the infantry to cross the canal successfully. Once some of them were across, engineers of the 409th company RE, rushed forward with lightweight personnel bridges and got the remainder of the men, across the canal. Yet others crossed the canal by swimming with life vests below and above the lock.

Ultimately, they were successful in driving the Hun out of the lock buildings and taking possession of them, themselves. It would still be while until they were ready to move forward. Capt. Woodward looked at the position the men were bunkered down in, and figured that the Boche artillery, would be aware of this depression they were hiding in and would eventually target it. He made the decision to move the section across the canal and shelter in the assortment of shell holes there. This decision, whilst not popular with either his men or his superiors, proved extremely wise. When the action was over, they found countless members of the BEF dead in that depression from artillery fire. His decision had saved potentially many lives.

After another hour or so, the signal came back to No 4 Section, to go.

"Right lads, get this gear loaded up, an' move forward. Girders off ye goe first," Bob ordered.

The men jumped to their feet and together, carried the 800 lb (364 kg) girders five on each side. By now they were prepared and practiced in the technique and it went smoothly. It was 0730 now, and there was an orderly stream of men and materials headed for the lock. Along the banks of the lock, was a culvert, so Bob got the men with the later equipment, to shelter in that culvert, until they were needed. At least there, they were safe from enemy machine guns, although the artillery continued to rain down. The culvert did give them some cover from the artillery though.

At 0800, the task of building the bridge commenced, even though in that position, at that time, they were under fire. Every now and then, Bob dashed forward, to check on the progress and to see if the next stage was required. Once the two main girders were across, it was a lot easier for the men to move backwards and forwards and build the remainder of the bridge. Each time one stage was finished, Bob would order the next to move forward and to get the men to stay, only as long as required at the bridging site and, if not required there, to return to the culvert and to provide covering rifle fire wherever they could. By 1000 hrs it was clear that the enemy had been pushed significantly back from the lock, so they moved forward to assist in the final phase of the bridge making. The last of the decking was being fixed and the approach ramps were being completed.

As Bob crested the lock, he was able to look around. The sight that greeted him was horrible. There were dead bodies floating in the water on the downside of the lock, whilst on the topside, where they were working, many bodies had been retrieved from the lock and were lying on the banks. On the east side of a lock the scene was repeated, except that this time, with two different uniforms, the khaki of the British and the grey of the German. The lock buildings were in extremely poor shape by now.

At about this time, Bob could see small groups of men in grey uniforms, with their hands above or on their heads being marched back towards the bridge. They were being escorted by one or two British soldiers, who marshalled them on the east side before marching them across the personnel bridges. The men of No 4 Section made to cover these POWs with their rifles and marshalled them on the west side until their British guards made it across. "Thanks, matey." came the call from the Brit.

"She's all right Cobber, Do the same for a white man's dog," came the reply from the Aussie. Bob supposed it would take the Englishman, a while to process that one. By then he would be far away.

The bridge work was completed by 1015 hrs and Capt. Woodward signalled back that it was safe for the tanks to advance. The first tank crossed the bridge at 1030. The Hun was now, well and truly, on the run. Despite the fact that it took the infantry, three attempts to cross the canal, to open the action, all infantry objectives for this stunt, were achieved by 0930 hrs and over 2000 POWs were taken.

By 1100 hrs, the captain, two lieutenants and eighty five ORs, made their way back to their temporary camp at Rejet de Beaulieu, collected their gear and marched proudly back to their lorries at Mazinghien, some two miles (3.2 km), from the lock. They had left five of their mates behind, dead. Five others had been taken to the CCS, with serious wounds. This had been one of their worst days for casualties, although the men did not really see it that way. They were surprised that the casualty list was so small, given the nature of the task, and the amount of fire they had been under. A long list, of honours and awards that would come out of today's action, for 1 ATC. The wet, tired and relieved men, arrived back at camp at 1700 hrs. They unloaded their gear from the lorries, casually walked back to the tents and crashed. Nothing was expected of these heroes tonight.

In fact, nothing was expected of these men for the next few days. There is no doubt that this had been a torrid few days for them and they had done such an exemplary job that they were given the next five days, to rest and recover. They certainly needed it. The roads on either side of the canal crossing, were built through marshy land and were unable to cope with the weight of equipment passing over them. No 1 Section was detailed for the next few days, to rebuild and shore up the road. The road they built is still in use today. Sections 2 and 3 spent these days on mine detection and neutralising. By the 10th, No 3 Section was called forward for road repair work by the village of Sain du Nord which is fifteen miles (26 km) east of the canal.

Of the five who never came home from this action, only four can be identified. The fifth remains unknown. Both the company records and Capt. Woodward's diary record five deaths in the action but only four can be found in the nominal roll:

8271 Spr Barrett, Charles. 40 yo

5518 Cpl Davey, Albert. 31 yo

7680 Spr Johnson, Arthur Robert Dudley. 43 yo

8279 Spr Knight, Frederick Nelson. 40 yo

Corporal Davey had spoken with Capt. Woodward only the day before, asking him to please take care of his personal effects and see that his wife gets them if he was killed the next day. Capt. Woodward spoke to him, telling him that they all stood a chance of that happening and that he was no worse off than anyone else. Cpl Davey insisted he was going to die, and said to Woody, "Captain, nothing you can say will remove the conviction that I will be killed.

Will you please do me the favour I ask?" Just to stop him making a scene, the captain agreed he would do that. This situation affected Capt. Woodward significantly, as Davey's premonition came to pass in the pre-dawn of that morning.

The following letter was received by the CO of 1ATC, two days after the bridging of the Sambre canal. It was a letter from the commander of the 1st Division BEF, to all units under his command that took part in what became known as "the forcing of the Sambre-Ouise canal." Whilst 1ATC is not a British unit, it was attached to, the first division BEF, for this action.

The task that the division was called on to perform yesterday, was one entailing the utmost forethought for every detail, the most careful and precise staff work in all branches, a thorough and precise organisation in Battalions, of the most minute detail and gallantry, tact and endurance on the part of all troops engaged.

The complete success of the operations is very greatly due to the skill, ability, rapidity and completeness with which the bridging arrangements were completed and perfected. I wish to pay special tribute to Lt Col C.E.P. Sankey D.S.O. His field company commanders and all ranks of the R E's, and section first Australian Tunnelling Company A.E. for the parts they have played in these operations. The cool gallantry with which they placed the bridge in position under heavy fire after long and arduous hours of labour, was magnificent. After their severe ordeal they were engaged for the rest of the day in bridge building under fire, without which the operations would not have been completed.

They have very worthily upheld the very high and traditions of the Royal Engineers.

I cannot sufficiently express my admiration and thanks to all branches of the staff and to all units in the division for their unsurpassed efforts of the last three weeks culminating in as fine a military achievement as any troops could have carried out.

The division on a whole has every reason to be more than proud of their record and they could not have done more than uphold as they have done the brilliant record of the 1st Division of the British army.

5-11-18   *Sgd E. P. STRICKLAND*
Major General Commanding 1st Division
And this from Lt Col Sankey
To C. O.

1st Australian Tunnelling Company

I want to bring to your notice the great gallantry and devotion to duty displayed by Captain O.H. Woodward, M.C. and bar, of your company, who was attached with his section to the engineers of this Division for the operations of yesterday. He had very little time for the preparation of his material, but in spite of this everything was complete, and his organisation and arrangement of work were so good that a bridge capable of carrying tanks was erected within 4 ½ hours after zero. The work was rendered very difficult by the very heavy enemy barrage, which I regret to say caused very heavy casualties. I am informed by one of my field company commanders, who was present at the site, that Captain Woodward carried out his detailed reconnaissance of the lock with complete disregard of personal danger, and superintended the erection of the bridge with great gallantry. He also came to the assistance of my Field Company when they were reduced by casualties and helped them complete their work.

(signed) C.E. Sankey, Col R.E
C.R.E 1st Division

(Nb. Again this is reprinted exactly as the letter was received by the company. Punctuation was not, apparently, considered important.)

Back in the camp at Busigny, through the 9th and 10th of November, everyone, officers and ORs, were elated at the news they were hearing that Germany wanted to sue for peace. Finally, it looked like this war, to end all wars, as they were now calling it, the was all but over. It had not come a moment too soon. Sitting back in their tent, the men were talking about what this meant, for them. The talk had gone round and round, reminiscing, reliving and questioning.

Bob spoke up, "But jus' wha' has it achieved? Wha' has it solved? Wha' was it all aboot in the furst place? Dae they even remember wha' it was aboot in the beginnin'? This has bin a worldwide war. There are millions o' dead. There are even many thousands o' dead people, who were naw even involved. Wha' aboot the civilians in all these towns we've seen. Wha' did they dae tae deserved this treatment? Were they jus' in the way? Were they jus' incidental damage, therefore they dinnae matter? I jus' dinnae get it. We've bin lucky all o' us. We came through unhurt. Wha' have we lost? Maybe a hundred men? For Wha'? For wha'?"

"Aye Bob, we ken tha' too. But wha' was the alternative? Jus' leave 'em tae it? Let em tek it all?" Bill wasn't sure what else to say.

"Noe Bill I dinnae mean why did we come. I ken that. Ye cannae let these bastards jus' walk in. They had to be stopped." The men all drew breath. They had never heard Bob swear before. He went on, "I mean, why the hell did it happen in the furst place? What were they hopin' to achieve?"

"Well, I jus' think the Boche suffered from a superiority complex," Bert commented. "They had bin wantin' a stoush for some years. Then that clown went and assassinated the Archduke Ferdinand, an' tha' gave 'em the excuse. The Austrians were in the Germans' pocket, an' they pulled all the Austrian strings, so they made the terms after the assassination, absolutely impossible. The poor old Serbs were on a hiding to nothing. They'd bin forced into a lose-lose situation. Then all these who's in who's pocket pacts, meant that everyone had tae jump tae everyone's defence. Like I've said before, everyone was just boiling for an excuse for a fight. Well, they got it, an' they copped a wallopin'." He gave a giggle. "See I have learned some Australian. I like that word, it's so descriptive." They all gave a giggle, even Bob. He was clearly upset by the whole mess though, and the boys knew it.

"Cheer up Bob," called Bluey, "It'll all be the bloody same in a hundred years. Besides, we ended up on top. That's what's important right now. And what's more, we finished on a bloody good note, didn't we? I mean, we done a good job on that last stunt. We sure as hell showed them pommies how to do it, anyway, don't you reckon?"

"Aye Bluey we did. I recon tha' was the best bit ye know," Bill added. "Anyone, who can show the poms they're naw the top dog, is worth their weight in gold. If there's anyone wi' more o' a superiority complex than the Germans, it would have tae be the Sassenachs."

There was general agreement around the tent on that comment.

The only entry in the unit diary for the 11th of November 1918 was: *Fine and cold. Lt Bates and Irving on leave to England. Armistice signed with Germany 11.00 hrs.*

And so it was, that, at 11:00 AM, on the 11th day, of the 11th month, of 1918, and not a moment before, the guns did indeed, fall silent, despite the fact that the armistice was actually signed, at 4:30 AM, but was to come into effect, at 11: 00AM.

In the second week of November 1ATC was seconded to the British Ninth Army, to whom they remained attached, for the rest of the month. They spent their time checking roads, bridges railways and buildings for mines. They were finding a mixture of electrical and delayed action mines. These had to be defused and removed and often the holes filled in. Some of these holes could be huge, up to 25' deep in some cases. During the rest of November, they moved almost daily covering a huge amount of both France and Belgium. Places like, Avesnelles, Hestrud, Thuilles, Wallcourt, Yves Gomez, Namur, Corenne, Rostene on the Meuse river, Charleroi and Marbaix. Often on these days, they would be out in front of the British infantry, checking for mines as they went. The infantry was not to travel on any road, unless they had been cleared first. They certainly had a ''Cooke's Tour' of north east France and south Belgium, in this time, even having time for a half day sightseeing trip around Charleroi. The work, however, was no sightseeing tour. Once they were at Marchiene au Pont, in Charleroi, they remained for a week, moving out daily to inspect and de-mine the area. As an example of just how dangerous this work was, below is a list of ordinances removed in a one-week period at the beginning of December:

610	6" (152mm)	Shells
64	8" (203mm)	Shells
69	12" (304mm)	Shells
14	9" (229mm)	Shells
27	77mm (3.1")	Shells
9	others	
81	Slabs Perdite (an explosive pre cordite)	

These former artillery shells usually had either an electrically detonated fuse, an acid / Metal, corrosive fuse, or some other kind of delayed action fuse. No one knew when they were meant to go off, or even whether they were meant to go off. It was hazardous work, but the men of 1 ATC managed it without any casualties.

The mail from Australia, took many weeks to come through. Bob knew this but still, was becoming impatient, waiting for reply from Jean to his proposal by mail. It was mid-November, when Bob finally received a letter from Jean answering his question in the affirmative. She wrote, "Of course, I accept your proposal of marriage. I'll be happy to be your wife, Mother and Father are delighted too. They put a notice in the Daily news on 18th September announcing it. I have enclosed a clipping for you to see."

Bob immediately rushed back to the tent. As he burst in, he said, "Bert, Bill, she said yes. I'm going to marry her when we get home."

"Congratulations Bob," each of them said, as they jumped to their feet and came over and grasped him firmly by the hand and shook it.

"Well, ye've got tae make it home now don't ye Bob?" said Bert.

"Aye laddie I dae," he replied. There was much merriment in the tent that day.

The moving around commenced again in the second week of December, with the checking of the Charleroi-Brussels railway line. The Belgian railway authority gave 1ATC an engine, carriage and two trucks for the duration to assist them with the checking. In the second week, No 4 Section were given the responsibility of checking the Nivelles section of the railway line. This took some time, as there was plenty of evidence of mining the rail lines, and even a complete section of the lines being removed. As an indicator, of how fast the German retreat must have been, whilst there was evidence of mining, not a single hole, had been filled with shells or explosives, even though they were stacked up, in the carts, alongside the lines awaiting use. They had not had time to actually lay the shells or set the fuses. This made the job safer, but not a great deal quicker. Every hole had to be treated as suspect until proven otherwise, and every hole had to be filled in.

Up until this time, November and the first ten days of December were bitterly cold, often wet and the sky was never seen. Once they were at Nivelles the weather started to warm up, to at least the mild setting. By now the men were sick of the cold and welcomed the warmer days. It also made working on the job much more pleasant. It helped that the men and the officers, were now billeted in the one place on the rue de Charleroi, in Nivelles. It was a most comfortable billet, one of the best they had had since been in Europe. One small party of men, from 4 Section, had to make a trip over to Stavelot, near the German border, to inspect a rail tunnel that a local official had reported as possibly mined.

A worker had noticed there were wires protruding from some concrete work. They took three days to travel over and back, only to find that whilst there were indeed wires in the concrete, when they were pulled the whole section of a concrete patch, fell out. They had been put in there years before, as part of a repair job on the tunnel.

Unfortunately for poor Bill, on the 1st of December while stacking the GS wagon, he managed to be in the wrong place, at the wrong time, when the load dislodged and he caught his hand, breaking his right index finger. He was sent off to the 53rd CCS for treatment but after assessment, they moved him on to London for treatment and recuperation. Once he was declared fit, he was retained in London and returned to Australia on the SS Lancashire, departing London on 7 February 1919 and arriving home 24 March 1919. He never got the chance to say goodbye to his mates before he left.

It was around this time that Maj. Anderson MC MID, CO of 1 ATC received the following letter from General Sir W.R. Birdwood. Birdwood had formerly been commander of all Australian troops at Gallipoli and of I ANZAC Corps early on the western front and from 1917 Commander of the British 5th army.

My Dear Anderson,

I write a line to congratulate you very heartily upon the distinction conferred on you and on our Australian Tunnelling companies in the terms of the commander in chief's special order of the day of the 4th December.

I so fully realise how well do you have deserved this honour, and none have done better work than an our tunnellers. It has always been a source of regret to me that it is more or less the fate of all the Tunnelling companies in France not to receive perhaps all the recognition they had deserved.

Working, however, on every front as they do, often makes it extremely difficult for their work to be fully appreciated – a fate, too, which I always think applies to scattered units like railway companies, etc. Being scattered, too, as you are, it is a great sorrow too me not to have seen as much of you as I should personally have wished to, and I am glad to have this opportunity now of writing to wish you a happy Christmas, and may many a happy and prosperous New Year be before you all on your return to Australia.

Yours sincerely
(Sgd) W.R. Birdwood.

In the lead up to Christmas 1918, once the pressure of the mine detecting was off, there was time for football matches and filling in of demob forms. A team was selected from the men of 1ATC to play Association Football (Soccer) against a Belgian team. The game ended in a fitting 2-2 draw. The barmy weather of the last two weeks was about to end though, with a vengeance. Christmas eve it snowed, and the men had a white Christmas. This was, of course, for most of the Australian born men, a first and a fitting reward for their efforts. Christmas dinner consisted of Duck and Christmas pudding. The men were ecstatic. Real food. Not out of a can food, and not only that but, there was enough for everyone to have seconds. Sheer luxury. That afternoon there was another football match against the Belgians which 1 ATC won seven – nil. The next couple of days were around zero degrees (32° F) and the year came to a close with more form filling in, and a move to the town of Liberchies, between Charleroi and Brussels.

The first two weeks of January were split, between checking the last of roads and rail for mines and sending some of the men off on courses, for retraining, in preparation for return to civilian life. The good part of the mine checking, was that for a nice change, none were found, just preparations. Mid-January saw each of the four sections, begin to relocate to Chatelet. The first draught of men, to return to Australia, occurred at this time too. It was only a small draft of four men, but it was the beginning of the breakup of the company. There were more soccer matches and rugby as well but the highlight of the month, was the ball, given by the company to the people of the town. The ball was held in a hall in the town and a great deal of effort went into this ball, to say thank you to the people of the area, for the hospitality and kindness towards our men. The ball was a resounding success, with so many people in attendance that it was almost impossible to get a spot on the dance floor, let alone dance around on the floor.

The day after the ball, saw medal presentations by Lt Gen. Orth, of the Belgian mission GHQ. He made two presentations of the Belgian Croix de Guerre, to S/Sgt Hutchinson, and to Sgt Curran.

On the 28th of January, company HQ also relocates to Chatelet and the company, is finally together again. Two more football matches are played, the first being a rugby match against the 9th battalion, which the 1ATC boys lose 9-0. The second is a soccer match where a combined 1 and 3 Section battled against combined 2 and 4 Section. The game was played on frozen ground, as the temperature, had been consistently below zero, for most of this month. The former won that match 3-2. The purpose of this match was to select a team to play the 11th battalion in the coming days. Two further draughts of men, of twenty nine and eighteen are marched out for return to Australia in the last two days of January.

At this point, company records cease. There is no record who won the match between the 11th battalion and 1 ATC but knowing both groups well, I hope the match ended in a fitting draw. Both groups, gave so much to the success of the campaign on the western front, with the 11th having already contributed from day one at Gallipoli, 25th April 1915.

1 ATC records finish with the following summary:

KIA	5 officers	
	94 ORs	
WIA	11 officers	1 DOW
	278 ORs	11 DOW
POW	5 ORs	
Honours and awards	21 Officers	
	43 ORs	

359 Members of the 3 Australian Tunnelling Cos and AEMM&BC lost their lives.

1   Died of burns
2   Drowned
6   Died whilst POWs
6   Died whilst at sea
7   Accidentally killed in train or motor vehicle accidents
72 Died of disease or illness
89 DOW
176 KIA

Some were never recovered and lie in Flanders Fields.

In Flanders Fields

In Flanders fields the poppies blow
Between the crosses, row on row,
That mark our place: and in the sky
The larks still bravely singing fly
Scarce heard amid the guns below.
We are the dead: Short days ago,
We lived, felt dawn, saw sunset glow,
Loved and were loved: and now we lie
In Flanders fields!
Take up our quarrel with the foe
To you, from failing hands, we throw
The torch: be yours to hold it high
If ye break faith with us who die,
We shall not sleep, though poppies grow
In Flanders fields.

Lieutenant Colonel John McCrae 3 May 1915 Ypres
KIA 28 January 1918

Part 4

Chapter 28
Home at Last

The last days of January witnessed the last of the search for mines and booby traps. The company had been highly successful finding and defusing these. It needs to be remembered there was no technology, such as metal detectors, available in 1919. It had been discovered that the needle of a compass, would deviate to one side or the other, when it came close to magnetic metal, such as steel used in artillery shell projectiles. This magnetic property had been adapted for use in assisting with the discovery of buried mines but had to be really close to the mine and was unable to be used along railway lines due to the metal rails.

Now, the focus of the tunnelling companies moved to reconstruction. It was important for the Belgians, to get their transport infrastructure back up and running. Engineering companies (which the tunnellers were now classed as) from all allied nations, worked tirelessly on roadbuilding, railway reconstruction, water reconnection, bridge building and any other transport or infrastructure related projects they were asked to do. They left the building reconstruction to the Belgians. This work would continue for most of the year.

The infantry, being there solely as fighting soldiers, were the first to be repatriated to their home countries. They all arrived home to tumultuous welcomes and parades. These were our conquering heroes and deserved the accolades of the community. The engineers, being the builders in the army, were tasked with remaining behind to assist wherever they were required. Only those members of the engineering companies that were needed back home were released in the early months. As time went on, more men from the engineering corps, were marched out to England, for return to Australia, if they would no longer needed in France and Belgium.

Bob and Bert were both marched out to England, on 23rd April 1919. They would spend roughly three weeks in England, completing their demobilisation preparations. In that time, Bob naturally wrote to Jean, to say that he was on his way home. He indicated to her that he would be landing in Sydney but would immediately get the train for Perth, to ask Robert for Jean's hand in marriage, if she still so desired. He would get the answer when he arrived, as there would not be time to receive a reply before he left Sydney.

On 12 May 1919, Bob and Bert boarded the SS SAUDAN, for the return trip to Australia. At least this time on the high seas, they did not have to worry about enemy submarines, so it was more like a cruise, even though it was a little on the cramped side. They arrived in Sydney, Australia, on 29th June 1919. There were no parades this time though. The world was wanting to move on from war now, they had had enough of it and returning troops were now old news.

Bob did not waste any time in Sydney. As Bert lived in Perth Western Australia, he was due to train straight back to Perth from Sydney, so Bob took the opportunity to accompany him, on that rail journey across the country. As soon as all the demobbing formalities were completed in Sydney, the two men booked their passage to Perth. The Trans Australian line had only been completed three years before this, so it was a new thing to be able to travel all the way across Australia by train. Prior to its completion, the only real way from Sydney to Perth was by ship, as the men of 1ATC had done in 1916. The train journey of nearly four days would cut three days off the journey from Perth to Melbourne and four off the trip to Sydney.

This trip would give them four days of relaxation before arriving in Perth but there would be three changes of train, as the different states used different gauge railways. The first leg was from Sydney, New South Wales to Port Augusta, South Australia and was around 800 miles (1300 km). stage two was across the Nullarbor Plain to Kalgoorlie, Western Australia, where many of his fellow 1ATC tunnellers came from, and that was around 1130 miles (1854 km). The final stage form Kalgoorlie to Perth was the shortest at about 375 miles (600 km).

The two had ample time to discuss the last three years whilst confined to the train for the four days. Many other people chatted to them about the war as well, but they were unable to convey to them, the sheer horror of what they had seen, and done. In their debrief in England before leaving for home, they were given the instruction to "go home and forget about it all. Don't discuss it with people who were not there." The utter stupidity of that statement echoes down through the years. How could anyone who had seen what they saw, forget it? The truly sad thing about this attitude is that it still exists today.

When Bob and Bert were alone, they could talk freely about their experiences, and they did.

"I dinnae ken how I'm goin' tae tell 'em all aboot all tha' we've bin through," Bob would say.

"Aye Bob," Bert answered. "I knoe we're naw supposed to talk aboot it but they're gonnae ask. Wha' tha blue blazes are we gonnae say tae that?"

"I'ma bit scared fo' ma Jean, because I dinnae sleep at all well these days. Wha's she gonnae say?" Bob was genuinely apprehensive.

"Aye I've noticed tha' Bob. Ye're no orphan there ma friend, no orphan indeed. Most o' tha fellas tha' were in our tent, are in tha' same boat. We've seen so much stuff that noe human should have tae see ever, an' we're suppose tae forget it? Nice o' them to say that, but ye think they could mebee give us a hint, on jus' how tae dae that." Bert was usually a rather mild mannered and quiet person, but he was frustrated and just did not understand how to accomplish this direction.

"Ye cannae jus' tell 'em nout. Ye gottae tell 'em somethin'. Doesnae feel right, tae noe tell 'em; but it doesnae seem right tae frighten 'em with the whole truth either. They probably wouldnae believe half o' it if we tol' 'em anyway. I'm not sure if I believe it masel'. I dinnae Ken wha' tae dae." Bob was beginning to get quite agitated by now. Bert was by now, used to seeing Bob work himself into a panic and knew that now, was the time to change the subject, to try and draw his mind off, the things he had seen. He knew that he was having enough trouble himself, coming to terms with what they had been through, but he also knew that Bob had seen one or two more things than he had. Particularly at Hill 60.

Bob had explained to him in detail, what he had seen, in the aftermath of that explosion. Bert was really grateful that he had not been asked to reconnoitre the hill afterwards. He was not sure, how he would have been unable to handle it. He managed to divert Bob's attention, to the scene passing them by, as the train rolled on. Neither man had experienced the vastness of Central Australia prior to this trip. Whilst there was no doubt that this area was barren, it still had a certain beauty about it that was hard to explain to anybody else. Especially, someone like their relatives, remaining in Scotland, who they were sure, would not understand what they were seeing, just as much as, they would not understand what they had seen in Europe.

"This part o' the country, isnae fit for man nor beast tae look at it. But survive they dae. I guess tha's why Australia's animals, are so different tae anywhere else in tha world. They have tae be different, jus' tae survive," Bert said changing tack. "Wha' dae ye think?"

Eventually, Bob answered him. "Aye, they dae. Indeed, they dae." He paused for a moment pondering the dilemma of living in this country and then added, "I wonder where they get their water from? I havenae seen any water at all today." The distracting technique had worked at now Bob's mind was on something different. Bert knew this would not last though. This war had occupied the last three years of their lives twenty four hours a day, seven days a week, fifty two weeks of the year. It was inevitable that their conversation would turn back to those dark days. It did, over and over.

Eventually, the browns and reds of the interior, gave way to yellows and browns and whites, west of Kalgoorlie and they in turn, transformed into the greens of the agricultural areas to the east of Perth. After a short stop in Northam, for water and coal, the train commenced its journey along the Avon River and through the hills of the Darling Scarp, before dropping off the edge of the scarp through the Greenmount National Park. It would not be until 1947 that this park, would be renamed, the John Forrest National Park, after the state's first premier.

Both Bob and Bert remembered the last 15 miles (25 Km) as it went right past Blackboy Hill camp, on through Midland Junction and into Peth Station. The last time they travelled that, was over 3 years ago. They were younger and much more naïve then. There was so much expectation of the adventure of the war, amongst the men then. That feeling, had most certainly been shattered. So much water had passed under each of their bridges since those days. Much of it, they wished they had not experienced. They had made some lifelong friends in these last 3 years, but equally, they had lost friends as well. As the train crossed the bridge over the Swan River in East Perth, the two men commenced their goodbyes. Bob promised Bert that if Jean still wanted to marry him, he would call on Bert to be his best man. Bert agreed, saying it would be an honour to stand beside him on that day.

The train pulled into Perth station, with a whistle and a rush of steam. Both men alighted, shook hands and went their own ways, Bert looking for his family, and Bob looking if any of the Chappell family were there. He was beginning to feel disappointed when he spied Jean over by the station building. She was standing there with a big smile on her face, just watching Bob. He turned and walked towards her and when they met, they gave each other the biggest of embraces. It drew the looks of several of the people on the platform. That was not something you did in public. Neither spoke for some time. Eventually Bob drew her back to arm's length and said, "Och Jeanie, I have so missed ye. I havenae stopped thinkin' 'bout ye, since the day I left. How are ye my dearest lassie?"

"Oh Bob, ye dafty man." Jean laughed. "It is just so good tae see ye again. I've missed ye a lot. I've prayed for ye every dae, tae make sure ye'll come through, and ye have. I'm well, by the wae, and I have tae say, rarely has a day gone by that I havenae though about you too. Ever since that card ye sent with the bit to mother on it, she's been preparing for this dae. I'll noe keep ye waiting. Of course, I'll marry ye. Mother and father knaw wha's happenin' and they are happy aboot ye, ye knaw that."

"Och that's grand lassie. My, ye have changed a lot in three years. I certainly ken I have. Has noe one else come to the station, wi' ye?" Bob asked.

Jean chuckled, "Noe, just me. Jess wanted to come too, but mother found a job for her tae do to keep her at home. Mothers obviously have particularly good instincts and knaw when one person is enough. We'll just get yer luggage and then we can cross the bridge to oor platform and get the next train to West Perth. Come on then."

They collected Bob's bag and headed back towards the bridge, when Bob spied Bert and his family, so they went over. "Hello Jean," said Bert. "How are ye?"

"Hello Bert, I'm well thank ye." Jean replied. "So, yer finally home then eh? Had enough of Belgium?"

"Just a little, I'm afraid." Bert said. "It's a lovely country, but in different circumstances please."

Bob jumped in now, "Bert, she said Aye, laddie."

"Well, congratulations to the both o' ye. Wonderful news. Wonderful," Bert grinned from ear to ear. He turned to his father. "Bob has asked Jean to marry him, and she said yes."

"Och tha's wonderful. Congratulations from us as well. I saw the notice in the daily paper last year," said Bert's father.

"I just hope Robert is oright wi' it anyway," Bob added.

Bert's dad laughed, "Och he'll be alright. A lot more bark than bite wi' that man."

"Aye," said Bob. "But this will be his first daughter tae goe, so I'ma little apprehensive ye knaw."

"Well come on Bob, we've only just got enough time to cross over tae catch oor train home," Jean said.

"There ye goe Bob," Bert added. "She's started on ye already."

"Oh, wheesht ye tongue Bert Carr. Be off wi' ye," Jean hissed at Bert, as she struck out with the back of her hand, a huge smile on her face. Everybody let out a huge laugh, then they all headed for their respective platforms. Bert and family headed east along the same platform, for the Armadale line, while Bob and Jean crossed the bridge for the Fremantle platform.

They made it to the Fremantle train, with just moments to spare. They were only on it for a few minutes when it pulled into the West Perth station. As they stepped off, Bob let out a cry as he spotted the whole Chappell clan standing there and waving madly. They hurried over and Bob shook Robert's hand vigorously, then gave Mimey a big hug too. Jessie and Berta both joined in. Unfortunately, Jack was not able to come to the station, as he was still on service in England. There was much babbling and carrying on, laughing and back slapping.

"Och how good it is tae see ye safe and back home again Bob," Robert was genuinely pleased Bob had returned safely. "And ye are a sergeant noo too, eh?"

"Aye Robert. Is grand to be here, I can say. I'm a CQMS, which is the same as a staff sergeant. It's a new position, they only created last year. Wasnae a grand way tae get the promotion though." Bob said.

"Aye laddie, I understand ye," Robert answered. "War's a horrible thing oright. Have ye heard how the lad is recently?"

"Aye I have," Bob replied. "I was able to check up on him on ma couple o' days in Sydney. Frank has pulled through oright. He still has a lot of recoverin' tae dae, but he is goin' tae mek it."

"Oh, that's wonderful Bob," Mimey spoke up this time. "Anyway, lets noe be standin' aroond here gasbagging, let's get walking. We've got a lovely dinner cooking for this evening. We dinnae want it burning noo do we?"

"And will ye look at ye two, Jessie, and Berta," Bob exclaimed as they took off. "Jess you're a real fine lookin' young woman noo, and Berta yer a young woman noo too. Jus' look. Yer, wha', fifteen noo?"

"Next month," replied Berta with a big smile on her face.

"Och, it's so grand tae see ye all again. I've thought aboot ye all nearly every day, jus' prayin' for the day I could be back here wi' ye all," Bob said.

"Don't worry, we've bin doing the same for ye too, Bob," Jess finally spoke. She had been so excited to see him again, she had been just dumbstruck, until now. "And it looks like our prayers were answered, ye've come through unscathed."

"Not so sure aboot that," Bob said under his breath. He just looked at Robert, who looked back and minutely nodded his head. Even though he had said precious little so far, Robert had already noticed the change in Bob's eyes. He knew a little of that look from the men who came back from the Boer war and the few he had met in the last few months from this war. He would say nothing for the moment, however.

As they walked the short distance back up to Florence St, Bob kept looking around seeing many a familiar sight. He felt like pinching himself, as it all seemed like he was in a distant dream. This did not feel one bit like reality. He had dreamt of this moment, many times and now he was here, it just did not seem real. After the black days of wartime Belgium and France, coming into this, well, paradise. There was no evidence anywhere of the war to end all wars.

Once they arrived at the house Bob was ushered inside and directed towards a seat. Jean sat with him, and the other two girls buzzed around asking all sorts of questions, mostly about the war. Bob did his best, to deflect these questions with vague, generalised answers. Mimey came in shortly with a cup of tea for them all.

"There ye go Bob, a nice hot cuppa tea. I'll recon ye'll be in well need o' that after that great train journey."

"Aye Mimey," he replied. "I havenae had a really good cuppa for the last 5 days."

"My goodness lad," she added. "Ye're tongue'll be draggin' along the groond ba noo."

"Aye, that be the god's truth noo," he said.

"So then Bob, how are ye?" she continued. "We have kept up on what ye've been doing, well as much our newspapers will tell us anyway."

"Well," he started, "well, I imagine, they didnae tell the whole truth aboot it all. They never do. I can say it was terribly, terribly horrid. I lost a few good mates over there. I saw a lot of stuff an' I cannae say much moor that that."

"Aye laddie," Robert offered. "We'll leave it at that for now. This is too good a moment tae spoil with ill news. We've waited a long time for this dae, we're only going tae celebrate it. Tell us aboot the train trip across the middle."

Bob told them everything he could think of, about the train ride across Australia. From the mountains of New South Wales, to the plains of the interior of that state. Even though, this was midwinter, much of the trip from the Flinders ranges, in South Australia, through to the wheat belt of Western Australia, was as dry as the desert areas he saw in Egypt, travelling through the Suez Canal. The Nullarbor Plain was the flattest, most treeless, part of the earth he had ever seen. It was so barren of trees, being covered only by a low scrub, and yet, there was something so innately beautiful about it. The unbelievable contrast, between the red and brown of the ground and the bright, bright, beautiful, blue cloudless sky, made for a unique picture that he would never forget. He said about being in Kalgoorlie and changing trains there. He of course, had heard of Kalgoorlie but never really expected to see the place. It was a hive of activity, but everything was dusty. It truly looked like a typical mining town to him.

He told them of his visits to his sisters in Scotland and of his times in London and of the time he caught up with Jack, in England, not long after Jack arrived. Jack had enlisted in late 1917 with the 11th battalion AIF, as soon as he was old enough to do so. He had completed his training, at Blackboy Hill, the same place that Bob had spent that month, over three years ago. He had sailed to England departing Albany WA on 29th July 1918, with reinforcements for the 11th Battalion, but had arrived in England, on 27th September, too late to see active service. He was sent to France in January 1919, to assist with the reconstruction efforts and was attached to the 30th Engineers. He would leave England, on 1st August and arrive home on 2nd September.

The whole time Bob was talking, Jean just sat next to him, quietly, hanging on every word he spoke. It was only natural that she had questions, about her decision, to accept Bob's proposal. She had only had three weeks with him, over three years ago, and then, only on occasional days. She had had three years of letter writing, between the two of them; but was that enough, on which to make a major life decision? Sitting, as she was, listening to his every word, she now had the answer to the question she had been asking herself, over and over, this past three years. She knew, this was the man for her.

They continued to talk about what had been happening back in Perth for the last 3 years and the sort of reports they got back home about the war. Bob had to laugh a little about the differences between the reported truth and what actually happened. After a while Mimey went to begin preparing the evening meal and got Jess and Berta to come help her, a calculated and deliberate move. Robert, Bob and Jean continued chatting for a while before they fell silent for a second or two. Bob took the opportunity to put the question to Robert.

"Aye Robert, there's something I've been wanting tae talk tae ye aboot. I know we, Jean and I, have agreed on getting married but I have never officially asked you. It's only right and proper that I dae that."

Robert let out a huge laugh, which sort of stunned Bob. "No need to dae that, laddie. She's a woman of age an' can mek up her own mind. Thank ye all the same and if it will help ye, of course, ye can."

Robert let out a sigh of relief and squeezed Jean's hand. He looked at her and smiled, then let out a little laugh. "Well, I guess that's it then. We're engaged ma dear."

"Mimey. Can ye come in here please dear?" Robert called to the kitchen. Mimey entered with a querying look on her face.

"Aye dear," Robert said with a smile on his face. "He asked."

"Och wonderful," she turned to Jean and gave her a big hug and then Bob. "Congratulations tae the both o' ye." Robert got up from his chair and went over and congratulated them both.

Jess and Berta came in now and sat around asking all sorts of questions about the wedding.

"Hold on girls," said Bob, "we've naw had time tae discuss any o' the details yet. As soon as we have decided what's happening, we'll let ye know."

"They've all been teasing me since we heard ye were coming home," Jean added. "I cannae believe it's all real though. Ye're actually home, safe an' sound. It's grand it is."

"Aye," Bob said, "I am home safe." He left out the sound bit.

That evening they all sat around talking and playing cards again. Bob had for so long, longed to be back at Florence St, just to spend the evening doing these normal things, talking, playing cards, listening to the wireless, listening to the piano playing. He had so missed all that day to day living. Robert went off to bed early still, needing to rise early to prepare for the day's baking. Mimey, Jess, Jean and Bob, playing cards again. Berta, reading her books as usual. His life, of the last 3 and a half years, seemed a million miles away now. His life of the next few years now looked bright too.

The following day, Bob and Jean sat out on the front veranda, on a cool but sunny day. They soaked up the warmth of the sun, as best they could and started to plan out their future.

"I would like tae get married, as soon as possible," Bob said. "Then I'd like us both tae train tae Sydney, back in ma house, and get back tae ma carpentry business. Ma dearest Jean, I'd like tae try and forget aboot the last three years. I dinnae ken if that's possible though. I have tae tell you my dear, that I'm noe the same person that left here in April '16. After wha' I've been through, I am now different, so I have tae tell ye that if you want oot, now's the time tae say. I have a horrible feeling in my heart, these days, and I don't know how it's going tae affect me in the days tae come. So, whilst I love ye wi' all ma heart, I'm giving ye this opportunity noo, tae opt oot, if ye want."

"Oh Bob," she replied, "I can tell ye're noe the same person that left here three years ago. I could tell that from the moment I saw ye at the train station. After a war like that, it would be impossible, tae remain the same as befoor. I wasnae sure, aboot us, until I saw ye get off that train yesterday. When I saw ye standing there, looking around that train station, tae see if anyone was there tae meet ye, I nearly burst with pride. That's when I knew, we were on the right track. So, naw Bob, I'll noe be backing oot. We'll get through this together, you and I."

"Och ye're a braw wee lassie ye are Jean," Bob replied. His eyes were moist at this point. Men do not cry, do they? So, the let us just say, moist.

Jean went on. "I thought we'd probably be heading for Sydney, so I have prepared masel' for it. Mother and father are both expecting it as well. It's just right, that's where yer business is, that's where we go. As far as the other matter goes, why don't ye tell me a little of what you experienced, so I can understand what ye're going through, a little better."

"Och I cannae Jean. I saw things, no man or woman, should ever have to see or experience. Maybe as time goes on, I can tell you a thing or two but right now, it's too raw. What we did to those Huns at Hill 60; I cannae believe I was a part of it. I Ken it was war, but…." Bob's voice trailed off, he was shaking his head and his eyes was staring into the never never.

Jean just sat there and listened. She reached out and took his hand in hers. She sat back and stared out into space, with him. She knew that when it was time, he would tell her what she needed to know. The fact that he had already started to tell her, without even realising it, was the first step. She was a patient person, she could wait. Support was what he needed right now. Bob completely took the wind out of her sails with the next comment. "Jeanie, there's somethin' tha' happened over there a lot. That I need to talk tae ye aboot. In a lot of the places we were, quite a few of the men, disappeared from time tae time tae, shall we say, seek the comforts o' some o' the locals, especially doon in France." Jean had a somewhat quizzical look on her face indicating her lack of understanding. "Jus' like doon in Roe St, if ye get ma drift," he added.

"Oh, that kind of comfort," she replied somewhat surprised. Roe St in Perth was the local brothel region in Perth. It was the street immediately across the railway line from the city centre. It continued right through to the 1970s as such. She went on, "So why would ye mention that?"

"Well, I cannae abide that kinda thing, at all. I believe that sort of thing, remains within the walls, o' a married couples house. I didnae associate with those kind o' men, while I was away, if it could be avoided, at all. I just need ye tae understand that." He could not look at her during this conversation. It was too embarrassing, but he felt he needed to say it all the same, to put it on the record.

"Well Bob the thought o' that never entered ma heid. I completely agree with ye. Ye can believe me on that score," she said to complete the conversation.

After what seemed like an hour but was more probably only 3 minutes, she said to him, "So Bob, when do ye think we should have the wedding?"

"The what? Och, the wedding. Aye." Bob was jolted back into the present. "We should get married before the end o' the month. What dae ye think?"

"Oh, that quickly? There's a lot tae do, between now and then. The kirk will need time, tae publish the intent to marry. I think we can get everything else done in that time, don't ye?" Jean was a hard woman to fluster. Come what may, she just took everything in her stride.

"Aye ma dear. I think we can. Shall we go and discuss it with yer mother noo?" Bob said this with a wink of the eye.

"Yes Bob. I think that's a very good idea," she replied.

They went inside and Mimey was busy in the kitchen as usual. She was kneading out the dough for the bread. Bob always thought this was strange given Robert was a baker, but Mimey always made the bread at home.

"Mother," Jean said looking directly at her.

"Yes dear. What's the matter?" Mimey replied.

"Oh, nothing's the matter. It's just that we have come to some agreements aboot the wedding," Jean said.

"Oh aye," Mimey replied.

"We havenae set an actual date yet but we want to get married by the end of the month, if it can be arranged." Jean sounded almost like she was asking a question. "That way we can get the train for Sydney after, so Bob can get back tae work as soon as possible."

"Aye lassie, I understand that," Mimey said. "I wish ye could set up over here, we'll miss ye both so much."

"I understand that, mother, but Bob's business is already started over there, so we have tae goe," Jean remarked.

"Aye lassie, I dae understand that. So what date are ye thinkin' aboot?" Mimey asked.

"We need a calendar to work that oot," said Jean as she reached for it. "It looks like the last Saturday is the 26th, how is that?"

"That should be fine," Mimey said, and Robert agreed. "Who's gonnae be your bridesmaid?"

"I thought I'd ask Jessie. What dae ye think?" Jean offered.

"I think that would be a lovely choice, dear. Wha' ye gonnae do, Bob?" Mimey asked.

"Och I've already asked Bert Carr if he would oblige, an' he has said he would," answered Bob.

"Wonderful. He's a lovely chap, is Bert. I tek it you two got on really well over there?" Mimey replied.

"Aye we did," Bob answered. "He has much the same in values, as I. I didnae get to ken him, until we were in Ypres, not long after we were put in the same section. There was also Bill McIvor, from Sydney as well. He runs a plumbing business just up the road from me, in Hurstville. I knew him before this lot, although not well. But we enlisted at the same time at the same place, so it kindae put us together, for the duration."

"Well, I suggest ye both go and see the minister at the kirk as soon as possible. I tek it, it will be the Ross Memorial Kirk?" Mimey asked.

"Of course, Mother. Do ye want tae tek a walk over there noo Bob?" Jean asked.

"Wait on ye two. We'll have to run this past Father first," broke in Mimey. "I'll tell him wha's happenin' when he gets home. Then ye can go and see Pastor Galloway."

"Ask him or tell him, Mother?" Jean said with a smile.

"Tha's right. I'll ask him and tell him wha' his answer is." They all had a good laugh at this. Yes, Robert was the household head, but Mimey made all the decisions.

Later that afternoon, they went and saw Pastor Galloway at the church and laid all their plans out before him. He knew Jean well by now. The family had been attending his church for the last 7sevenyears, ever since their arrival in Australia. The 26th of July was too soon, he told them, as he had to publish the banns for the marriage for three weeks prior. He suggested they look to 9th of August, as that was the earliest he could do it. They agreed with this date and he was pleased to allocate that for them and would prepare the notifications. He bade them farewell and offered up his best wishes.

When they got home, they told Robert and Mimey of the new date and Jessie was home, so Jean asked her to be her bridesmaid and she instantly agreed, throwing her arms around Jean and Bob. They spent the rest of the evening making all the wedding plans.

Chapter 29
I Do

The 9th came around so quickly, no one could believe five weeks had passed since Bob returned. The wedding was attended by a small group of family and friends and well-wishers from the church. It was a simple ceremony, with little fuss, and that suited everyone. Bob and Bert looked really suave in their suits, white shirt white bow ties and topped off with button up white gloves. A bit of a change from his uniform, Bob thought. A nice change too.

Jean looked radiant and happy to be pledging herself to Bob, even though she knew it would mean uprooting herself from her family. She had her man to support now. She wore a white three quarter length dress, with a high but loose rolled collar. The upper part of the bodice was embroidered with a small and delicate area of white satin piping. Down the front were two panels, one on each side, of similar white satin piping embroidery, adorned with false pearls. The sleeves were elbow length but covered with tulle to the wrist. Her veil was a simple bonnet adorned with two rows of pearls, cascading down to a moderate train. Her shoes were white and low healed.

Jessie wore a pale blue, three-quarter-length dress with a wide round collar and embroidered bodice. It was tied with a wide belt of the same material as the dress, which was allowed to fall to the same length as the dress, the end being fringed. She wore an extra wide brimmed hat of dark blue velvet adorned with a white band. Both ladies also carried large bouquets. After the ceremony, they all headed back to Florence St for an informal afternoon with family and friends.

They spent a few days in Perth after the wedding and then embarked on the long train journey across Australia. Bob tried to explain to Jean what it was like, but she was still, unprepared for the sights. She was glad this was winter, as it would be excruciatingly hot through the centre in summer. She saw what Bob saw in its beauty though. She agreed that its massive expanses of scrub held a certain fascination, but was extremely glad she did not live out there.

It was obvious that lots of families did indeed live out there, principally to service the train, but it was not for her. She thought sunrise and sunset were the best times of the day. The sky took on an endless variation of colour. From the reds and oranges at the horizon through pinks, purples and various shades of blue, the likes of which she had never witnessed before. She clung to Bob's arm and marvelled at the sight. She was happy, that was for sure. She snuggled into his side and thanked him for showing her this wonderful vision.

Arriving in Sydney in late August, they had all their luggage delivered direct to their house, except for a few things for the train trip. They transferred to the domestic station and caught the train out to Hurstville station in south west Sydney. The house in Illawarra Rd was about a mile (1.6 km) from the station, so Bob called for a Taxi to take them home.

Jean loved the house. It was small, but with only the two of them, it was ideal. It had a four foot high (1.2m) scalloped white picket fence, with pale green posts topped with spherical finials. The house itself, was of a federation style timber ship lap construction with the metal roof. Centre front of the building was a small, gabled, portico, extending over the front, wooden steps and topped with a small finial. It had a small front veranda, with white posts, filled in the long the top, with federation style, filigree ironwork and the ends were filled in with latticework. Inside there were two bedrooms, a lounge room, and a kitchen dining room complete with a Metters wood stove.

Out through the back door, on the right hand end of the back veranda was the washhouse complete with copper, for boiling the clothes, and a mangle for wringing the water out of the clothes. The backyard was relatively bare just a grassed area, with the privy down the path and a clothesline between two posts, with a long diagonal prop, to raise the line, once the clothes were pegged.

"Oh Bob, it's lovely," Jean said with a smile. "Love the front fence too. The yard is enclosed so we could hold a dog in there, couldn't we?"

"Aye Jeanie, that we could," Bob replied. "Come on in and see the inside ma dear. Oor luggage will arrive soon I expect. As ye can see we'll need tae purchase some moor furniture. In the couple o' days I was in Sydney last month I got some, but I didnae wannae get too much yet. I wanted ye to have some say in oor choices."

"Oh, thank ye Bob. It's nice inside too. Good size rooms. Nice big kitchen dining. No trees in the yard though. Well, we can plant some then, can't we?" she commented.

"Aye, that we can. If ye wan', we can plant fruit trees, like in the Perth backyard too," he replied.

"That would be nice Bob," she said. "Oh, I do like it Bob. I think we'll be able to set up a nice home here, do ye noe?"

"Aye I think so, bonnie lassie."

At that moment there was a knock at the front door, as the luggage had arrived. They helped to unload and bring it into the house. They spent the rest of the day unpacking suitcases and boxes and sorting out how the house would be set up. One of the first things Jean did, was to unpack the jewellery box, Bob had made for her in Ypres and it took pride of place, on the dressing table. They discussed what furniture would be needed, to complete the house. They would spend the next few days finally getting everything set up and working. Then, Bob could get back to his carpentry business. After all the money from the Army was not going to last forever.

Bob's discharge papers came through and on 25 August 1919, was finally discharged, from duty with the AIF. At that time, he was advised that the army was offering the former troops, a demob equipment allowance, to get them off and running, in their chosen area. Bob filled out the applications and was allocated a sum of ten pounds ($20), to spend on whatever equipment was available for his trade of carpentry. These articles that he chose, would remain the property of the government, for a period of five years and provided they had been used for legitimate purposes and kept in good condition, ownership would pass to the former soldier, after that period. On the 9th of September, he made the selection of tools as per the following list:

2	Canvas tool bags
1	Mortice gauge
1	8" Steel square
1	Trying Plane
1	Stanley Combination Plane No 55
½	doz Chisel Handles (lge)

1   Set Hand Drill Bits

1   10" Steel Square (Wooden Stock)

2   Aprons

½   doz Pencils

Total cost, 10 pounds. ($20)

During this first month in Sydney, Jean noticed that Bob did not sleep at all well. He took a long time to get to sleep and when he did, he was often woken by bad dreams. They discussed what was happening, and Bob assured her that as time went on, things would surely settle down. Little by little, Jean was made aware of some of the things that happened in Europe during those three and a half years. He told her, of as many of the good things that happened, as he could remember, but little of the trauma, death and destruction that he had witnessed. He told her that they were encouraged to forget about what went on and not to discuss in any detail what they had experienced.

Jean was not sure this would help in her understanding of what Bob was going through. She knew he was struggling, but was unable to really help as she had no idea what demons were playing in his mind. As the end of the year approached, Jean tried to encourage Bob to go and see the doctor, to see if there was anything he could do, to help him sleep. Eventually, he did see the doctor, and one thing the doctor said to him was that he was not alone. In the last six months, he had seen many former soldiers who reported symptoms similar to what Bob was experiencing. He said he understood that it was a reaction to the things, they had seen and done. The army had coined a term for this condition, that of "shell shock."

Bob indicated that he knew of this, as they had discussed that whilst in Belgium and France, but he did not think it applied to him. He had none of the twitches or strange walking gaits or indeed what they knew as the thousand yard stare.

"Besides which," Bob stated, "the other army term for it, is LMF. Lack of Moral Fibre, and a can tell ye right noo doctor, tha' doesnae apply tae me."

"I have no doubt you are right Bob," said the doctor. "I do not for one second, believe the LMF argument. I think, and many of my colleagues think, that it is your brain's subconscious reaction to the things you've seen and experienced. Also, to the percussion of the shells going off in your near vicinity. Many of the men I have seen, have told me of some of the things you boys saw and even did. I for one, do not believe you can go through that stuff and not come home without some problems. Did you experience any near shell explosions Bob?"

"Aye," he replied. "So many, I cannae count 'em. Dozens and dozens."

"I see," replied the doctor. "Well, we think that this will pass, with the passage of time, so if you can hold on for a little while longer, you should be as right as rain before you know it."

"It were often different for officers, if they were suspected o' shell shock," Bob remarked. "They were legitimate cases, but us ORs, well, we were jus' cowards on the whole. Wilfred Owen, the great poet, was a lieutenant in the British army, an' he got shell shocked, and they sent him to Craiglockhart, in ma home country tae recuperate. He came back, right as rain, as ye put it, an' I was with him, at the Sombre Canal in the last week o' the war. He was one o' the many British casualties that day, so Mrs Owen didn't get tae see her son again. So many dead, an' what foor?"

The Doctor could see that Bob was suffering the aftereffects of the war. Naturally, he wished there was something to do, to help him, but no one knew how to treat shell shock. (what we know today as PTSD, Post Traumatic Stress Disorder). Not only did they not know how to treat it, but the experts also were not even really sure if it existed. There were many theories on the topic, but they were just that, theories. It would take many years, before the medical fraternity even came close to describing, what this condition was.

In the end, the doctor told Bob the best thing he could do was to get plenty of rest and try and concentrate on the good things in life, putting the war out of his mind.

Aye, thought Bob. *Truly spoken, by someone who was nowhere near the war*. He went home and told Jean, the bulk of his conversation with the doctor. "All I need is rest and tae avoid stressful situations, apparently. Huh, a lot of good that'll do."

"So, he wasn't much use then, Bob?" asked Jean.

"Noe really." He paused for a moment then added, "Och, he wasnae too bad. He was very understanding. He said he's seen a lot o' fellas like me, in the last few months and he thinks ma brain may have been a bit injured from the shock waves from the artillery shells exploding nearby. I tell ye it's definitely possible, coz the shock waves were somethin' else at times."

It was about this time that Jean's health appeared to deteriorate. She felt nauseous most of the time and had difficulty keeping her food down. In the January of 1920, the boot was on the other foot and it was Bob encouraging Jean to go and see the doctor. She could not argue against it, given her attempts to get

Bob to the doctor in the first place. When Bob came home from work, one afternoon in early January, he said to Jean, "So wha' did the doctor say tae ye? Can he help ye with ye're sickness?"

"Oh aye," said Jean. "I'll be fine. This sickness will wear off shortly, apparently, and the whole problem will be sorted oot by aboot August."

"Och tha's a long time," remarked Bob. "Wha's the problem if it's gonnae tek tha' long tae sort oot?"

Jean smiled a big smile and answered him, "The kind o' problem that will end with the delivery o' a baby. I'm pregnant."

Bob sat for a minute, trying to process what he had just heard. "A, a baby? Och ma lord, we're gonnae be a family?"

"Aye Bob, we are," Jean said. "The baby will arrive sometime in August he thinks. So wha' dae ye want? A boy or a girl?"

"Och, bonnie lassie, it doesnae matter so long as she's healthy," Bob said with a huge smile. His problems were relegated to the back of his head for the moment. He was elated.

"Oh, so it's a girl, is it?" Jean ribbed him. "Tha' would be nice, but a boy would be nice too, would it noe?"

"Och aye, it would. Did I say it were gonnae be a girl?" he asked finally realising what Jean had said.

"Oh, aye ye did," she said as she reached over and gave him a huge hug.

They embraced for a while, and then Bob said, "Och, tha' means I better get on an' mek a crib for the wee bairn. Do ye noe think?"

"If tha's what ye want tae do, feel free. Whatever ye do will be lovely, I'm sure." Jean hoped that the impending birth of their child would take Bob's mind away from his difficulties. Initially it did, but it was not long before the dreams and the mood swings came back. The doctor's opinion that they would lessen over time did not seem to be happening, however. In fact, if anything, they were getting more frequent. She did not say anything, however, as he was still being the gentle, wonderful man she fell in love with, and the doctor should know how this goes. Bob did return to the doctor on a few occasions, for follow up, but he was unable to provide any remedies.

On occasion, Bill would drop around to catch up and he and Bob, would sit out on the front veranda chatting. Jean would join them for a cup of tea, but after that was over, she would go inside, leaving the two of them to go over old times. She knew they needed time together, to cover the old ground again. In doing this, she hoped she would give Bob an outlet to let go of old memories. To a degree it did work, but the nightmares and night sweats, would start again soon after. She would try in the evenings, to get him to open up about his experiences, but being the gentleman he was, there was no way he was going to burden her, with his problems. He had been told, to go home and forget about it and not to discuss it with anyone who had not been there, and that is what he would do. Even so, Jean began to build a picture, piece by piece of at least some of the things that were worrying him. Tiny pieces that he would let slip in conversation with her, all pieces she would overhear from Bill and Bob's conversations.

As time went on and the pregnancy started to show, she began to notice some subtle changes in Bob's condition. He was becoming less tolerant of some people. He became more irritable. The frequency of his headaches increased. The further her pregnancy progressed, the more paranoid he became. He started distrusting fellow workers. He wanted to know what Jean did every moment of the day. The nights were worst. He would see figures in the shadows, figures that he thought were out to get him. Jean was thankful that Bob was a good Presbyterian boy and due to this, he did not turn to the drink. She knew that their local pastor had been in the AIF, so she went to him to ask for his advice.

He was particularly understanding, having seen many similar cases over the last three or four years. He indicated to her that there was precious little she could do other than to support him and wait. He did offer to speak to Bob and arranged to come and see him the following Saturday afternoon. Whilst Bob was a trifle irritated by the interference in his affairs, he did understand that he needed help and seeing the pastor had been in the AIF himself, he was prepared to talk to him.

That Saturday afternoon, the pastor arrived, and they had a lovely afternoon tea. As soon as the tea was over, Jean excused herself and left the two of them to their discussions. They talked for a good two hours. Occasionally, she would hear fits of laughter coming from the lounge room. She was glad, this meant they were getting on and were covering some ground. When the pastor left, they waved him goodbye, from the front gate and then turned to walk inside. Bob put his arm around Jean's shoulder as they climbed the front steps.

"I'm sorry I got upset the other dae when ye said ye'd spoken tae the pastor," Bob said. "In fact, it was good tae talk tae him today. He had seen much o' the same things that I have seen and had a good understanding o' wha' we went through. I didn't know him then, but he was in some of the same places as I was.

He was in Ypres and Albert, so he knows what we did. He has given me a little more perspective noo, than I have had befoor. I know ye're trying tae help, and I thank ye lassie. I dae love ye, and I'm looking forward tae havin' a family with ye."

"Oh, I'm glad ye had a good talk," Jean remarked. "He's a very nice man, isn't he?"

"Aye Jeannie, he is. He's a man o' the world," Bob replied. "The other thing he did say, was that perhaps, I should tell ye a little o' what went on. Mind ye, there's a lot I could never tell ye, as I don't think it's fit conversation for anybody."

"I understand that Bob, but I would like tae know a little. It may help me tae understand ye better."

"Right then, lassie. Shall we make another cuppa and sit?" Jean agreed, and Bob directed her to sit whilst he put the kettle on.

They sat at the kitchen table, and Bob told her of the Hill 60 campaign. He told her about the tunnels, about working underground, about camouflets and crumps. He told her of the day they detonated the hill and described the conflagration, but did not go into any details, of what he saw, when he surveyed the hill, after the explosion. He simply said that many of the Germans on that hill, did not survive and many of them are likely, still there. He told her about Hooge and the death of his mates. He told her of the many installations he had worked on around Zonnebeke, of what was left of the towns, or more correctly, what was not left.

He went on to describe their transfer to the Somme and how once they were there, the pace picked up to drive the Germans back to their fatherland. Although he had written to her about Capt. Woodward, he now told her in detail, the sort of man that he was and how they had formed a good bond. Bob said, he had hoped to go up to Tenterfield, to see the captain marry his girl, early next month, but his priorities, lay with Jean, as she was about to give birth around that time.

Then he told her about Frank and how he had gotten his promotion to CQMS. He told her that he still did not understand how he and the men in his own tent escaped without injury, but those next door, were killed and maimed. He finished off with the preparations and execution of the job at the Sombre Canal, of how he had seen Wilfred Owen that evening and twelve hours later, he was gone. The whole time he described what went on, he would intersperse the statements with, "it's just not fair" or "I dinnae understand it" or "it's just not right."

Jean sat and listened without interrupting. She would nod her head or shake it, as the situation demanded. When he was finished, there was silence for a while. Finally, she spoke, "Well thank ye, Bob, for telling me these things. I knew ye'd had some bad experiences over there, that goes without saying, but now I can understand a little. I'll be here to support ye through both the good and bad. We've only got a few weeks left with just the two of us. Soon, we will be three, and we're both going to need you then."

"Aye Lassie. I'll be here for the both of ye. Ye can be sure of that," Bob replied. He finished with, "Jeannie, I have stared three o' the four horsemen in the face. The bible tells us tha' the 1st, the white horse, is conquest an' I saw wha' trying that brings tae people. Nothin' but pain an' sorrow. The 2nd, the swordsman on the red horse, brought war tae those unfortunate people and destroyed their country and property. The 4th horseman, on the green horse, was death, an' I have seen way too much o' that. I dinnae wish tae be here, when the 3rd, the black horse completes the prophecy. It's all jus' too much."

"I understand what ye are saying, Bob, but all that is over noo. Ye can put all that behind ye noo, surely," Jean answered.

"Tha's wha' they told us tae dae. It's easier said than done. I jus' cannae get the pictures oot o' ma heid. They just won't leave me alone," Bob replied.

"Well, mebee we can work on that together, then Bob. We'll manage, dinnae ye worry noo," Jean said with a comforting touch of his hand.

Bob squeezed her hand tightly and patted it with his other hand and added, "Aye lassie, we'll work on it together, bu' I dinnae like the chances. They're just always there. Always there."

Chapter 30
Joy and Desperation

August came around and by now, Jean was having difficulties moving around. This baby was making life difficult for her. Jean was only a slight woman, so the added weight of the baby put a lot of strain on her. She was uncomfortable, in pain much of the time, and yet still, she was worried for Bob. Since his chat with the pastor and then with her, things had definitely improved, but it was not fast enough for Bob and he was becoming agitated again. Jean was starting to experience contractions and they had a couple of false alarms, thinking the baby was on the way. But it hung on. They were both looking forward to the day, the bub would arrive. Both of them hoped the baby would give them renewed focus and enable them to move on.

On 20 August, Jean called Bob late afternoon and told him that this time it was for real. Bob organised a taxi to take them to the hospital nearby, and Jean was admitted. As soon as she was comfortable there, they turned Bob away, as was the custom of the time. He was told that this would take all night and should come back in the morning to check on the progress. He walked the mile or so to his home, wishing he was able to stay. He felt he needed to be near her, as much as she probably wanted him near, during this time. That evening Bob took an age to get to sleep and again, his dreams plagued him and woke him through the night.

Morning came around and he breakfasted then headed for the hospital. Jean was still in labour and yes, this time it was for real. He was not allowed in but was kept informed of her progress through the morning. Mid-afternoon, a nurse came out and informed Bob that he now had a baby daughter. "Can I go in and see ma Jeannie noo, nurse?" he asked.

"Of course, you can now. Just follow me and I'll take you through to her," the nurse said to Bob.

"Is she oright, nurse? I mean, are they oright?" Bob asked.

"They are both fine, Mr Hood. Your wife has had a tough time of it, so be gentle and don't expect too much out of her just yet," the nurse told him.

"Okay, thank ye, nurse," he replied. They walked into Jean's room and she was lying in bed, half propped up with pillows, the sheets and blankets pull right up to her chin. Her eyes were shut, she was resting. Bob darted a look at the nurse. "Are ye sure she's oright?"

"Yes, Mr Hood, she's fine," the nurse smiled at the look he gave her.

"Hello Bob," the voice came from the bed. "We have a beautiful baby daughter." Jean had opened her eyes at the sound of Bob's voice.

"Och Jeannie, tha's wonderful. Where is she?" Bob asked looking around. He was expecting the baby to be there too.

The nurse answered him, "Oh, she's in the nursery for the moment. That way, we can keep an eye on her, to make sure everything is fine."

"Why, is something wrong wi' her?" Bob was beginning to panic.

"No Mr Hood. She is doing very well. We always keep the babies in the nursery for the first few days," she explained.

"Come here, Bob, and sit ye doon," Jean said. "How are ye, ye poor man. Ye havenae been able to see, what's been going on have ye?"

"Naw," he replied. "It's noe been much fun, not knowin' wha's happenin'. Ye're mind plays all sorts o' tricks on ye. Och it's grand tae see ye again Jeannie. How are ye?"

"Oh, I'm sure I'll survive," she said. "I think us women, have done this once or twice before and survived ye knaw."

He smiled. "Aye, I guess ye have." He was settling down now.

"Ye go with the nurse and see her and see if ye still want to call her, what we decided on," she said as she pointed to the nurse.

"Och aye. I shall. Is that oright wi' ye nurse?" he said as he got out of the chair.

"Of course, it is. What do you think I've been waiting here for? The Prime Minister?" She laughed as she finished. She was a jolly nurse. Not at all the kind he was used to. In his experience, they were always bossy and wholly matter of fact, with no time for frivolity. Mind you, most of his experiences with nurses, had been in the army. He guessed they probably did not have the time to be jolly in the army. They were nearly always dealing with life and death situations too, so were not likely to be in a good mood then.

She took him down the corridor and around the corner. He knew they were getting close to the nursery when he heard the wailing coming down the passage. She led him into a room, with a big window, in front of a row of 4 babies. He looked along the row and saw on a cot, "HOOD." "I tek it tha's ma Bebe is it?" he asked.

"Yes, Mr Hood. That is your baby. Isn't she beautiful?" She said.

"Aye! She's a brawl wee lassie. An' ba the soond o' it, she's got a good set o' lungs too," Bob replied. He could not get the smile off his face. Not that he wanted to. This was the happiest day he had had, since the day of his wedding. He stood looking at her for a few minutes. She lay there alternatively staring back at him and then crying aloud. When she stared at him, he could see straight into those beautiful big blue eyes. They were beautiful he thought, but at the same time, something in those eyes disturbed him.

The nurse said to him, "Maybe tomorrow we can let you have a hold of her. For the moment, she needs her rest too. She's had a tough time too, you know."

"Aye, I guess she has too," he replied.

After a few minutes he returned to Jean's room. There were three other new mums in the same ward. As Bob sat down next to Jean, she said, "Well Bob, what do ye think?"

"Aye Jeannie, she's a brawl wee lassie," he replied.

"What do ye think aboot the name?" she pressed him.

"Och aye. I think it fits perfectly. Enid Hood. Aye, that'll dae nicely," he said.

"That's what I thought," added Jean. "So apparently, they will bring round the paperwork tomorrow, for us tae fill oot, tae mek it official."

"Och," laughed Bob. "I hadnae thought aboot that. I've noe done this befoor."

They both had a good giggle at his comment. They chatted for a short while, as he was not allowed to stay long. After a bit of backwards and forwards, Bob made a strange comment to Jean.

"I dinnae who she looks like. She doesnae look like ye much and she doesnae look like me at all."

Jean laughed and explained, "Its early days. The baby's gone through a very difficult process and they're always a bit squashed, for the first couple of days, apparently. The nurse tells me that she will settle down, over the next few days, besides, I actually think she looks like you. She's got your eyes."

"I canna see it," he said, "but I'll tek ye're word for it. We'll see how it goes eh?"

"Aye we shall," replied Jean. At that moment, the nurse came in and told Bob that he had better be on his way. Jean needed to get her rest. He said his goodbyes to Jean and headed out the door. Once again, he walked home, only this time, it was more like he floated home.

He visited her every day for the next ten days, usually after work. Each day was the same thing. He thought it strange that Enid did not look like him. Eventually he agreed that she did look like Jean, but he was taking some convincing that he had anything to do with her. Some of the things he was saying, gave Jean some cause for concern. Bob was starting to see things that were just not there, almost to the point of paranoia. By the time Jean came home from hospital, he had worked himself into quite a state. He was convinced that Enid was not his child. His dreams at night were getting worse, to the point that it woke him several times a night. With the new baby and his dreams, neither of them was getting enough sleep now.

Jean also seemed now to be suffering from "Melancholia", what we now know as Post-Natal Depression. The lack of sleep, Bob's condition and getting used to the new baby sent Jean lower and lower. To the point that a nurse was assigned to check on her on a daily basis at home. She would come in each day and make sure the baby was seen to and then check on Jean. The doctor had prescribed medication for Jean to assist her, so the nurse ensured that was taken at the appropriate times, as it was now apparent that Bob was unable, or perhaps unwilling, to see to that.

It seemed that Jean was not improving, despite the active intervention by the medical staff, and the nurse was becoming quite concerned by her lack of progress. By the time Enid was 1 month old, things appeared to be getting to the critical stage. By now the nurse was living in, to keep a close eye on them both.

Before dawn on the 21st of September, the day the baby turned one month old, Bob was in the kitchen talking to the nurse. She was particularly concerned about Jean. She had a heart to heart with him, in the attempt to snap him out of his depression. "I am very worried about your wife's progress, Mr Hood. She is not doing as well as we would like. I fear you may have to prepare yourself that she may waste away. Unless something happens soon, I fear we may lose her."

"Och noe," he replied. "I cannae live without her. She is the only thing I've got."

"That's not true, Mr Hood. You have a beautiful baby girl there, that's got to be something to be worth living for," the nurse answered.

"It would be if it were mine," he said, and he got up to go down to the bedroom to see Jean.

"I'm at the end o' ma tether, Jeannie. The baby cannae be mine. It's in the eyes. She's noe got my eyes. She's somebody else's." Bob was absolutely distraught by now.

"Noe Bob. She is your daughter. Yours and mine. Nobody else's." Jean answered as best she could. She struggled to get the words out through the tears now. She had known Bob was unwell since returning from France, but now it was beyond question. There was definitely something seriously wrong. The nurse managed to get Bob out of the room and calm him down. He was so agitated, and it was not long before he returned to Jean's room and had another conversation with her.

"Och Jeannie," he started, "Ye're just so sick. Ye're noe mentally right. Ye're noe right in the heid. I dinnae wha' tae dae. I need ye so much."

"Oh, noe Bob, I'm alright. It's ye who is sick, ma darling. Ye need tae get help," she replied. "Ye need tae get it now."

Once again, the nurse dragged Bob out of the room and encouraged him to go to the neighbour's house for a sleep, which eventually, he did. The neighbours had been in earlier and had offered to help out, if there was anything they could do. The nurse went next door to ask if they could put Bob up just for the day, just to give Jean a rest. That evening back at his house, Bob was given a dose of "morphia", as ordered by the doctor to keep him calm and sent to bed. It appeared as though he was then having, a peaceful night. The nurse checked in on Jean again and made sure she was comfortable for the night.

At about 4 am, Bob woke and went to the kitchen for a drink. Once he had that, he sat down at the kitchen table, to think through the events of the previous day. As he sat, he was spinning his toiletries bag on the tabletop, in front of him. It had been left there because of sleeping in two places yesterday. The questions just went round and round in his head:

"Jeannie says the baby's mine, but she doesn't look like me."

"Is she mine or has she been playing aroond?"

"She says she hasn't, but can I trust her?"

"Of course, I can trust her."

"So why can I not believe her?"

"What am I going to do?"

"What are we going to do?"

"I don't know what tae do."

"If the baby is noe mine, I couldn't keep going."

"But if she's noe mine, whose is she?"

"She says I'm the one who is sick. Is she right? Mebee she is."

"Maybe it's all just a product of the last 4 years."

"I just dinnae know anything anymoor."

"Maybe everyone would be better off without me."

"If ma Jeannie's noe gonnae mek it, mebee I need to get to the other side to greet her when she gets there."

These thoughts went spiralling around in his head just like a tornado, until he was so worked up he lost contact with reality. Nothing seemed to make sense any more. Then the visions of the war came back into his head. There were fireworks, explosions, darkness interspersed with flashes of light. He was looking out of a barn, surrounded by the darkness, to see these flashes and mountains of dirt rising high into the air, and his mates dying around him, blood on his hands. By now his heart was pounding, and he felt he was running short of breath. "This is noe right," he thought to himself. "It's noe right and it won't go away. Please go away. I cannae stand this."

While all these thoughts and more were going through his head, he was fiddling with the contents of that bag. He pulled them out and spun them on the table one by one. The last item he pulled from the bag was his razor. His cutthroat razor. He opened it out and studied it carefully. He had taken that with him to the war and it had groomed him throughout. It had kept him looking his best, even when things got really tough. It had a lovely ivory handle that was now showing signs of wear. He opened it, swinging the blade back so the finger hook was in its usual position for a shave. The blade was crafted from the best "Sheffield" steel. It was a piece of art as well as a useful implement. He took it in his hand, as if to shave himself and...

The nurse got up early that morning to fetch a glass of milk. She walked into the kitchen and saw that Bob was sitting at the table. He looked to be asleep, with his head down on the table. She went in. "Good morning, Mr Hood. How are you feel..." Her voice trailed off as she spied the mass of blood all over the table and the floor. On the floor, next to Bob, was the razor. She immediately went to check his pulse, but realised it was way too late.

His throat had been cut with a 6" (15 cm) gash. There was no colour in his skin, he was cold, and she just knew. She called the neighbour, as they owned a telephone, and he came over, but it was obvious there was nothing to be done to help Bob. The neighbour's wife who had heard a commotion when the nurse came, had followed her husband over. She was already by his side, standing with her mouth open wide and clutching at her throat. The three of them just stood and looked. Nobody said anything for some time. "Is… Is… He… " stuttered the wife.

"Yes," answered the nurse. "I'm afraid he's gone. Poor man. Poor silly man. I'm going to have to call the police and let them know, so I suggest you go and get changed. Probably be a good idea if you stay at home until they ask for you as well," she added.

When the police arrived, they examined the scene and interviewed the three of them. They wanted to go and interview Jean as well, but the nurse managed to talk them out of it, by explaining just how sick she was. She indicated that she would not tell Mrs Hood about this, until she was better. She would make up some excuse for him not coming in to see her. The police were convinced it was a case of suicide anyway, so they were prepared to accept the nurse's explanation. They arranged for the removal of the body and advised everyone that they would probably be required for an inquest into the death at some future date to be advised. The nurse cleaned up the scene after all the formalities and went about nursing Jean. I do not know if the neighbours stayed on there, or what happened to them after this episode. One could understand if they no longer wished to live there, but no one seems to know the outcome of that.

The nurse went in to see Jean as soon as she managed to clean up and told her that Bob had contracted a cold or flu, and felt it was best if he stayed away for the moment. The nurse did not want to burden Jean with anything else at this stage of her recovery. There would be plenty of time to fill her in on the happenings from overnight.

She had Jean's mother's contact details and sent a message through to Mimey and Robert about what had happened. When they heard the news, they were devastated. They too knew that the Bob that came back from the war was not the Bob that they had farewelled four years ago. They were not however ever expecting anything like this. They were certainly concerned with his condition, but this; this never entered their minds. They told the rest of the family what had happened, then Mimey immediately set about making arrangements, to get to Sydney, to bring Jean home.

The nurse stayed on for the week and arranged for the neighbour to look in on Jean as well. Jean slowly but surely started improving. It was like, without the weight of Bob's health issues pushing her down, she was able to concentrate on her own health. She loved him dearly, but his problems were holding her down. She felt that if she could get better herself, she would be able to help him. Jean was unable to attend the inquest the following Monday. The combination of her medical state and the loss of her husband, made her unable to leave her bed. The police, the nurse and the neighbours attended the inquest and gave evidence that supported the findings—that Bob had committed suicide.

MAN CUTS HIS THROAT

Robert Hood, 36, was on the 22nd inst found dead in the kitchen of his residence, in Illawarra-Street, Hurstville, with his throat cut. At the City Coroner's Court yesterday, a verdict of suicide was returned.

Sydney Morning Herald. Tuesday, 28 September 1920

A SAD TRAGEDY

Robert Hood, a carpenter, aged 36 years, was found dead at his home in Hurstville, on Wednesday of last week with his throat cut. A nurse, who was attending his wife, stated that deceased seemed depressed about his wife who was suffering from acute melancholia, and feared she was going to die. Witness advised him to go and have a rest as he had had no sleep for some time. He was given some morphia as directed by the doctor, and he had a quiet night, but on the Wednesday morning as she went into the kitchen she found him lying on the floor with his throat cut, and a razor lying beside the body. A verdict of suicide was returned.

Wellington Times, NSW-Thursday 30 September 1920

Back in Perth, Mimey and Robert organised tickets for her to travel across Australia by train to Sydney. As distraught as she was, Mimey was a strong woman and she knew she had to remain so, for her daughter's sake. She had her moments when she was alone, and she cried. She cried for her daughter and her baby and she cried for Bob. Mimey was a religious woman as well, so she prayed too, again for Jean, Enid and Bob, but she also prayed for the strength she was going to need over the next few months and years. Enid would not be the only child in Australia being brought up by a single mother, the war had seen to that, but this one was in this family, and this family was going to do the best job they could, for Jean and Enid.

By the time the inquest was over, Mimey was already on the way. She got quite a surprise when they left Perth because there was quite a crowd there to see the train off. They were there to see Dame Nellie Melba, depart Perth for the eastern states. For four days Mimey had the honour of travelling with Dame Nellie all the way across Australia. She even got to sit and talk with her. She maintained that whilst Dame Nellie was a world class star of the opera, she was just a down to earth normal person like the rest of us. She seemed unspoiled by her fame. Dame Nellie gave Mimey, her sincerest condolences on the need for her journey.

Mimey arrived in Sydney four days later, she had enjoyed the crossing for what it was and what she had seen but not for the reason she had to travel. The nurse was at the Sydney station to greet her. She had promised to do so to explain everything she could. She helped Mimey with her luggage and getting her to the correct train, for the ride out to Hurstville. Along the way she explained as best she could remember the details of both Jean and Bob and the situation, they found themselves in. She told Mimey that while Jean was still understandably low, her health was definitely improving. She had been suffering from acute melancholia, and Bob was afraid she was going to die. Today we would probably call it Post Natal Depression.

"At least now Mrs Hood is taking some notice of the baby. That is a positive move I believe," the nurse told Mimey.

"Is the baby alright, nurse?" Mimey asked her.

"Oh yes. Make no mistake; that baby's a survivor. She's a strong one that one," came the reply.

"Thank heavens for that," Mimey answered. "How long dae ye think it will be, befoor she's well enough tae travel back tae WA?"

"Oh, I would think not for some while. You might be here for a few weeks at the current rate," she told Mimey.

Well, that won't be happening, thought Mimey to herself. "We'll have to see," she said. "Jean's a tough one, an' when she sets her mind tae it, there's noe stopping her."

"Jean you say. I thought Mr Hood called her Jenny?" the nurse quizzed her. She had told at the inquest that Bob had been calling her Jenny.

"Oh noe, it's definitely Jean," Mimey told her. "What ye heard was probably him calling her Jeannie. He did that. The accent probably made it soond tae ye that it was Jenny."

"Yes, now I hear you saying it, I think that must have been the case. Ours is the next stop, so we better get organised," the nurse said, standing up.

They picked up a taxi at the station to take them to the house. As soon as they were inside, the nurse directed her to Jean's room. She went in and Jean immediately sat up and gave her mother a big hug. There was much wailing and consoling over the next few minutes and Jean was asking her mother things like "Why? What did he have tae dae that?" Questions that Mimey had no answer for. She would listen to the same questions from Jean for years. Still, she would have no answer for her.

By the end of the following week, Mimey felt Jean was strong enough for the trip back home, so she booked the tickets for the three of them. On the Thursday, they packed the bags they needed for the trip and left Sydney for Perth. All the other baggage had been sent on ahead of them as freight.

When they arrived at Perth station four days later, Robert was there to meet them with the car. He tried his utmost to retain his composure when they met on the platform, but he was unable to hold the tears in. He too, cried with Jean and Mimey. He was going to miss Bob.

"I'm so sorry, ma darling Jean. I dinnae understand it at all," he told her.

"Noe father, I cannae understand it either. I knew he was sick, and I wasnae able to help him. He had soe many demons. I guess he just couldnae beat them all. They must have gotten jus' too much for him." She had had time to think, on the train and this was the conclusion she had come to.

"Aye, I guess so," Robert said. "I mean, we knew he was damaged by the war, but I didnae realise he was that bad." At that moment he saw the baby in Mimey's arms. "Oh, Jean she is a braw wee lassie that one is she noe?"

"Aye she is, father. I think none of us realised he was that bad at the time, Father, he got worse over the last few months," Jean explained, "but let's noe talk aboot it here. Can we go home please?"

"Of course, my darling, let's get all your bags loaded and get oot o' here," Robert replied.

He brought the T Ford Tourer around to the front of the station and loaded the car with the luggage. They all climbed aboard for the ten minute drive back to Florence St.

When they arrived at the house, Jess, Berta and Jack, ran out to meet her and they threw their arms around Jean and just cried. They were both happy and sad at the same time. They loved having their sister back but missed Bob so much. Jean then just looked at the house and cried. She was home. She loved being with Bob, and she would have gone wherever he went, but this felt like home. The conversation went along the same lines as every other greeting had done. The same questions, the same non answers. They all went inside then, each of them carrying a bag, and the girls cooing over the now seven week-old baby.

Mimey called out, "Anyone for a cuppa?"

Epilogue

Jean and Enid settled down nicely in Florence St. Enid was a spoiled little one. She had four mothers and two fathers to bring her up. She had a particularly happy childhood. Over the next few years, Robert opened a bakery in Bencubbin, in the Western Australian wheatbelt, and Jean and Enid moved up there for the two years they had it. Unfortunately, the shop next door caught fire one night, in somewhat suspicious circumstances, and they lost the entire bakery along with it. The only reminder, of its existence, was the lone brick chimney left standing.

After that, Robert opened another bakery in Beaufort St in North Perth and Jean and Enid would stay there sometimes, over the shop.

Robert died in 1929 of a ruptured stomach ulcer at age 58.

Jemima, Mimey, my great-grandmother, was a rock of the family throughout her life. Her religion was her staff throughout her life, and she instilled her values throughout the family. She passed away in 1967, at age 94.

Jack was married in 1923 to Ellen (Nellie) Wagner. She was an artist, who painted with watercolours. She became famous for her pictures of Western Australian wildflowers. She passed away in 1966 at age 67. Jack re-enlisted for WW2 with the 2nd AIF but transferred to the VDC in 1943. He took command of the defensive installation in Albany WA (now known as 'The Forts'), overlooking Princess Royal harbour. March 1944 he was promoted to Lieutenant Colonel, remaining there until August 1944. After the war, Jack continued with the law office for some years and ended up working for the Perth City Council. He passed away in 1991 aged 92. They had four children.

Jack spent many years fighting to have Bob's death recognised by the Government and the Army and to get Jean the pension she deserved. It took until 1948 for Bob's name to be added to the nominal roll of casualties of the Great War. Twenty eight years of letter writing and talking to officials finally paid off. Finally, recognition that these men who took their own lives after returning were casualties of the war, just as much as those that still lie in the fields of France and Belgium.

Jessie never had children of her own and married much later in life to David Ross, also a Scotsman. He passed away in 1959 at age 77. She continued to look after her mother, Jemima, until her death. Jessie passed away in 1971 at the age of 71. (Oh, and she made the best meringues!)

Roberta also had no children of her own and married later in life too. She married a Baptist minister, Rev Harry Reeve. Harry was 19 years older than Berta and passed away in 1968 at age 87. Berta passed away in 1973 at age 69 from breast cancer.

Jean, my grandmother, was always there for us kids, my two sisters and my brother. She lived about a mile away from us in Applecross, in Perth, WA. As kids, we stayed with her every weekend until we grew up and flew the nest. She was always there. She never lost her Scottish accent. In fact, none of the family from Scotland ever lost their accents. She was like a second mother to us. She remarried in 1970, at the age of 73, to Wing Commander O.G. (Greg) Gregson, OBE ex-RAF. His is another story that needs telling. He passed away in 1979. Jean's health slowly started to decline after that, and she passed away in 1993 at age 96. She did last through the night though, didn't she? I still miss her.

William Archibald (Bill) McIvor RTA on 24 March 1919 and resumed his life in Sydney. He married in 1922 and continued to live and work as a plumber in Ryde, Sydney, NSW. He had three sons and a daughter, and passed away in 1951, aged 61.

Robert Lawsen (Bert) Carr, RTA 21st June 1919, and returned to his life as a carpenter in Perth, WA. Bert regularly dropped in on the Chappells, at Florence St, over the next few years. He remained a friend of Jean's for many years. Enid can remember him coming to see her from time to time, as a child, but never knew why. She just knew him as a friend of the family. They lost touch after a few years. He married Blanche Fowler in 1921 and they had three children. He passed away in Perth WA, in 1963 aged 69.

Capt. Oliver Holmes Woodward MC and 2 bars, RTA May 1919 and took up a position with Mt Morgan Mining in Queensland. He married his sweetheart, Marjorie Waddell in 1920, in Brisbane, Queensland, and not long after moved to Port Pirie South Australia with BHP. There they had a daughter and two sons. In 1935 he became General Manager of North Broken Hill and became a board member in 1944. In 1958 he was awarded the C.M.G. by Queen Elizabeth II. He was president of the Australian Institute of Mining and Metallurgy in 1940 and president of the Australian Mines and Metals Association from 1952-54. He retired as manager of North BHP in 1947 but remained a director until 1961. After retirement he and Marjorie moved to Hobart where they remained until his death in 1966. Part of his exploits during the Great War have been immortalised in the Will Davies book and the 2010 Jeremy Sims movie "Beneath Hill 60".

Enid, my mother, grew up in a loving family that set the course for her life. She met my father, William (Bill), whilst they were still young, but had no real interest in him. He was three years younger than her. (Little Billy Hill she used to call him.) At around the commencement of WW2, they connected and started dating. Dad joined the RAAF when he was old enough, as a communications technician.

He served at various installations around Australia, from Perth to Melbourne to Jacky Jacky, on the tip of Cape York (now known as Bamaga). His longest post was two years in Cairns. It was then a secret transmitter station in the hills above Cairns. Between the half dozen or so men posted there, they built it from the concrete up. It was there to send radio transmissions from South West Pacific Area Command (US General McArthur and Australian General Blamey), to the troops in the Pacific region.

They married in 1944. After the war, they raised a family of 4 children in Applecross, WA. Bill worked for the one organisation throughout his working life, although it went through a variety of name changes as each business bought out another. Vox Adeon was the company, which disappeared after it was bought out by Harvey Normans. He retired just before the takeover. He also was active in the church as well. He became a Bishop in the Liberal Catholic Church and at one point oversaw the church, Australia wide. He passed away in 1993 at age 70. Not a day goes by I don't miss him.

Enid, well, she was indeed made of strong stuff. Last August 2021, she clocked up 100 years on this earth and she is still going strong. Her eyesight has mostly gone, but she has not lost a single marble. She has lived alone since my father died, looking after herself until 2020, when her eyesight failed. My sisters have played a pivotal part in keeping her as independent as she wanted to be. Without them, well, who knows?

Her one regret, apart from losing her husband too soon, was that she has known little to nothing of her father. This is where this journey began. A quest to find answers for her and, I have to admit, for myself as well. Whilst we will never know in this world, the answer to the biggest question—why—we have been able to find many answers as to why he ended up the way he did.

I now find myself asking myself a new question. I wonder what he would say now, if he could? I have pondered that question for a while now and I think I know what he would say. Do whatever it takes to help someone in need, even when they do not think there is any hope. I know he would finish with, "I am sorry, so sorry. It is not your fault. It is not anyone's fault. If I had known then, what I know now, I would never have done it. Please forgive me."

WHATEVER IT TAKES

Abbreviations

A&GAC	Ayrshire and Galloway Artillery Company
AE	Australian Engineers
AEMM&BC	Australian Electrical Mechanical Mining and Boring Company
AIF	Australian Infantry Force
ANZAC	Australian and New Zealand Army Corps
ATC	Australian Tunnelling Company
AWL	Absent Without Leave
AWM	Australian War Memorial, Canberra, ACT
BEF	British Expeditionary Force
Bel	Belgium, Belgian
BHP	Broken Hill Propriety (Limited)
Capt.	Captain
CCS	Casualty Clearing Station
CO	Commanding Officer
CoS	Chief of Staff
Coy or Co	Company
Cpl	Corporal
CQMS	Company Quartermaster Sergeant
CRE	Commander Royal Engineers
CRC	Canadian Railway Company
CSM	Company Sergeant Major
DAC	Divisional Ammunition Column
DCM	Distinguished Conduct Medal
Div.	Division
DL	Deputy Lieutenant
DOW	Died Of Wounds
FAB	Field Artillery Brigade
Fr.	France, French

Ft or '	Foot or Feet (measurement)
Gen	General
GHQ	General Head Quarters
GOC	General Officer Commanding
GSW	Gun Shot Wound
G S Wagon	General Service Wagon
HE	High Explosive
HMAS	His Majesty's Australian Ship (Navy)
HMAT	His Majesty's Australian Transport (Ship)
HQ	Head Quarters
IJA	Imperial Japanese Army
KCB	Knight Commander of the order of the Bath
KCMG	Knight Commander of St Michael and St George
Kg	Kilogram (2.2lbs)
KIA	Killed in Action
L/ Cpl	Lance Corporal
lb(s)	Pound(s) weight
LCDR	London, Chatham and Dover Railway
LMF	Lack of Moral Fibre (Cowardice)
LP	Listening Post
Lt	Lieutenant
Lt Col	Lieutenant Colonel
MC	Military Cross
MGS	Machine Gun Section
MID	Mentioned In Dispatches
MM	Military Medal
MSM	Military Service Medal
NCO	Non Commissioned Officer
NSW	New South Wales
OC	Officer Commanding
OIC	Officer In Charge
ORs	Other Ranks
POW	Prisoner of War
PT	Physical Training
Pte	Private
QM	Quarter Master

R&R	Rest and Recreation
RE	Royal Engineers
RSM	Regimental Sergeant Major
RTA	Returned to Australia
SER	South Eastern Railway
Sgt	Sergeant
SMLE	Short Magazine Lee Enfield (rifle)
VDC	Volunteer Defence Corps
WA	Western Australia
WIA	Wounded in Action
Yds	Yards (measurement)
YMCA	Young Men's Christian Association
yo	Years old (age)

Glossary

*Bairn	Child
*Bonnie	Nice, beautiful
*Braw	Good, very nice
Camouflet	Small charge detonated underground to explode the oppositions mine workings
Canny	Wise, understanding
Coppers	Police
*Couldnae	Could not have
Crump	Term used to describe the damaging of above or below ground workings
*Dae	Do
*Dafty	Silly, stupid
Demob	Demobilisation. Released from the Army
*Dinnae	Did not or Do not
Divvy	Division. Army unit, consisting of around 15 000 men
Duck board	A ladder like walking platform of 2 rails and cross pieces of timber to allow walking through muddy areas
*Fouter	Messing about
*Glaikit	Dumb, silly, foolish
*Hasnae	Has not
*Havena	Have not
*Heid	Head
*Ken	Know, understand
*Kirk	Church
Mates Rates	Special discount price for friends
*Mawkit	Dirty, filthy
Minnie	Short for Minenwerfer, a German mortar like armament, slow-moving, short range

Palliasse	Canvas bag stuffed with straw, usually used as a mattress
*Peely-wally	Pale and weak looking. Often used to describe someone's character
Privy	Loo, dunny, thunderbox, toilet, W/C
Salient	A bulge in an otherwise straight line
Sap	Trench dug either above or below ground for troops to shelter in. Dug by the...
Sapper	Lowest rank in the engineers (equivalent of private)
Stunt	A term given to a planned military action
*Tae	To
*Tatties	Potatoes
Tea	Dinner, evening meal (when used to refer to a meal, not the drink)
*Wheesht	Shhh. Be quiet
Whizz-Bang	Faster than sound, artillery shell. The first you knew of it was when it whizzed past you and went bang. Long range.

*Scottish terminology

9 781398 477261